D1478285

Economic Origins of
Roman Christianity

Economic Origins of Roman Christianity

ROBERT B. EKELUND JR. AND
ROBERT D. TOLLISON

THE UNIVERSITY OF CHICAGO PRESS   CHICAGO AND LONDON

ROBERT B. EKELUND JR. is the Catherine and Edward Lowder Eminent Scholar Emeritus of Economics at Auburn University. He is the author of numerous books, including *The Marketplace of Christianity* with Robert D. Tollison and Robert F. Hébert.

ROBERT D. TOLLISON is the C. Wilson Newman Professor of Economics at Clemson University.

The University of Chicago Press, Chicago 60637
The University of Chicago Press, Ltd., London
© 2011 by The University of Chicago
All rights reserved. Published 2011.
Printed in the United States of America
20 19 18 17 16 15 14 13 12 11   1 2 3 4 5

ISBN-13: 978-0-226-20002-6 (cloth)
ISBN-10: 0-226-20002-7 (cloth)

Library of Congress Cataloging-in-Publication Data

Ekelund, Robert B. (Robert Burton), 1940–
    Economic origins of Roman Christianity / Robert B. Ekelund, Jr. and Robert D. Tollison.
        p.   cm.
    Includes bibliographical references and index.
    ISBN-13: 978-0-226-20002-6 (cloth : alk. paper)
    ISBN-10: 0-226-20002-7 (cloth : alk. paper)   1. Church history—Primitive and early church, ca. 30–600.   2. Church history—Middle Ages, 600–1500.   3. Christianity—Economic aspects.   I. Tollison, Robert D.   II. Title.
    BR163.E34 2011
    270.1—dc22

                                                        2010046171

♾ The paper used in this publication meets the minimum requirements of the American National Standard for Information Sciences—Permanence of Paper for Printed Library Materials, ANSI Z39.48-1992.

For Mark Thornton, for everything!
RBE

For my coauthor, who never takes his oar out of the water, with respect and affection, on his seventieth birthday
RDT

Contents

Preface

This book chronicles the evolution of Roman Christianity from its origins to a full-blown monopoly of belief in Western Europe on or about the year 1100 CE. Our motivation in telling this story is twofold. First, we seek to add economic perspective to the origins and development of this movement, and as such, it completes our previous work on the development of high medieval Christianity (*Sacred Trust* [Oxford University Press, 1996]), the Protestant Reformation, and the "competitive revolution" of Christian religion to the present day (*The Marketplace of Christianity* [MIT Press, 2006]). The current investigation is completely unique and stands alone with respect to previous studies in two important respects. *Sacred Trust* was concerned with monopolistic manipulations over the medieval period *once the monopoly had been established*, and *Marketplace* was centered on the retreat of the Roman Catholic monopoly and the advent of mature Christian competition down to the present day. The present book is a "prequel" to these developments. It analyzes in economic terms how a monopoly of Pauline (Nicaean) Christianity emerged out of competition with Judaism, Roman-Egyptian cults, and other Christian sects over a long historical period. More specifically, it demonstrates how a *Roman* monopoly on Christian belief slowly evolved over large parts of Western Europe and how it prospered from vertical integration as many modern firms do. Further, the present book is theoretically distinct from our previous efforts in the following sense: while the principles of competition, market structure, industrial organization, and microeconomics have been applied in our earlier and present work, we here emphasize religious preferences and risk, entrepreneurship, product differentiation, cartel behavior, and the quest for monopoly power to analyze the history of Christianity over the first millennium.

Our second overall aim is to show that there is a kind of "natural" evolution of Western monotheistic religion—based on exclusivist claims that there is but "one true way" to salvation—which tends to lead to monopoly. This has not been true of other religions, including Judaism, Islam, and Eastern Orthodox Christianity. This development may have had untoward consequences for states, individuals, and society or even promoted violence, as in theocratic marriages of church and state in the West. While we utilize the "dark ages" evolution of Roman Christianity as an example, the principle may apply to other religions and to present-day conditions in some parts of the world as well.

Our book is descriptive of events over the first millennium of Christianity rather than prescriptive. We in no way wish to downplay the role of "faith" in religion—rather, we argue that it is at the center of providing credence in religious belief. Further, we intend this work to supplement, certainly not to replace, the many social and historical research efforts in the area. Indeed, we rely on the many excellent accounts of first millennium developments in Christian religion, including those of Rodney Stark, Keith Hopkins, Ramsey MacMullen, Roger Collins, and others to illustrate our thesis that modern microeconomic theory—particularly the theory of industrial organization and markets—may be a useful explanatory component of key historical processes. We would never claim to be specialists in medieval history. Thus we do not attempt to provide a history of the so-called dark ages or of religion in general (Asimov 1968). (Indeed, even though the term "dark ages" has become somewhat passé given recent research concerning the significant economic growth, trade, and development that occurred over the course of the first millennium, we nonetheless use the term interchangeably with the "early medieval period.") Our aim is far more modest: to show how during this period a Roman Christian monopoly developed due to exogenous events as well as by an evolving "economic strategy." The latter occurred by defining and selling a unique and well-defined product through keen entrepreneurship, networking, manipulation of civil governments, and the creation of forms—violent and otherwise—of entry control. The economic carapace we explore is not intended to be an excursion into "medieval history," and we acknowledge that medievalists may provide a different interpretation of points covered in this book. We do argue that economics may be a fruitful avenue for uncovering complementary hypotheses concerning the emergence of Western Christianity.

This book is a product of a three-decade-long quest to understand how monopoly can be created and destroyed within particular institutional structures. Our initial investigation involved the rise, heyday, and declension of internal mercantile policies in England and France (*Mercantilism as a Rent-Seeking Society* [Texas A&M Press, 1981] and *Politicized Economies* [Texas A&M Press, 1997]). As such, the present work continues the study of the process of monopoly creation but, unlike our former study, analyzes a special and unique institution—the Roman Catholic Church. Combined with *Sacred Trust* and *The Marketplace of Christianity*, this volume rounds out our previous analyses of later periods of Church history by offering an economic explanation of the rise, spread, and monopolization of Christianity.

We are grateful for the contribution of Octavian Vascilicu to the econometric work reported in chapter 4 and to an appendix at the end of the book on the impact of Saint Paul as an entrepreneur of Christianity. He should be considered a full coauthor of the appendix. Ekelund is deeply and forever grateful to the late Peter Guenther of St. Mary's University, San Antonio, for having instilled in him a deep appreciation of Roman and medieval history as well as the history of art. His astonishing knowledge of and devotion to human culture is a gift to many generations of students. We are also grateful to seminar and workshop participants at Harvard, Wake Forest, and Clemson Universities for suggestions at presentations of parts of this book. Randy Beard, James Buchanan, Audrey Davidson Kline, Kenneth Elzinga, George Ford, Robert Hébert, Dennis Mueller, and Mark Thornton also contributed valuable comments. Medieval scholar Thomas Kuehn of Clemson University gave most valuable advice on particular points of fact and interpretation over the entire manuscript, and we are deeply grateful for that. Discussions with friends Chad Parish and John and Mary Jane Roper of issues raised at various points were fruitful. Rachel McCleary of Harvard University, more than any of our initial readers, offered trenchant and important comments on the manuscript. Her influence has been of enormous benefit. We sincerely thank her and all who have provided good advice. We thank our editors, David Pervin, Maia Rigas, and two unidentified referees for extensive and helpful comments. The book has been greatly improved by their reviews. We, of course, bear full responsibility for the final product.

Robert B. Ekelund Jr.
Auburn University

Robert D. Tollison
Clemson University

CHAPTER ONE

Roman Christianity:
An Evolving Monopoly

Introduction

The longest-running institution in Western culture and arguably one that has had an enormous influence on Western civilization has been the Roman Catholic Church. The Roman Church, as the "point of origin" for all Christianity, has been the subject of intense attention over the centuries. That attention is not misplaced: the history of the past two millennia of Western civilization cannot be understood apart from the development and dominance of this form of religious belief. The Roman Church has been a pivotal player in Europe for over a millennium and a half through its impact on European institutions, society, culture, and politics. The flowering of economic growth emanating from Europe to the rest of the world could not be analyzed apart from the evolution of the Christian church. We believe that simple economic principles help to shed light on this fascinating institution, both in the past and in the present. Previous studies, including our own, have primarily focused on the economic and social implications of church dominance in the High Middle Ages. Our goal in the present work is to chronicle in economic terms the successful rise and rapid spread of Roman Christianity, from its humble origins when it faced persecution and multiple forms of competition through the turn of the twelfth century, at which point it had become the dominant religious and economic institution in many parts of Europe.

Beyond the sheer success of an institution lasting for 2,000 years, a host of amazing facts surrounds the development of the Christian religion. First, there was the rapid *rate of adoption and expansion* from a tiny sect to become the state religion of the Roman Empire in a bare three hundred years. While all estimates derived from both Christian and non-Christian sources are necessarily speculative, a well-executed study estimates the growth of Christianity at approximately 3.4 percent per year between 40 CE and 350 CE (Hopkins 1998, 192–193). Under these estimates the number of Christians grew from about 7,400 members in 100 CE to 1,100,000 in 250 and to 32 million members in 350 CE. Other estimates give similar approximations.[1] If these data are even approximately correct, a small religious movement developed relatively quickly into a nascent monopoly over parts of Europe that began to dominate the empire that once sought to destroy it. Second, and even more amazing perhaps, is the subsequent development of the Christian church up to the early and late Middle Ages—a time when the *Roman* (or Latin) branch of that church held a veritable monopoly (with only fringe competition) on the belief system of much of Europe and England. This development—occurring through the decline of the Roman Empire and the multitude of social, economic, and political developments throughout Europe and elsewhere including the rise of nation-states in the Middle Ages—has been analyzed both historically and within the realm of religious history. Church monopoly and behavior, as is well known, led to the Protestant Reformation of the sixteenth century and the plurality of Christian sects today, numbering in the thousands worldwide.[2]

Beginning with Adam Smith, economists have been interested in the organization of religion. Contemporary economists have in fact created an entirely new field called the "economics of religion" in both macroeconomic and microeconomic terms. Beginning from initial theoretical perspectives on religious behavior (Azzi and Ehrenberg 1975), the study of cult behavior as a theory of clubs (Iannaccone 1992, 1995, 1998), and religion as a study of economic organization (Ekelund, Hebert, and Tollison 1989, 1992), investigations have taken scholars in a number of directions, primarily rooted in microeconomic theory.[3] Theories of doctrinal strictness (Barros and Garoupa 2002) and the role of sainthood (Ferrero 2008) are also examples of this latter approach. Aggregative or macroeconomic theories, including those related to religious participation and economic growth (Barro and McCleary 2003, 2004, 2005; McCleary and Barro 2006a, 2006b), are extremely interesting and valuable contributions to the field.[4]

A contemporary economic analysis of the historical evolution of religion has also been underway as well. This project builds on existing contributions to the field and features market theory, industrial organization, and modern microeconomics to plumb the organizational structure of Christianity and its effects over time. In this spirit, the current book on the evolution of Christianity from the time of Christ through (approximately) 1100 CE is a continuation of two earlier books on the medieval church and its evolution to the present day. In *Sacred Trust* (Ekelund et al. 1996), the analysis focused on the time period of roughly from 1100 CE to the advent of the Reformation. In *The Marketplace of Christianity* (Ekelund, Herbert, and Tollison 2006), the central topics were the Reformation and entry of Protestant religions into the marketplace, along with many of the consequences of competitive Christianity. In the present work, as in the two previous books, we apply economic analysis to consider the rise and spread of early Christianity from the time of Christ until the Roman Church emerged centuries later as a powerful purveyor in the marketplace for religious services (roughly between 1000–1200 CE) over much of Western Europe.

The present book is fundamentally differentiated in theme and theoretical application from our earlier endeavors. The book *Sacred Trust* studied the activities of a monopoly that had already *been achieved*— how it manipulated doctrine, invented Purgatory and auricular confession, and used the Crusades and other methods to protect itself from competition. The study *The Marketplace of Christianity*, on the other hand, examined the consequences of successful entry into the Christian market by Martin Luther and other Protestants, many of which benefited from state-sponsored religious monopoly as well. The latter depicts the mature competition that the Christian market has undergone in the post-Reformation period. Indeed, thousands of Christian sects exist today. *Economic Origins* analyzes how traditional (Nicaean) Christianity emerged out of the competition with Roman cults, Judaism, and other Christian cults and, most importantly, how a *Roman* monopoly over Christianity developed thereafter. Again, we employ the tools of modern microeconomics, but in the present work we place special emphasis on cartel behavior, the search for monopoly power, religious preferences, and risk and product differentiation theory. The tripartite approach of the present book is to analyze economically and discuss the emergence of the early "competitive phase" of the Christian movement up to Constantine; then, to examine the fixation of doctrine under Constantine at the Council of Nicaea; and finally, to show how the vertical integration of church theology, ritual, and practice was, slowly and sometimes fitfully, accomplished from (roughly) 400 CE to 1100 CE as the church emerged as a *Roman* monopoly.

The various dates bracketing our current study are no doubt inexact, and it is not our intent to engage in a search for the exact moment when the church reached the pinnacle of monopoly power over the spiritual and over a not inconsiderable part of the temporal life of Western Europe. Many historians argue, correctly, that the "Christianization" of Europe was incomplete well into the Reformation era. Rather, one aim of this book is to explain how the church rose from a small group of believers at the time of Christ to a vast, supranational, quasi-monopoly religion some ten to twelve centuries later over vast parts of Europe. We offer this analysis as a foundation and complement to our earlier work dealing with later periods of church history. In this endeavor we do not (and could not) present a complete historical account of these centuries, as would a medieval historian. Rather, we seek to describe only some of the essential features of Christian development over this time. The fact-based and Christian- and non-Christian document-based approaches of many historical and sociological accounts (e.g., Hillgarth 1969; MacMullen 1981, 1984; Hopkins 1998) are central to understanding this millennium-long process. The social-scientific method of understanding Christianity and its growth, largely undertaken by Stark (1997, 2001, 2003, 2006), while open to criticism (Klutz 1998; Hopkins 1998), is yet another means to understanding the emergence of Christianity, and we owe much to Stark's many inquiries. Drawing on all of these approaches, we would stress that economic concepts and arguments, when added to these historical and sociological accounts, have much to contribute to this multidisciplinary endeavor.

A completion of the political economy of the Roman Catholic Church as one of the longest-running institutions on record is only one of the two central aims of the present study. We believe that it is critical to understand, in the expanding domain of economic theory, how the drive to monopoly on the part of religion is but one example of the natural desire of institutions (and businesses) to eliminate competitors and competition as they develop over time. That was as true in the Roman and medieval period as it is today. A fundamental expression of a religion's monopolistic tendency is to claim to profess truth and to see contradictory beliefs as heresy. A religion's proclamation that there is only one "true" system of supernatural belief—a claim of exclusivity made by Christianity from the beginning—may and has led to strife, bloodshed and war. Our study therefore has implications for all religious movements, historical and contemporary. It is important to note that this analysis is not pejorative or normative in any sense relative to religion or to religious institutions. We are not discussing theological issues per se; rather, we are presenting a positive analysis of how religious institutions behave with respect to given events and under certain motives and constraints. A firm grounding in issues relating to monopoly organization *and its evolution* is therefore central to our study.

Aspiring to Monopoly

Textbook treatments of monopoly simply assume that a monopoly is a single seller of a unique product and trace the effects of such a structure on price and output. The basic economic concept is definitional and static in nature. A pure monopoly is said to exist in an industry composed of a single seller of a product with no close substitutes and with high barriers to entry. Prices are higher and output lower than under competitive (or intermediate) market models. Naturally, this definition must include the definition of the product or service; the meaning of "no close substitutes"; and, in context of a particular market, the meaning of "high" barriers to entry. The requirement of "single seller," moreover, may be broadened to include a concept of a group of sellers acting as one—a cartel. But in this static conception, the *process of monopolization* is basically ignored.[5] The emergence of the theory of rent seeking (Tullock 1967) has changed this situation somewhat and such interesting and important questions as how monopolies come into existence and why they sometimes go away (deregulation) are addressed (Ekelund and Tollison 1981).[6] Sometimes the answers to these questions are easy (as when a patent is granted or when a collusive agreement is unstable), but in other cases, like that of the Christian church, answers are more difficult to uncover. So, given that a product and a market may be defined for religion, several critical questions emerge. How did a monopoly emerge from a competitive environment to begin with? What were the effects of monopolization on the behavior of the Christian church, and how did the Roman Catholic Church (from now on generally referred to as "the church" or the Roman Church) consolidate and protect its monopoly power?[7]

Monopolies have been one critical form of political and economic organization throughout recorded time just as authoritarian or monarchical regimes have dominated democratic or market-based systems. The approaches of sociologists, historians, and political scientists have been important and applicable to understanding long-term processes. The masterful (if often challenged) views of Arnold Toynbee (1889–1975) created a lengthy and often dense theory concerning the rise and fall of civilizations with multiple causes for cyclic activity.[8] Religion, of critical importance in Toynbee's conception, was the factor that bound civilizations together, a point that is not in conflict with our analysis of the interactions of church and state. We are, however, far more focused with the Christian church itself and its means of ascendance to monopoly power over the first millennium.

Other scholars in sociology and political science also offered trenchant insights into the progress and decline of societies. The eminent historian Paul Kennedy emphasized (1987) that the rise of the Great Powers is intimately related to relative resource availability and to economic sustainability. Conversely, decline is related to overextension and imperialist adventures. Such military challenges put unbearable pressures on the resource base of societies and create ultimate relative decline. Sociologist, political scientist, and historian Charles Tilly (1929–2008) examined the related rise of the nation-state as the dominant form of political organization from the Middle Ages onward (Tilly 1990). High resource costs of military innovations are emphasized in Tilly's explanation, as is the high taxation necessary to finance competition between states. The summary observations of these two thinkers are not directly applied to the period we consider in this book but are undoubtedly relevant to the rise and fall of Rome and early medieval ("Dark Age") dynasties. We argue, in complementary rather than competing fashion, that an understanding of how a *particular* emerging monopoly—the Christian church between (approximately) the first and twelfth centuries—helps provide insights into the course of European history over that period and beyond. In our view, history is not only explainable in terms of competition, resource endowments, or fractionalization; it is also about ideas, philosophies, or innovations that can lead to monopoly and monopolization. Most famously perhaps, nation-states—China, Japan, England,

Spain, France, Portugal, and the Netherlands included—attempted at various times in history to gain world domination through a variety of means reducible to the process of "competition for monopolization." Tribes, ancient temple societies such as Egypt or Assyria, trading companies, empires, colonialism, robber barons, mercantilism, Microsoft, the Organization of the Petroleum Exporting Countries (OPEC), and myriad other examples indicate that aspiring monopolists are a prominent aspect of economic history. So, too, are the occasions of the deregulation and dissolution of monopolies, as in the declension of mercantile policies in sixteenth- and seventeenth-century England.[9]

The historical Roman Church fits well within this perspective. As noted above, we have previously shown how monopoly and monopolization were the hallmarks of church behavior in the High Middle Ages, and how Protestantism broke the hold of the Catholic monopoly in large parts of Northern Europe during the Reformation. In the present book, we complete an analysis of the long history of the Roman Church from its origins as a competitor in the market for religion, both Christian and otherwise, to its emergence as a vertically integrated, multinational, monopoly enterprise circa 1000 to 1200 CE.

We will stress the *process* by which the church became the sole supplier of religious and other secular services, with only fringe competition, over the first ten or so centuries of its existence. Key features of these developments are:

the early spread of Christianity in the Roman Empire, fueled by the entrepreneurship of Paul and other disciples of Christ;

the adoption of a particular form of Christianity as the official religion of the Roman Empire (Constantine);

the homogenization of the doctrines of Christianity (completed at the Council of Nicaea after a long waiting period for Christ's return); hereafter there was a monopoly over the *theology* of Christianity, if not over the interpretation of it;

the spread of Christianity throughout Western Europe and liaisons with secular leaders (e.g., Charlemagne); this movement began the vertical integration of the church in the West;

schism between the Eastern and Western Churches over the powers of the pope;

expansion of the economic and tax base of the Roman Church and establishment of the balance of power between the church and secular rulers;

extension and entrenchment of the vertical organization of the Roman
Church with the *Roman* papacy and Curia at the upstream level providing
doctrine and interpretations, regulating the "downstream" level (geographically local parishes, monasteries, and so on) to ensure "uniformity" of teaching and product to the laity;

ultimate triumph of the Roman Church as a religious monopoly in the High
Middle Ages, the competitive breakdown in the sixteenth century, and
briefly, the implications of these and earlier developments for contemporary
Christianity.

The long and arduous journey to monopoly in the Middle Ages was,
in addition to the early confrontations with Rome, naturally accompanied by great conflict as well as cooperation with the entire evolution
of European society and culture itself. The barbarian invasions of the
late Roman era were interspersed with strong and Christian-protective
"European" governments, the rise and onslaught of Islam, which threatened all of European civilization, and Viking raids and the development
of feudalism culminating in strong nation-states. These challenges were
met by a Roman Church that was not a temporary or Schumpeterian monopoly until the *late* Middle Ages.[10] Its monopoly power was ultimately
restrained by the Reformation in the sixteenth century, but it lasted for
many centuries and, in fact, still constitutes a partial or practical monopoly in some parts of the world. With certain exceptions, it may possibly
be the longest-running example of monopoly that history affords us.[11]

A Word on Method

We employ an economic approach to explain the evolution of monopoly
church behavior. We discuss this method in chapters 2 and 3 and defend it
as we have elsewhere (Ekelund et al. 1996; Ekelund, Hebert, and Tollison
2006). Modern microeconomics is based upon the idea that all choices
can be analyzed as being economic in structure, and this is the method
we employ in the present and other works on religion. This is not controversial as such. The issue is whether the economic approach contributes to our understanding of church and religious behavior. Historians,

anthropologists, and sociologists have contributed much to the under-standing of religion and its evolution and characteristics. Our approach in no way supplants the important analyses, past and present, of social scientists such as Paul Kennedy, Charles Tilly, Arnold Toynbee, and many others interested in the progress of European history. It is rather an analysis of how the progress of a single institution—the Christian church—fits into the overall institutional structure of early Europe. The reader will have to judge for herself whether the economic approach is helpful as a complement to general social science in the overall analysis.[12]

One advantage of the economic approach is that it can offer refutable hypotheses about church behavior. For example, one important null hy-pothesis is that the church was in the business of serving the public inter-est by propagating and enforcing doctrines that led to the production of certain public goods such as a lower crime rate ("Thou shall not steal"). An alternative hypothesis is that the church provided doctrine and en-forcement to believers in order to raise revenue. As we have argued in earlier work on the medieval church, the doctrines associated with pur-gatory and the payment to absolve one's sins or the sins of loved ones acted in principle to lower the average price of "sin" in the Middle Ages. The invention of purgatory led to a system of first-degree price discrim-ination in which payment for forgiveness and position in purgatory was based on the income of the petitioner and not on the severity of his of-fense. So the average price for sins fell under purgatory (a varying con-tribution to the church rather than a uniform price of eternal damna-tion), an action in clear contradiction of the church as a public-interest organization. This is not the only example. A public-interest organiza-tion would arguably provide its services at minimum costs of produc-tion or be staffed by low-paid, volunteer managers. A public-interested church would be decentralized to increase its flexibility to respond to lo-cal issues. A church bent on monopoly and revenues as a major part of its goal would behave in a different manner. As we will see, the theory of monopolization and monopoly are helpful in understanding the rise, spread, and ultimate dominance of the *Roman* Catholic Church.

The Roman Church as a High Medieval Monopoly

Before we turn to the early history of Christianity, it will be useful to characterize the church as the monopoly that it became in the 1000–

1200 CE timeframe. Why do we argue that the church was a monopoly and had monopoly power by this time, and how are these characterizations a useful way to analyze the church?

Establishing a Monopoly

As a purely factual matter, the church was a "dominant firm" in the medieval economy. By "dominant firm" we mean that the Roman Church became a monopoly but that it always had "fringe competition" from other belief systems, that is, from Jews, pagan sects, other forms of Christianity, and of course, from nonbelievers. As a dominant firm, however, it had the power to set the full price of membership in the Christian church. The competitive producers were "price takers," not "price makers," and their competitive activity had to take place around the price that was set by the Roman Church. Thus we say that it was a monopoly in all essential respects regarding the behavior and outcomes of its members. The church owned a third or more of all cultivated land in Western Europe (and a substantial amount of uncultivated land as well). If land is the basis of taxation and medieval production, the church was by far the largest economic entity in Western Europe. The organization and employment of the church was massive. In 1300, for example, church officials constituted 1 percent of England's population. On the Continent there were a large number of sects, bishoprics, monasteries, abbeys, and cathedrals.

Maintaining a Monopoly

To maintain monopoly power, the incumbent monopolist must be able to deter the entry of new competitors. Throughout the period prior to the Reformation, the church dealt with potential entrants harshly. The Crusades are perhaps the best example in that not just Muslims were targeted for extinction, but Eastern Christians as well. Any doctrinal differences that came forward were dealt with sternly and decisively by the church. Both insiders (sects) and outsiders (infidels) were targeted in an effort to deter entry and defection from the church and its doctrines. The tactics employed in their efforts included heresy, excommunication, and violence (e.g., the inquisitions and periodic torture and burnings of heretics and "witches").

Homogenizing the Product

An important aspect of the entry issue facing the church was what econ-omists call "entry from within" an industry. From early times there was a movement in the church to homogenize and come together to agree upon a common and *exclusive* framework for belief. Creating a homogeneous product is part of establishing a monopoly, particularly when it comes to doctrinal issues. The Council of Nicaea, which laid the foundation for traditional Christian belief for all time, is a fundamental example of this process. As traditional Christianity progressed over the centuries, one either accepted the principles laid down by the Council of Nicaea (as amended in very minor ways by later councils and as interpreted by the church) or one was not a Christian.[13] Over time, various sects would ap-pear and take issue with church doctrine or behavior. Consistent with retaining its monopoly over Biblical interpretation and doctrinal issues, the church systematically and sometimes violently stamped out such crit-ics. The reason is easy to see. Monopolies and cartels tend to eschew product differentiation since, other things being equal, it facilitates en-try by competitors. While product homogeneity is not unique to monop-oly (e.g., consider grain or egg production under competition), it opens the door to competing interpretations and "belief contracts" that were a threat to the business of the church and were dealt with accordingly. In-deed, the church would then point to its monopoly position as proof that it was the one true way to the blissful afterlife.

Inelastic Demand

As in the normal case of monopoly, the market demand curve for re-ligious services was inelastic along its relevant portions. Inelasticity means that believers (buyers) were relatively unresponsive to full price changes for the church's main product—assurances of eternal salvation. There were few substitutes for the services of the church, all the more so since competitive visions of the Christian life and afterlife were vig-orously outlawed by the church. The structure of medieval life proba-bly required church membership as a condition of operating in the lo-cal economy. For such reasons, the church fathers were able to exploit a relatively inelastic demand function for their services. Over time, the church sought to shift its demand curve to the right and to make it relatively more inelastic. This was done through investments in advertising or brand-name capital. Relics, miracles, and cathedrals fall into this category of behavior.

Price Discrimination and Territories

In our earlier books we extensively model and discuss purgatory and related doctrines as a system of first-degree price discrimination. Price discrimination is the practice of charging one buyer or group of buyers a different price than that charged to others for the same product (belief system). The price difference is not due, moreover, to differences in costs of servicing consumers but (often) due to the differing income of the buyer-believers. In what is called "first-degree discrimination," individuals or groups are charged the maximum demand prices for atonement services. This was possible because such services could not be resold by purchasers. The church also historically practiced geographic or market division of services. As a vertically integrated enterprise, it also formed policies to maximize enterprise revenues by limiting the ability of local units to monopolize at that level. The point is simply that price discrimination and territorial divisions go hand in hand with monopolistic behavior.

Organization

The church was vertically integrated with geographic divisions. The church in fact *perfected* the downstream-upstream vertical monopoly structure in order to achieve its monopoly over the first millennium (a development we discuss at length in chaps. 6 and 7). The church's organization and governance structure were based on the model of a strong central authority, which ultimately had the power to run the institutions of the church. There were collegial procedures in the church, but these were and are, in practice, *advisory* to papal authority. Unlike the Eastern Church, the church at Rome did not rely solely on collegial decision making. In terms of organizational economics, the church at Rome adopted a model with a clear residual claimant at the head rather than a collegial or "conciliar" model in which coalitional politics held sway.[14] A residual claimant is the individual (or group of individuals) that share in the profits (net of cost) of a firm. Predictably, the church at Rome was more successful in economic and other terms as a result.

The pope and other church officials were in part residual claimants to church revenues. To the extent that revenues were not taken out of the church, a good prediction is that they were dissipated through the cost function of the church. The church was analogous to present-day athletic departments at universities, which are always decrying "deficits" in their operations at the same time that athletic facilities grow in size and grandeur, coaching salaries rise, and the carpeting in athletic offices gets thicker. The size, scale, and grandeur of the cathedrals may possibly be an expression of cost inflation and the degree to which the church monopoly was producing its religious services at inflated costs. One may witness, for example, the behavior with respect to church buildings, ceremony, dress, and relics of the Protestant churches that began operation during the Reformation. These were clearly lower-cost suppliers of religious services.

Plan of the Book

That Christianity can be seen as a long struggle from competition to monopoly power is not surprising. Western monotheistic religion with an undifferentiated and *exclusive* main product—establishment of the conditions for eternal salvation—has a natural predisposition toward monopoly. This does not mean that all monotheistic religions, even in the West, have this natural predisposition. (Greek Orthodox Christianity, monotheistic in character, did not adopt the vertically integrated model of Roman Christianity.) If a particular religion represents the essence of the good life and the road to salvation, there can only be one true "way" whatever the sect. Other points of view complicate and contest this vision and must be dealt with voluntarily (conversion), involuntarily (coercion), or uneasily (coexistence). The medieval church, at the height of its powers and its sphere of influence, applied *all three* policies to various degrees at various times. And it must be remembered that Christianity, along with Judaism and Islam as one of the three Abrahamic religions, was monotheistic and exclusivist in character. Stark (1997, 204–205; 2006, 3–10) and Iannaccone (1995) elaborate on the development of monotheism and underscore that religious firms fare better in the market when they are monotheistic. We would make the observation that these firms tend to monopoly by methods of expansion as well when they are in non-zero-sum circumstances.[15] The manner through which the Roman

Catholic Church achieved and applied monopoly power is the subject of this book, although not all monotheistic religions follow the path of Roman Catholicism as vertically integrated monopoly firms. (Other than the Anglicans, most Protestant sects utilize a "bottom-up" strategy of firm organization.)

Chapter 2 presents an overview of the literature that is related to our study. This includes contributions by economists, sociologists, historians of religion, and others who have made important contributions to our understanding of religious institutions and processes. Some of these scholars are historical figures (e.g., Adam Smith and Max Weber), and some are modern-day pioneers of the economics and sociology of religion (e.g., Rachel McCleary of Harvard University).

Chapter 3 prepares the reader for the historical analysis by providing a brief introduction to the economics of religion, particularly embellishing upon the rational choice approach and monopoly business organization discussed briefly in the present chapter and on the tools used in discussing the historical evolution of Christianity in this book. It develops a simple model of rational choice of religious type on the basis of uncertainty concerning an afterlife or "assurances of eternal salvation"— the essential (but not the only) product supplied by Christianity. This analysis is based on utility maximization under uncertainty, where individual decisions take place within a multicontract competitive environment. The nature of the religious good is analyzed, as is the method through which such a good spreads and gains credence among demanders for it. An even more fundamental issue is addressed: the nature of the demand for religious contracts and the manner in which the characteristics of the essential religious good (assurances of an afterlife) relates to those contracts.

The principles discussed in chapter 3 prepare the reader for an enhanced explanation for the rapid initial adoption of Christianity in chapter 4. Previously restricted to the efforts of historians and sociologists, we initiate an integration of the economic theories of entrepreneurship and networking with these perspectives and discuss, without technical jargon, the results of simple statistical tests of the early development and spread of Christianity.[16] We conclude, with the aid of simple tests, that the early spread of Christianity was the result of the interplay between entrepreneurial activities and network effects spawned by the teachings of Paul to the Gentiles and through the Jewish Diaspora.

The rapid rise in the number of Christians between the time of Christ and the emperor Constantine in the early fourth century is well established. Cycles of persecution came to an end with the (probable) conversion of Constantine and his legitimization of Christian belief. An economic theory and evidence for it of the rise and ultimate cartelization of the Christian religion in Rome supplements traditional sociological and historical explanations in chapter 5. We theorize that efficiency considerations (which include rent seeking and cost savings) led the Roman state to at first adopt and then cartelize the religion under the emperor Constantine and other state leaders in the fourth century CE. The provision of a unified Christian religion in that century may be described in economic terms as an arrangement that reduced agency costs to the state and provided rents to the Christian church. The adoption of Christianity by the state lowered its "agency costs"—the costs of maintaining order and a stable, functioning society—and increased "rents" or enhanced revenues in excess of costs to the unified church.

Chapter 6 carries the discussion to the period after Constantine up to the coronation of Charlemagne as Holy Roman emperor in 800 CE. The church's application and promulgation of forward vertical integration is at the center of our discussion in both chapters 6 and 7. Vertical integration is the combination in one firm of two or more stages of production operated by separate firms. The upstream and downstream activities of the religious or other firm may be combined into one firm or separated in ownership and operation. Events of the fourth century—Constantine's legitimization of Christianity and Theodosius's elevation of it as the official state religion—was only the beginning of the hegemony ultimately acquired by the Roman (Latin) Church as a dominant force in the upstream church and as a vertically integrated firm. As such, the "business model" of the church was forward vertical integration, which simply means that the upstream church (wholesale) came to "own" the downstream parts of its operations (retail). This necessarily entailed the development of monitoring and auditing functions at the center (later administered by the Roman Curia), which were used to insure that the church's revenue and other policies were coordinated in a fashion that roughly led to maximum net revenues and to policy outcomes that helped the church create and later maintain its position of monopoly in the Western European religious marketplace.[17]

The church was, of necessity, part of a geopolitical gambit between

the eastern and western parts of Europe and in the center of the barbarian invasions of Europe and Italy, but it sought to establish a vertically
integrated monopoly both before and after Roman hegemony. The Roman Church, if it was to make good its claim of primacy over all Christianity, had to deal with the opposition of the Eastern emperors and
patriarchs as well as myriad other problems and conflicts. Chapter 6 outlines how the Roman branch of Christianity was able to do that. Fundamentally, the Roman papacy and its product definition and claims of
primacy were rescued by affiliation with the Frankish kingdoms, culminating in the good offices and protection of Charlemagne. At the same
time, the church established a downstream sale of its main product, assurances or probability of eternal salvation, with monasteries, local prelates, and missionary activity. The downstream church, in its demands for
reform by individual clerics, orders, and monasteries, contributed to the
church's organizational structure. It was also aided by the good fortune
of an otherwise occupied Eastern Church that had to deal with political
and military challenges of their own from Islamic pressures. These factors, along with the great success of the Roman Church at evangelizing
the barbarians in Western Europe, permitted the Roman monopoly to
move forward. The "business strategy" of the church was to proselytize
pagans, barbarians, and whole societies that would defend the Roman
papacy and would recognize its legitimacy.

Property holdings of the Roman Church were vast even by the time of
Charlemagne, as was its power to enforce behavior that was deemed unacceptable given the monopoly it asserted over the content and interpretation of scripture and other rules and regulations. But even after Charlemagne, the church had to face competition and conflict with political
regimes for revenues and matters within the Christian religion. In particular, the Roman Church had to deal with internal corruption and again
with the Eastern Orthodox view that the bishop of Rome, while deserving special honor, did not hold primacy over the entire church. These issues, together with the all-important property and investiture disputes
with civil governments, again manifestations of forward vertical integration with the church replacing civil controls, are discussed in chapter 7.

The Roman Church, which divorced itself from the eastern branches
of Christianity in the middle of the eleventh century, had become a
loosely vertically integrated monopoly in all practical senses by the year
1100 CE. In our concluding discussion (chap. 8), we first review the path
that Roman Christianity took to medieval monopoly from the birth of

Christ to the Middle Ages. We then discuss the impact of this monopoly on the religious life of the medieval period. What were the effects of the monopoly on religious belief in Europe of the time, and what was the impact of that monopoly on later developments in the Christian religion? The answers to this question are not merely of historical importance. They lay bare the structure of a universal tendency to monopoly or, more accurately, the means through which religious institutions attempt to gain monopoly control over markets and, when having done so, elicit competition for that control. The rise of Protestantism and competitive Christianity rounds out our discussion of the power of monopoly, its dissolution, and its implications for society.

Our quest to understand the implications of church efforts to achieve monopoly over the first millennium does not end here, however. The journey to and success of monopoly over the course of the first millennium and the tools used to achieve it *have implications for modern developments in Christianity*. Thus we conclude in chapter 8 by focusing briefly on contemporary aspects of church behavior, finding that the Roman and other Christian churches defend traditional doctrines, but that this is and can be only partially successful in the competitive and scientific environments of advanced contemporary societies. Most particularly, we focus on how the organizational structure developed over the first millennium Roman church remains in place and adjusts (however slowly) to changing conditions. Vertical control has created problems for that brand of Christianity but it is, in the main, defended throughout the hierarchy in the modern world. In sum, the aims and analysis of this book are simple but, we believe, remain highly interesting in a modern context. Our argument presented here may be summarized in three steps.

First Step

After our review of the literature, as a first step we show how modern economic concepts of risk and reward help explain a demand for religion. The use of these concepts—risk aversion, networking, entrepreneurship, and industrial organization among them—help explain the rapid and dramatic rise of Christianity in the Roman Empire and the "Dark Ages" and the tendency to monopoly (and possibly violence) in the sale and maintenance of a religious product in the case of the Roman Christian religion.[18]

Second Step

Having shown how economic concepts can explain the rapid growth of
Christianity, we demonstrate how, through religious and political interaction and competition, the *Roman* side of Christianity created quasi
monopolies of spiritual and temporal power over early medieval Europe
between 400 and 1100. These "business strategies" included the spread of
Christian religion by evangelization and the assertions of spiritual power
over temporal authority. The organizational features of this monopoly included a vertical tension between the upstream church—which delivered
doctrines, interpretations, and directions of ritual—and the downstream
church—geographically local parishes and monasteries that delivered a
final product to the faithful. With a monopoly in place, we explain how,
through the extension of the monopoly power over Christian belief in
the High Middle Ages, the Roman Catholic Church was able to consolidate its power by inventing doctrines and imposing aggrandizing regulations that enhanced its wealth but that also ultimately created entry of
new varieties of the Christian product.

Final Step

Despite competition in the product line to create and recreate monopoly
conditions in parts of the world, religious pluralism imposed by a state
through nonestablishment constitutional clauses and growing "secularism" in most *advanced* nations of the world constrains the Roman Catholic Church and, implicitly, all other Christian religions from establishing monopoly conditions and results.[19] Ecumenism—the cartelization of
Christian (or any) religion—is a most unlikely outcome under these circumstances since the incentives to "cheat" on a common catechism exist with religious doctrines and practices as they would under the sale of
any product or service.

CHAPTER TWO

Religion, History, and Social Science

Introduction

The drive to monopoly has been the goal, if not the result, of many institutions, including governments and suppliers of religious products as well. This was unquestionably the case in so-called temple societies of ancient Egypt and Mesopotamia. Roman religion, much of it derived from Greece and Egypt, held to a pantheon of gods with different worshiping requirements. The Romans, indeed, tended to absorb and allow the conduct of alternative religions of the peoples they conquered, including the Jews, *provided* that the sect members were willing to worship the emperor in the imperial period. (Jews were generally considered "exempt" from this requirement.) Christians, however, were often in danger of persecution if they refused to pay such homage.

But the other side of the supply of religion is, of course, an explanation of why, throughout recorded history, most individuals have demanded the services of religion. Economists have been interested in this critical matter for several centuries, with most of the interest being of recent vintage and in various specializations. In general, they have studied religious behavior by inculcating the work of historians and sociologists in order to understand and describe the evolution and effects of the market for religion, which includes both supply and demand matters. They have also attempted, in the modern era, to appreciate how particular religious policies affect magnitudes of interest to economists (safety, crime, and so on). And, in an essentially macroeconomic endeavor, they have attempted to understand how differing patterns of religious belief and policies affect variables that are keys to economic growth. Studies of the economics of religion have grown steadily over the past quarter century.

The present chapter briefly analyzes *how* economists have approached the study of religion and, chiefly, expresses our view of the nature of the product "religion" and the source of quantities of this product or service that consumers want to purchase or the "demand" for it. The particular quantity of the service that an individual will want to buy is determined by many factors, including income, an individual's risk profile, the satisfaction an individual gets from the service, the price of alternative services, and the full price—the money and time costs associated with consuming the service—charged.[1] Clearly, the economics of religion uses a variety of economic tools to analyze many aspects of religious behavior, historically, descriptively and as prediction. This long-standing quest—stemming from Adam Smith and before—seeks to understand how demander-consumers of religious services of all kinds (including "assurances of eternal salvation") are motivated to purchase religious products and how sellers supply these services in alternative market environments (e.g., monopoly versus competition).

All of the tools of the economist, which include self-interest and rational consumer behavior (including risk preference) on the demand-consumer side and the economics of the firm, public choice, evolutionary monopoly theory, and industrial organization on the supply side, are brought to bear on the study. Specifically, we argue that the economics of religion is best studied utilizing a modified neoclassical approach that includes a contemporary conception of rationality and risk preference. By "neoclassical approach" we mean the traditional analysis of how individuals and firms behave to maximize their own objectives (e.g., maximizing satisfaction or profits) where activities are coordinated by a price mechanism. Often this neoclassical system is presented in purely static terms where equilibria occur in markets all the time, clearly an unrealistic proposition. But neoclassical economics has been supplemented by behavioral and other forms of modeling that includes how economic behavior is molded by institutions (and how behavior, in turn, alters institutions). Further, this "neo-institutional economics" has attempted to modify the standard role of the rationality assumption. We discuss the interface of these views within the context of the economics of religion after a brief review of the economic contributions, primarily of the recent past, to the economics of religion. The principal part of the present chapter deals with our perspective on the nature of the religious good—which we argue is a unique one involving "assurances of eternal salvation"—and its impact on the demand for the good and on the application of that demand to the Christian religion, which is the focus of this book.[2] Recent studies of demand have dominated economists' interests in the subject, but microeconomic studies have a long pedigree in both economics and in the broader social sciences.

Adam Smith and Max Weber

Without doubt, the two best-known progenitors of what we now call the economics of religion are economist Adam Smith (1723–1790) and sociologist Max Weber (1864–1920). There were plenty of theologians and religious apologists who preceded Adam Smith, but it was left to Smith to first put religious outcomes on the clear basis of self-interested incentives and efficient or inefficient outcomes for demanders. His fundamental *ideal* can be expressed succinctly: Smith supported complete separation of church and state on the basis that individuals' preferences and precepts (e.g., conditions for salvation and basis for temporal morality) were different. These heterogeneous demands *required* different brands of religion (Christianity) in order to maximize individual satisfaction. Thus optimal satisfaction of demanders *requires* competition in the market for religion. These principles were Smith's ideal. He fully realized that governments had co-opted religious beliefs in states that were theocratic in nature. Unlike the contemporary United States, most European national governments had established religions (as did most of the American colonies until the introduction of the establishment clause of the Constitution).[3]

Adam Smith, ever the keen observer of institutions and international practice, knew quite well that establishment religion was a basic feature of many European states. How could the efficiency of such organizations be analyzed? Smith believed that state religions limited choice and were not optimal, but noted that the form of organization was the key to suboptimal efficiency. Efficiency of religion meant good preaching, a lack of indolence and greed, and the maintenance of consumer choice and sovereignty. Suboptimal efficiency meant that more of these "products" would be provided under some forms of religious organization than under others *given state-sponsored religion*. That is, religions could be hierarchical or more decentralized where the selection of local preachers occurred. That explains Smith's qualified praise of the Presbyterian clergy. Even within a state-imposed Presbyterian religion, the church established an internal organization emphasizing freedom, equality, and voting rights, features that promoted consumer satisfaction. Less-centralized, denominational churches continue in this decentralized tradition to this day.

To be sure, a plethora of great thinkers were concerned with religion and its effects, and only a few can be mentioned here. One of the penultimate Enlightenment philosophers, David Hume (1711–1776), argued, in contrast to his friend Smith, for establishment in the conduct of religion if religion had to exist at all. However, he believed that social morality existed *independently* of Christian or religious morality (Hume 1976). Theism, Hume believed, while contributing marginally to social cohesion, was prone to intolerance and persecution, but most damagingly, it stood in opposition to liberty. Early "functionalist" views of religion—that it contributed to cohesive societies—were espoused by Auguste Comte (1798–1857) and later by Emile Durkheim (1858–1917). Durkheim abandoned methodological individualism and believed that institutions, such as religion, were to be evaluated on the functions they provided to the society (Durkheim 1915). This view was later adopted by the great twentieth-century sociologist Talcott Parsons, who perhaps most clearly promulgated this view of institutions and religion (Parsons 1951). Parsons's view underscores the point that societal cohesion depended on a common morality among its members. Further, cohesion depended on the common purpose and identity that was achieved by religion. The positivist philosopher Auguste Comte (1968) taught that the most primitive stage of society was the "religious phase," but he allowed that the advance of mathematics and science would soon reduce that influence, ultimately eliminating it altogether. He described a declension from this phase to the "scientific" phase of society, a belief undergirded by a theory that the laws governing society were totally analogous to physical or natural laws, creating what he ultimately called a "religion of humanity" with "scientists as priests" and all manner of positions that mimed religious administration.[4]

Possibly the most famous thesis in social science is that promulgated by sociologist Max Weber. Weber's famous work *The Protestant Ethic and the Spirit of Capitalism* has been interpreted as having several meanings (e.g., Protestantism caused capitalism by making "pursuit of gain" legitimate). Whatever its interpretation, however—and it appears clear that Weber did not espouse some unified single determinant of capitalism—his was clearly a *preference-based argument* for the demand for religion. Weber was interested in "the influence of those psychological sanctions which, originating in religious belief and the practice of religion, gave a direction to practical conduct and held the individual to it" (Weber 1930, 55). Acceptance of a "calling" in this world was a task set out by God for man. The impact of this change in preferences had both microeconomic and macroeconomic implications. We are primarily interested in how Weber's argument flows from the demand side of religion—how Protestantism altered preference sets that led to saving, investing, and capital formation. In reality, however, the advent of Protestantism in the early seventeenth century unleashed a supply-side revolution as well. Simpler churches, simpler rituals, fewer "feast days," and many other factors reduced the requirements of religious capital, which helped bring about economic growth.[5] Clearly, therefore, the advent of Protestantism led to both supply- and demand-side changes in behavior within the context of Weber-like preference changes.

Contemporary Theoretical Approaches to the Demand for Religion

A plethora of approaches and directions has developed within the economic study of religion since Adam Smith. These contemporary studies, rooted in microeconomics, have taken a number of directions. Virtually all of them stem from assumptions of rational behavior, but that assumption—in particular, in its application to religion and religious behavior—has come under scrutiny and attack by those who believe that metarational assumptions must be made about matters of "faith." In particular, behaviorists posit alternative sources of behavior with respect to the more standard rational approach to religion. In the present section we consider these approaches.

Empirical Studies

The early modern studies (Azzi and Ehrenberg 1975) originated in empirical studies that analyzed which variables determined religious participation behavior, on the one hand, and how religious participation in turn affected economic variables such as crime or regional growth, on the other hand. For example, Azzi and Ehrenberg, utilizing a framework of economic rationality, studied some of the same issues that have occupied sociologists in their quest to understand the effect of religious behavior. Participation by sex, age, income, and ethnicity were analyzed but within a "Beckerian perspective."[6] Beyond simply examining the facts—which occupied the activity of traditional sociologists—the Azzi-Ehrenberg paper allowed individuals to allocate their full resources (goods and time) to temporal and afterlife consumptions (an idea promulgated by Gary Becker). Their results, while using rational economic behavior as a ground, do not differ in substance from the traditional sociological interpretations of religious behavior. In high-income countries such as the United States less time-intensive religions and self-administered Christianity have in the main undergone rapid growth especially if one includes atheists as well as believers in Christ who do not participate in organized religion (Pew Forum on Religion and Public Life 2008). The reverse is true in low-wage, low-income households (Evangelicals).[7] Azzi-Ehrenberg found that religious participation rates increase with wealth, being female, and with age. Some of these particular conclusions have been reversed over the decades since Azzi and Ehrenberg's pioneering efforts, but the attraction of using rational and empirical methods to analyze many aspects of religious behavior has not.

The tradition of studying the empirical impact of particular religions and religious behavior has become a cottage industry in economics as well as in the field of sociology (see below). For example Heath, Waters, and Watson (1995) estimated the impact of four religions on state per capita income. Including control variables for each state, they find that both fundamentalist and Catholic versions of Christianity have negative, significant influences on per capita income over the years 1952, 1971, and 1980. These results do not conflict with other studies showing that religious participation is associated with high incomes, lower divorce rates, and lower welfare participation (Gruber 2005). A number of empirical studies utilizing purely "economic" variables reach important conclusions regarding religious participation and marriage rates, criminality, and crime rates. There has been, in short, since Azzi and Ehrenberg's initial study, a flow of research devoted to the empirical effects of religion.

Religions (Cults) as Clubs

The study of religious behavior and its foundations utilizing economic rationality has been employed in modern work in economic theory. Specifically, religious goods have been characterized as club goods—goods that are not consumed individually but where there is selective association with provision of the good (Buchanan 1965). The methods of selection may be as simple as membership fees in the case of certain club memberships or rituals in other cases. Depicting religious organizations as "club goods" was trenchantly developed within the framework of Beckerian economics in 1992 by Lawrence Iannaccone. A predetermined stock of religious capital (often identified in Becker's analyses of behavior) is the foundation or "quasi-constraint" upon which religious behavior is built in this model. After all, one would not expect a person born into a pervasively Buddhist society to be anything but a Buddhist (although "conversion" is possible). An addiction to religion may also grow over time, although "switching," though costly, may be more likely in youth, and marriage is more likely within one's own religion.[8]

A theory of "club behavior" may be superimposed upon these considerations. Adam Smith recognized the existence and possible outcomes of club behavior.[9] While cults could be dangerous to civil society according to Smith, he understood that certain "club effects" attached to particular religious organizations. Specifically, the fact that one's satisfaction or utility received from participation in some organization is a positive function of the number of other individuals participating is a foundation for cult or religious behavior. One's utility depends upon and also affects the utility of other members of the religion or sect.[10] The problem is one of the free rider—an individual who receives the benefit of consuming a public good or service without paying for it. This "shirking" (receiving the utility of membership but not paying for it) must be controlled. Strictness, according to Iannaccone (1992), is the means used by religious sects to control the free-rider problem. Individuals, within a perfectly rational behavioral context, may choose stricter religions, where strictness entails the *demand* of stigmatizing behavior by religious sects to exclude participation by free riders. This might include, for example, shaving heads, particular (and often peculiar) dress, dietary restrictions, and so on, that makes free riding more costly to those who would receive benefits without paying the cost. Thus, Iannaccone rationalizes screening mechanisms such as celibacy or geographic isolation and therefore provides a rationale for membership in cults, clubs, or certain religions.

A problem arises, however, when large or pervasive religions are considered. Consider Catholicism. Who is to know if Catholics attend weekly mass in anything but a small-sized city and congregation? Such attendance would be quite difficult to monitor. Financial contributions in larger congregations are also difficult to monitor. Belief systems and the whole structure of faith become important ingredients in any explanation of religious participation (e.g., the specification of sin for missing Sunday mass). Under competitive conditions, a whole continuum of theologies are produced. Iannaccone assumes but does not specify a demand function for membership in a sect or religion, but what is the product that individual's demand? It must be connected to some product offering. Clearly, some afterlife consumption motive may be part of the specification. Moreover, within the constraints of Iannaccone's model, if the demand function were to be specified, it would apply primarily to a club good with individuals' benefits determined by the number of adherents.

The "club good" approach emphasizes strictness and homogeneity of demanders within a context of static analysis. Naturally, resource commitments must be made in the religious "club" as a condition of maintaining membership, but the extraction of these resources will be from *differentiated* demanders. As noted by Kent D. Miller (2002), dynamic efficiency in markets therefore requires different kinds of organizational characteristics in religious markets. Thus "strictness" must itself become a variable. Strictness is adjusted by suppliers as an outcome of religious participation, not as a cause of it. Miller argues that competition creates efficient resource allocation and efficient religious organizations in a competitive context.[11]

Religion and the New Institutional Economics

Neoinstitutional economics is the product of the application of modern neoclassical microeconomic analysis to institutions and institutional change. Thus, the approach applies to religion and religious institutions and flows from the proposition that rational choice (under particular constraints) creates and alters institutions, including religion and religious forms or "brands" of religion such as Christianity. (Other institutions subject to such analysis include property rights structures, law,

contracts, government forms, and regulation.) Institutions, including religions and the organizations they help create, provide incentives or establish costs and benefits that, for a time, govern economic activity and
economic growth. Intertemporally, however, institutions are themselves
altered through economic activity either due to feedback mechanisms
or because particular institutions create economic incentives for change.
Within such a model, any change in an exogenous variable—for example, the state of scientific knowledge in biology or genetics—could alter
the configuration of religious demands, eliciting alternative demands for
religious products.[12] Religious competition, laws surrounding marriage,
and theocratic marriages of church and state could all change.

The neoinstitutional paradigm expands the bare-bones Marshallian
model (standard utility-based microeconomic theory named for Alfred
Marshall [1842–1924]) to include positive transaction costs and uses insights from the new industrial organization economics, law and economics, public choice, and rent-seeking literature. In short, neoinstitutional economics seeks to establish a theory of institutional change using
a modified static theory of rational choice very much like that used in
the neoinstitutionalist literature (Furubotn and Pejovich 1974; Furubotn
and Richter 1997), which emphasizes *the costs of rational behavior*. Depending on the focus of the analysis and with appropriate specification
of both endogenous and exogenous factors, institutions that have not tra-
ditionally been regarded as "economic" in character—religion (in our
case), law, traditions, habits, tropisms, and many others—may in fact be
analyzed with the neoinstitutionalist framework. Such investigations
lend a "dynamic" quality to the study of the economics of religion. Religious doctrine is often employed to invalidate the use of new technologies, directly or indirectly, using biblical interpretations or exegesis as
a ground. Religion may attempt to directly and violently suppress technological change (e.g., the printing press) so as to maintain the integrity
of the religious institution and its "monopoly" over interpretation of received scripture. For example, the printing press was a major element in
changing the institution of medieval-Renaissance religion.[13] Thus, do institutions determine technical change, or does technical change determine new institutions? The only way to settle or shed light on such questions is the methodology of positive economics, including contemporary
microeconomics, public choice, industrial organization, interest group
economics, and rational behavior.

Sociological Approaches

The long lag between Adam Smith and Gary Becker–inspired work (Azzi and Ehrenberg 1975) on the economics of religion was filled with work on religion by both historians and (especially) sociologists. We have already seen that Max Weber worked on the impact of religious competition (Protestantism)—constituting a preference change—on economic growth at the turn of the last century (1904–1905). The great sociologist Émile Durkheim, the father of sociology already mentioned, began to study the impact of religion and secularism on social order in his 1915 book *The Elementary Forms of Religious Life*. Economic historian Richard H. Tawney challenged Weber's thesis concerning the effects of Protestantism, and historians Henri Pirenne and Ernst Troeltsch analyzed religion within the context of church history in the 1930s. Extremely valuable scholarly work focused on diverse topics such papal finances, medieval banking, and the role of usury in the evolution of the medieval church. Armies of sociologists and historians developed a vast literature on religion with particular emphasis on the development of Roman Catholicism and Protestantism regarding marriage, property, the Inquisition, the Crusades, the Roman Catholic response to Luther, and myriad other issues.

Contemporary sociologists are clearly divided on the issues of rationality, the role of economic methodology, and religion. Many if not most contemporary sociologists freely acknowledge the impact of Gary Becker's insights into the economics of human behavior. Granovetter (1985, 2004) theoretically (but nonformally) joined the neoclassical view of the rational actor with social context.[14] Some (e.g., Ellison and Sherkat 1995) believe that sociology is the "core discipline" to study religion and seek to integrate particular investigations in areas such as community psychology, church history, and theology (as well as economics) into the discussion. Others studies (e.g., Sherkat and Wilson 1995) more closely identify with Becker's views of religion as a rational marketplace with cultural elements affecting choice. One study (Sherkat and Wilson 1995) develops an interesting theory of religious mobility or "switching" within a broadened context of family and organizational variables. But the primary researchers in this area have been sociologists Rodney Stark and William Sims Bainbridge and sociologist/economist Lawrence Iannaccone. Stark, in particular, writing alone and with others (including Iannaccone), has studied the impact of secularization in religion (Stark and Iannaccone 1994), cult formation, fundamentalism, religion and magic, religion and science (2003, chap. 2), and as previously noted, the origins and development of Christianity (1997, 2006).

Stark places the rise of Christianity within a sociological and cultural context but attempts to do so in a scientific manner. He attempts to "identify adequate, quantifiable indicators of key concepts and then to properly test important hypotheses," arguing that "given adequate contexts, testing well-formulated hypotheses through quantitative analysis of adequate indicators will put historical studies of the early church on firmer footing" (2006, 22–23). This approach has not met with universal acceptance. There have been several broad objections. The pushback to his approach has centered around particular allegations he makes relating to the societal elements that had an impact on Christianity's adoption (e.g., Hopkins 1998; Castelli 1998). Other criticisms have been more basic and of a methodological cast (Klutz 1998). While we will take a more direct economic approach in this book, attempting to show how additional economic factors might improve the discussion, we note that Stark and others, who have established the rational and empirical nature of a sociological economics of religious inquiry have, along with the critical work of historians, bolstered the foundation of the economics of religion and had an important impact on our own research.[15]

Monopoly, Rationality, History, and Religion

The vertical integration of the Roman Catholic Church as an evolutionary process was discussed briefly in chapter 1. However, an approach that is useful both as a foundation for analyzing the historical evolution of Christianity and for use as a contemporary predictive tool may be termed a partial or modified wealth maximization hypothesis. This theory, which includes elements of both supply and demand for religious services, analogizes the religious firms as having a market, which supplies "products" that are demanded by individuals on the basis of full price, the price of substitutes, income or wealth, the level of education, including scientific education, and other variables.

The chief elements of economic theory used in explanation and prediction according to this model are the economics of the firm (originated by Hull and Bold 1989), interest group analysis and public choice, industrial organization, the economics of information, and the modern economics of implicit markets (à la Becker). With these tools, sometimes combined with empirical analysis, key moments in the history of Christianity may be described and analyzed. Some of these moments include the incredibly rapid adoption of Christianity within the Roman Empire, the buildup to the medieval monopoly of the Roman Catholic Church about the eleventh century, the medieval monopoly of the Roman Catholic Church, the market entrance of Luther and Protestantism, the evolution of contemporary competitive Christianity, and possible directions that might be taken by Christian religions in the future. But there are dissenters to this view.

The areas of experimental economics and the very modern field of neuroeconomics (Glimcher and Rustichini 2004; Camerer, Loewenstein, and Prelec 2005) have attempted to expand the scope of factors influencing human behavior. Individuals may have very different views on what policies are "fair" (consider the policy prescriptions of the two major political parties in the United States), be unable to calculate probabilities of particular events (whether a stock will go up or down), or have quite different "endowments" in terms of social norms or religious preferences. Thus, behavioral economics, most often emanating from laboratory or classroom experiments, may find apparent anomalies in the prevailing rational approach to economics and to the economics of religion.

Naturally, these studies, as are analyses of the hardwiring of the brain for religion and other behaviors (Newberg, D'Aquili, and Rause 2001), are important, but they are designed for laboratories.[16] As Gary Becker has noted, the economic theory of behavior relates to market, not laboratory, behavior (Becker 2002, 8). The demonstration that preferences are not transitive might be made in a laboratory experiment, but if that held in the real world, an individual could be easily fleeced of her assets. Individuals may not be able to calculate probabilities exactly, but those who must calculate them for a living (actuaries, blackjack dealers) either learn to do so or find other work. Further, while individuals might be behavioral outliers (Mother Teresa. founder of the Roman Catholic Missionaries of Charity who cared for the poor and destitute? Gandhi?), aggregative behavior may yield "rational results." As Becker suggests, "Broader preferences and 'bounded' rationality are part of a more relevant model of rational behavior."[17] Institutions clearly matter and shape individual behavior within such a model. Further, institutions change over time. We therefore hold, presumably with Becker, that culture and institutions matter and that broader preferences and decisions bounded by cultural and other constraints are embedded in decision making.

We do not and cannot argue that churches (e.g., the Roman Catholic Church) always behave as wealth maximizers in the post-Constantine era. Pre-Nicaean sects were unlikely to have been so. Other tools may apply to religious organizations, but they are not much different from those of modern price theory. Sports leagues, labor unions, and political parties have all been analyzed as collectives. These organizations, like religious organizations, are maximizing some objective function that may include wealth.

Conclusion: Economics and Religious Behavior

Our general point concerning behavior is that there is no such thing as "noneconomic" behavior so long as individuals are responsive to changes in relative prices (relative costs and benefits). Religious behavior may be subjected to such tests. When the costs of religious products rise (fall), individuals generally demand less (more) of it, and suppliers supply more (less) of it. It is possible that some individuals (e.g., Mother Teresa or Gandhi) may be completely irresponsive to changes in relative costs and benefits—that is, one may have perfectly inelastic demands for certain types of behavior (at least over the relevant range of the demand curve). And not everyone is necessarily good at rational calculation, and there may be anomalies in behavior. Individuals are in fact complicated, and behavioral economics is studying such forms of behavior. But that does not suggest that the study of religion requires a completely different theory of behavior in order to be productive. In positive terms, in other words, it is clear that an increase in the price of some religious good—ritual or money required of members, for example—will reduce the quantity demanded of it. We argue, therefore, that at least generally, religious behavior follows rational economic principles. In short, it matters not *what* religions actually maximize. Wealth, utility, and saved souls are all possibilities. Our point is that they behave purposely in seeking their goals, even considering a broadened conception of "rationality." An economic approach to human behavior remains a useful and potentially fruitful method of examining the relevant tradeoffs that both organizations (suppliers) and believing individuals (demands) face. A major part of that approach is the definition of the religious product and an analysis of the source of demand for it.

CHAPTER THREE

Economics of Religious Belief

Introduction

The demand for a belief system—a religion, philosophy of life and/or death, or cult-like behavior—is ancient and, for the most part, pervasive in ancient as well as modern societies. Naturally, particular beliefs may be specified and called "religion," but that does little to pinpoint the nature of the religious good let alone how and why that particular product is demanded. An investigation of these two critical matters is the subject of this chapter. In so many respects (but not in all), the demand for religion may be analyzed as one would demand insurance—that is, it would appear to be related to risk and uncertainty. The analogy is extremely attractive, and we use it here, but there are reasons why it is formally inexact, as will also be explained. In addition, as we suggested in chapter 2, an individual's demand for a religious product can be related to cult-like behavior. Sacrifices may be demanded of adherents and stigma may be attached to those who "free ride" on other demanders (Iannaccone 1992). Further, most individuals develop a "stock" of religious capital in the early and youthful years of life, often of an extremely particular type (Roman Catholicism, Mormonism, and so on), so that at least a part of the choice of religious belief at adulthood may be influenced or determined by such habituation (Stigler and Becker 1977). We will, in the present chapter, consider these and other aspects of the demand for belief. First, the nature of the religious good must be specified.

Nature of the Religious Good

How, in the terminology of economics, might the religious good be described and characterized? Of use here is the economic theory of information, developed in the latter part of the twentieth century, which established a tripartite distinction categorizing the nature of goods. Economist George Stigler created the "economics of information" (1961 [1968]) while Nelson (1972, 1974) first argued that goods and services may be divided according to information costs into search and experience goods. In the now-familiar distinction, buyers know the qualities of a search good before (and naturally after) purchase. Experience goods, on the other hand, are those whose qualities are not known or known completely prior to purchase but are readily discernable after purchase. Examples of the former might include restaurants or pharmacies, and of the latter, men's clothing, travel agencies, or carpet cleaning. In an important contribution to this literature, Michael Darby and Edi Karni (1973) identified yet another type of good called "credence goods" (Klein and Leffler 1981). Quality of these goods cannot be determined prior to sale. The exchange of such goods is particularly subject to fraud. The correct and logical conclusion concerning such goods is that they will be the subject of warranties in the form of licensing, money-back guarantees, or many forms of quality assurance. Examples of such goods and services are health services, psychiatry, home security systems, transmission repair, or addiction counseling. In reality, however, these goods—with time and/or resources expended—are actually extreme examples of experience goods. But the quality of such credence goods as tax services, psychiatric counseling, home security systems, or marriage and family counseling—goods or services for which quality assurances or licensing are routinely given—could actually be determined. Over a relatively short run, for example, we might believe a service such as addiction counseling or psychiatry to be "working," but it takes more time to discover its benefits (or failures).

It is obviously impossible to determine the quality of the product either before or after purchase even with an expenditure of time or resources with regard to a product such as "assurances of eternal salvation" or promises of an afterlife. Some acutely ill or injured people claim to have had near death experiences and to have been driven to "the light," but no hard evidence exists on these matters, which may be, after all, neurological in substance.[1] Thus it is the case that no one has returned from Shakespeare's "undiscovered country" with credible evidence to tell tales about what qualities, including its existence, an afterlife might possess. We therefore label such assurances of an afterlife a *meta-credence good*. A metacredence good is one whose qualities—despite warranties or investments in quality-assurance claims—cannot be discerned over the short or (lifetime) long run. No church or religion or claimant of any kind can offer a money-back guarantee to a soul dissatisfied with his or her afterlife experience. Naturally, this fact has not prevented the existence, emergence, and continuous evolution of myriad forms of spiritual belief and religion in thousands of forms, and one major reason for the success of religion is the successful establishment of credence in the metacredence product of an afterlife. Just how is this accomplished? The mechanism is the establishment of an entire *structure of faith* based upon ritual, dogma, rules, and doctrinal imperatives for "right living," creation of physical and personal capital that inspires awe and grandeur, and provision of corporeal products (some jointly supplied) that complement the tenets of faith and many other factors. For example, in most Christian sects, "grace" is a part of the structure of faith—that is, as Thomas Aquinas noted, God's grace is a supernatural gift that helps create corporeal virtue and faith in a world to come. As such, it is a doctrinal imperative and part of the product of most Christian religions.

This extreme in information asymmetry created by the metacredence quality of the afterlife element of the religious good is mitigated by *demanders* as well as suppliers. While neurology and genetic "hardwiring" for spirituality and belief in an afterlife may play a role (Boyer 2001; Newberg, D'Auili, and Rause 2001), factors relating to demand for the religious product also provide credence for the metacredence product offered by religions.[2] Externalities occur when the demands of one individual are affected by the demands and actions of other individuals. Networking technologies in supplying particular goods or services and the so-called superstar effect on demanders (Rosen 1981, which will be explained below) are in the self-interest of each individual who either attaches himself or herself to a network or who recruits individuals into the network. Preferences are shaped by social factors or infrastructure.

More formally, the utility of one consumer in consuming a product or service is a function of the utility obtained by other consumers of that product or service.[3]

This concept has been used in a variety of applications in analyzing the spread and durability of technological innovations and demand behavior such as the telephone or Microsoft software. The utility of one's use of any of these technologies is a function of its use by other consumers. Note that the implications of these technologies are that when a superior technology appears, it will spread due to the consumption externalities effect. While there is a tendency for monopoly markets to emerge in the cases described, superior technologies would be able to compete successfully with earlier ones, just as a new set of religious beliefs may replace established ones. A "competition for the field" could emerge, and other networks could and have materialized in the past.

A more purely *consumption* (rather than technological) effect might be the adoption by an individual of an element of fashion, a composer, a country music singer, or the like. This is the "superstar effect," meaning that there is an extreme consumption externality when an increase in the number of customers or adherents increases the utility of each consumer. My utility for Bach's music or French cinema increases when others demand and consume such products and services. Consumers, for example, can find more people with whom to talk about music and cinema. As a consequence, such markets will be naturally concentrated.

Networking and Establishment of Credence for Religious Goods

The concepts of networking and metacredence may be readily related to the religious good "assurances of eternal salvation." In our categorization of the ultimate religious product, an afterlife, Valhalla, happy hunting grounds, heaven, hell, nirvana, paradise, and so on, we emphasize that some, but not all, of the aspects of religion are explained. Most if not all religious firms are multiproduct firms, and it is important to understand the nature of these characteristics. As a multiproduct firm, the typical modern megachurch offers social services, personal counseling, rituals, recreation, sports, bookstores, cafes, community activities (Boy Scout meetings), and shelter for the poor. Many of these products or services are also supplied in openly competitive markets. Some of these products are search goods—possibly in the form of regular services or bowling activities—or experience goods, such as music performed at services, and ordinary credence goods, such as marriage counseling. But we argue that a principal offering—*solace for the transience of human life with promises of something better to come in return for some worldly costs*—is different from all the other multiple products offered by most religions, including early Christianity. Importantly, one of the primary attractions and products purportedly sold by early Christianity—"social welfare"—was certainly not unique but was produced in competition with other groups (Muir 2006).[4] Naturally, the provision of some nonreligious goods and services may add to the perception of credence of the main product as observed by economic researchers on religion (Eilinghoff 2003), charity, and social welfare certainly being among them.

Assurances of many kinds are typically offered for credence and metacredence goods. In the case of experience or ordinary credence goods, such as auto repair or tax services, money-back or buyback guarantees can be offered. The greater the credence required for purchase (the more "meta-" the credence good), the more massive the investment in assurance must be. The institution of highly ritualized services, including confession of and absolution from sins (mortal and venial), provides assurances for demanders in the Roman Church, as do the existence of educated and sexually abstaining priests.[5] Many of these assurances—some shoring up brand-name capital—come invested with "magical" qualities (Barb 1963). The extensive and pervasive use of relics invested with magic-like properties helped build brand-name capital and provide assurances to demanders and prospective demanders. Bones or severed fingers of saints and apostles, pieces of the True Cross, the tears of the Virgin Mary, and many other objects were (and are) used to provide credence for pilgrim tourists (and monetary returns) in the Middle Ages (Geary 1990). Contemporary Roman Catholic basilicas also contain such relics. Miracles, apparitions, and the "holy places" where they were alleged to have taken place also take on the character of assurances. These pure credence goods supported and continue to support the metacredence aspects of the product sold by the Roman Catholic Church. Physical capital investments of enormous magnitude also can provide assurances of both eternal salvation and commitment on the part of the religion providing them. Medieval cathedrals may be viewed as having provided "awe and grandeur" capital designed to invest demanders with confidence in the dogma and teachings of the medieval church (Bercea, Ekelund, and Tollison 2005). These structures were ocular evidence of the power of the Roman Church's vision of God and the conditions it set down for attaining the ultimate product of religion.[6]

It is important to note how our metacredence characterization of religion helps us understand some of the differences between magic and religion before examining the contracting process for such goods. Magic and religion are of course inseparable. According to one observer, "Magic cannot develop without religion—without the belief in the supernatural—and to that extent it cannot be separated from religion" (Barb 1963). Magic—a belief that some concrete promised occurrence will take place given some act or omen—in fact remains part of religion. The predictions of a soothsayer or palm reader, however, may be called simple credence goods. Whether one will find a lover or have good luck at the blackjack table is, ultimately, a disprovable proposition. Other forms of magic require faith. The doctrine of transubstantiation, through which the wafer host actually becomes the body of Christ in Roman Catholic ritual, or the miracles required in order for sainthood to be bestowed, are sometimes given as examples of magical elements wedded to ritual.[7] These elements, ultimately not provable in a corporeal or positive sense, differ from "rougher" forms of magic but only in degree.[8] But, fundamentally, we argue, magic is a credence good, whereas the principal product of religion—eternal salvation or some facsimile—is a metacredence good, one that no amount of corporeal time and/or resource expenditure can prove or disprove.[9]

There are empirical implications with respect to religious goods and advertising. A metacredence good requires more brand-assuring investments. But in the terms of commerce, we would expect experience or ordinary credence goods to have higher advertising-to-sales ratios. Organized religions would be expected to "advertise" in far higher proportions relative to sales than automobile dealers or cereal companies.

Religion and Faith

Faith in an afterlife and in the promises of Jesus Christ is the ultimate form of credence building. First, there is the matter of the witnesses to the life and miracles of Jesus as told in the New Testament. These miracles (Christ healing the sick, raising Lazarus from the dead, turning water into wine, and so on) were tales of Christ's divinity and his divine powers. But perhaps adding the most credence to Christ's messages and most importantly, to *belief in an afterlife* were his reported appearances after his death. All four of the Gospels adopted at Nicaea and the Acts of the Apostles provide accounts (Matthew 28; Luke 24; John 20–21; Mark 16) of Jesus's resurrection from the dead and his various appearances after death. Thus, accounts of Jesus's appearances include those reported in the New Testament to Mary the mother of Jesus and to Mary Magdalene, to disciples at the "supper at Emmaus," to the eleven disciples on a mountaintop in Galilee when they were told to spread the news, to Peter, to Thomas (the doubter), and in other examples as well.[10] This reportage, written at some distance from the actual events, tells of firsthand witnesses to Christ's divinity and resurrection.

A crucial link in establishing credence in these accounts was the testimony of Paul of Tarsus who was "blinded by the light" on the road to Damascus (Acts 9: 3–9) and converted to Christianity. (We will see in chap. 4 that the role Paul played in the entrepreneurship of Christianity cannot be overestimated.) Paul's account of several eyewitnesses to the resurrection of Christ (1 Cor 15: 3–7) is a key element in the "chain of evidence" of Christ's divinity and promise of an afterlife. Although there is much debate and discussion over the nature of this "chain"—whether the essence of Christianity had been taught to Paul by early Christian forebears or whether it was taught to him by Jesus—the entrepreneurship of Paul and other progenitors of the Christian creed was erected on faith— that is, it was a metacredence good.[11]

Paul and the other disciples of Christ (writing and preaching after Christ's time) had to establish faith as the foundation of the metacredence good of Christianity or the belief in Christ's teaching, which included an afterlife. Paul and the other apostles were not revenue maximizers. Rather, they were membership maximizers. They were given housing and food of course by Christian (and Jewish) communities, but it was belief that motivated them. Faith is motivated on the "demand side," as we will see in the following sections of chapter 3, by demander's risk profile, by the full price (the money price plus the "time price" of ritual) of particular belief systems, by education, by political and personal stability, and by other factors. Entrepreneurship and the development of credibility in a particular belief system (in this case, Christianity) on the "supply side" were provided by apostle-entrepreneurs. They gave witness and thus credibility to Christ's life, death, resurrection, and promises of an afterlife. In this role they were credibility agents. In sum, Peter, Paul, and the other disciple-entrepreneurs were extraordinarily adept at designing a "faith product" that effectively competed with pagan religions and Judaism.

Demands and Contracts for the Religious Good

Standard utility theory in economics supports the notion that choice, including religious choice, is made individually. Most certainly, however, utility functions are interdependent, as has been recognized by a host of economists from Thorstein Veblen (1934 [1899]) to Robert Frank (1985). An individual's utility for a given religion is conditioned, often to a large degree, by his or her "endowments" and constraints—including the environment of institutionalized state religion, the religion of one's parents, the preferences of others about what we do, and so on. Network and "superstar" effects, where there is a joint interest due to additional individuals to communicate and work with, discussed above, also play a role in forming an individual's utility function. Detailed modeling of these effects has not been pushed very far, but there are clearly interdependent aspects of individual religious choices. But, all other influences and costs considered, the individual may be portrayed as making a decision on religious preferences based upon a set of demand determinants including risk. Demand is a function of the full price including time, money and "ritual" costs, education (including the state of science), political and "social" stability, risk, and other factors.[12] We emphasize at the outset that no two individuals—even individuals facing the same price of alternative religious services, education, or similar risk profile—will have *exactly* the same demand for a particular religion or for a set of religious services. While some general product may be offered by a supplier, for example, Roman Catholicism, nuances of belief will obtain among members. The same applies to all religions and religious systems (the same is likely true of atheist beliefs and nonbeliefs).

Following precedent in the literature, our primary focus is on risk associated with "brands" of Christianity, but interdependent utility functions and risk profile are also operative when religions of any kind are monopolized when the state is a theocratic regime. Government-sponsored religion and theocracy are very much like the medieval model of the Roman Catholic Church. For example, one's personal security (job, social standing, and so on) is at stake in some Muslim regimes, and some individuals may find themselves in situations of "forced" rather than voluntary exchange in religious contracting. For such demanders the full costs of recontracting with some other religious supplier are high indeed, as would be, for example, a shift from Islam to Roman Catholicism within a Muslim society (a move from Saudi Arabia to Brazil). However, many of these religions (e.g., Muslims) have evolved into alternative sects or brands with alternative rituals and requirements reflecting different risk profiles. (The same feature applies to modern Judaism.) Naturally, forced exchange, where costs are nearly prohibitive, may take place under theocracies, but there are degrees of state-sponsored religion.[13] Less cult-like state religions such as those in northern and other parts of Europe exhibit low participation rates, reflecting changing risk profiles.[14] In short, while Christianity is the focus of this chapter, risk profile and networking analyses, explained below, would, in fact, apply to other major faith divisions as well.

Demand Determinants in Christianity

The seemingly elusive nature of the product of religion is rendered more concrete when the nature of the primary good sold is identified. While it is undoubtedly correct that all of the non-metacredence goods add substance and temporal credence to the ultimate product, that part of the religious product dealing with assurances of an afterlife or salvation is the primary object that is "purchased" by demanders. We therefore focus in our discussion of risk on afterlife consumption, which is, as identified by Stark (1997, 37), the "essential supernaturalism of all religions." The product, like all others carrying credence (and in our case, metacredence) characteristics, is characterized by risk and uncertainty (which are costs and therefore to be rationally avoided by demanders).[15]

Previous research has established a standard result (and formal models often based on Pascal's wager[16]) that "a rational individual chooses an optimal level of faith to both improve the quality of the afterlife and increase lifetime utility and found that, interpreted in this light, faith has many of the characteristics of insurance" (Durkin and Greeley 1991, 193).[17] Thus we argue, behaviorally, that an individual's rational choice of a brand of assurance has many of the same characteristics as the demand for insurance. Further, following practice in the literature, we argue that an individual's risk preferences are of a similar form to the rational approach to purchasing other products (e.g., a financial portfolio).[18] Choice of the stringency of religious affiliation in this view and the payment of some full price for that affiliation is akin to the risk of an ultimate bad out-come in the afterlife. If individual's *known attitudes* to risk in temporal situations such as financial risk can be related positively to revealed risk determinants in religious choice, we can characterize religious affiliation as being affected by risk aversion. (A pool player may not understand the intricacies of calculus but he plays as if he does). Thus we model the contract between the individual and religious belief as a function of the risk profile of individuals and, underlying this profile, are elements that contribute to the individual's profile and her demand for the degree of religious stringency. As a basis for understanding religious choice and secularism, consider several aspects of religion: the nature of the good, religion and risk profile, and the underlying demand and supply conditions for the religious good.

Traditional means for alleviating risk for such products include insurance, licensing, buyback arrangements, and so on. Selling related products—social services and liturgical music in the case of religious services—may also lend credence to the main product. But the afterlife metacredence good is essentially different from all other goods sold by religions (or self-generated by suppliers). Proof or disproof of an after-life, let alone the quality of it, cannot ever be objectively attained, no matter the quality assurances of auxiliary or related goods. Thus a *contract* must balance the marginal or average cost of risk with the marginal or average benefit of risk mitigation. Just as one takes out insurance against temporal risks of all kinds, an individual will buy assurance against supernatural risk, which is essentially an enhanced probability of a better afterlife outcome.

The full price of that assurance will be equal to the money price plus the time-ritual-doctrinal price for some degree of certainty. Payment of that price will assuage some level of risk by providing a level of certainty. We hypothesize that as the full price of religious participation rises, so does the probability of a good afterlife outcome or assurances against risk for certain believers. There is a positive relation between the probability of a "good" afterlife outcome and the full price of religious services demanded. Further, the amount that demanders of higher probabilities will be willing to pay depends upon their risk profile. We hypothesize that an individual's risk profile may be expressed as a function of a number of variables and that those demanding higher probabilities of afterlife happiness are more risk-averse. Level of risk aversion may be expressed as a function of income, education, age, social cohesion, political stability, and so on. Clearly, income and education are positively related so that as educational levels rise, the level of risk aversion falls. Risk aversion relating to ultimate reward and punishment rises with age and falls with increased social cohesion—tight family units or social networks reduce risk aversion. Naturally, other macroeconomic elements enter an individual's risk profile. Political stability, growth in gross domestic product (GDP), the inflation rate, and a host of other factors affect levels of risk. The usual caveats must be noted, of course. Many of the independent variables explaining risk may be highly correlated.[19] The degree of political stability in a country is a major factor in GDP growth rates, employment levels, and inflation. But the direction of causation in the risk function above is fairly obvious. Also obvious is the stock of religious capital that an individual carries into adulthood (Iannaccone 1995; Becker 1981). Those, for example, who are "cradle Catholics" (Baptists) are presumably more likely to remain Catholic (Baptists) in adulthood, although recent evidence (*Per Forum on Religion and Public Life* 2008, 2009b) appears to suggest that "switching" (from "birth religion" to other or no religion) as well as adopting multiple faiths is rising. Nevertheless, each individual reaches adulthood with some stock of religious capital, and that obviously influences demands for brands of religion.

Traditional-conservative Roman Catholics and Evangelical Christians (both of which are similar in requiring belief in the literal divine authority and inerrancy of scripture—at least as interpreted by church leaders), for example, are in general more risk-averse (less inclined to accept risk), so more certainty applies to their contracts.[20] These individuals, equivalently, seek less variance in outcomes where variance is simply a measure of the range of possible outcomes (positive and negative) around the predicted outcome. (Thus a risk-averse person is less willing to accept the likelihood of a bad result or what is the same thing, will buy a more expensive insurance policy against a negative result).[21] There is without doubt somewhat lower risk for Roman Catholics because an individual can be physically absolved of sin in this life through auricular confession, whereas Evangelical Protestants (like other Protestants) do not have an "intermediary" to validate sinful repentance and provide assurances of salvation (McCleary 2007). However, *traditional-conservative* Roman Catholics and Evangelicals are alike in a crucial respect: The full price that these believers are willing to pay is typically high in ritualistic terms, where ritual includes dogma—beliefs necessary to be a Southern Baptist or a traditional Roman Catholic relating to abortion, sex-related issues like gay rights, strict interpretation of the Bible, and so on. Auricular confession in the Catholic Church, for example, required once a year of all members, provides representation on the seller's side of the contract—giving assurances to the buyer.[22] The numerous interpretative and primarily invented hurdles to attain salvation arising in the medieval and contemporary policies of the traditional Roman and Protestant Evangelical churches give assurance (and more ritual, including mandatory beliefs and practices) to the buyers. Mandatory church attendance, marriage regulations and rules regarding sex, strict or literal interpretations of the Bible, the subordinacy of women, adherence to sacraments, and so on are examples. A higher level of monitoring a commitment is associated with the higher full price. Most mainline Protestants, on the other hand, are charged a lower full price for the supernatural afterlife contract. In contrast to the traditional Roman Catholic–Evangelical contract, these Protestants pay a lower full price. These contracts represent higher levels of risk or less certainty with respect to afterlife outcomes. In the mainline Protestant contract, where "every man is a priest," there are no intermediaries, and faith and good works are ordinarily sufficient. The traditional Roman Catholic hierarchy, on the other hand, creates uncertainty and risk by emphasizing, more in some periods than others, hell and damnation to help create fear, uncertainty, and risk to collect rents. (Examples of the latter are provided below.) Evangelicals are more difficult to categorize in this regard though it seems clear that such individuals opt for more certainty and a higher full price in their religious contracts.

Risk, Uncertainty, and Contract Details

Fundamentally, religious contracts are agreements with both formal and explicit provisions for the path to heaven. As economist Oliver Williamson (1975) argued, however, there are formal and informal elements to all contracts. Problems arise when there is an inability to specify actions or contingency claims in contracts. For example, in the standard Roman Catholic contract, certain actions or adherences are clear—observing the Ten Commandments, adherence to marriage regulations, observance of the sacraments, and so on. Thus, a formal requirement for Catholics is to be baptized. But the contract is informally filled out as well. The observance of the commandment "thou shall not" kill" is not formal or lit-

eral. Some churches interpret the commandment in nonliteral fashion
when self-defense or a "just war" is involved. This, for example, is the
manner in which the so-called Holy Crusades, chiefly against Muslims,
heretics, and any enemies of the *Roman* Church were undertaken in the
early Middle Ages in efforts to maintain its monopoly. The ambiguity of
an unfilled contract may lead to opportunistic behavior on the part of
buyers and/or sellers. The church—claiming the right to interpret holy
writings—can and does manipulate demanders by filling out details that
provide revenues. The history of the church is replete with such examples.[23] And, on the demanders' side, the church has at times taught that
members should, within strictly defined limits, let their consciences be
their guide to behavior vis-à-vis attainment of the afterlife. While this
reduces the latitude exercised by the seller, it allows demanders, both in
the Middle Ages and in contemporary practice, to "fill out" the incomplete or implied part of the contact. The important point is that, in addition to fixed rules promulgated by the papacy, a *degree* of uncertainty is
built into all religious contracts—with attendant levels of risk aversion—
and that a higher full price may be exacted from demanders for higher
levels of probability of the "good" afterlife outcome.

Demanders will consider a risk-adjusted rate of return when purchasing a contract for religious assurances of eternal salvation. As we have
noted, the willingness to pay a high full price means that the risk profile
of the demander contains risk aversion, and the buyer will purchase a
contract with more certainty. These contracts will likely contain a good
deal of ritual with detailed explicit and implied rules and regulations
with the monopoly over scriptural interpretation being left to the supplier of the religious good. Credence is established through performance
of rituals, through elaborate church services, through "testimonials" of
other adherents, and so on. Free rider problems—involving individuals
who do not "pay up" for membership and its privileges—are mitigated in
collectively provided religious goods in the manner described by Iannaccone (1992) by required rituals, contributions, and so on.

Many traditional and mainline Protestant providers offer lower-priced
religious services to demanders with less risk-averse profiles.[24] These
services—where every man is his own priest—do not require intermediaries to provide assurances of attainment of the ultimate good. The low
price, however, is accompanied with less certainty in outcomes. The ratio
of the formal part of the religious contract to the implicit part is low for
these Christians. Such contracts typify the liberal wings of many contem-

porary traditional Protestant churches, including most of the Episcopal Church in the United States and the United Church of Christ. The solace required for such demanders of assurances comes at low cost.

One might speculate that contracts with the lowest full cost of all are self-generated contracts. Surveys always contain persons who self-identify as "no religion" or "spiritual but not a member of a formal religion" or "Christian but not a member of a church." These individuals create their own theology, a characteristic of some ultraliberal churches as well. ("Create your own theology" has been, for example, an *actual* advertisement of the Universalist Unitarian church in Auburn, Alabama.) These individuals—said, in some survey polls, to be a growing number—are the least risk-averse of all. Full price, quite literally, is self-imposed.

Risk, Uncertainty, and Return: A Theoretical Perspective

These observations may be expressed in the simple terms of risk preference and return. From an individual's perspective, there is a trade-off between the average rate of return and risk. Higher risk must be associated with higher mean rates of return.[25] Assuming a continuous spectrum of religious choices, alternative risk and return scenarios are provided. Over the relevant spectrum of alternatives, risk (variance) is positively related to the rate of return. Decision makers must be compensated to take more risk, which is a "bad" from their point of view. A highly (perfectly) risk-avoiding individual will adopt highly ritualized and fundamentalist religions or cults. Alternatively, those willing to take on greater risk will align themselves with traditional Christian faiths and with more "philosophical" forms of spirituality and religion. In the limit, some individuals will "self-spiritualize"—for example, those claiming to be Christian or "spiritual" but who belong to no formal church or religion. In the most extreme case, some individuals such as confirmed atheists will not consider such "choices" at all.

In terms of religious belief, we hypothesize that traditional-conservative Roman Catholics and those belonging to other highly ritualistic and rule-driven churches and cults will prefer greater certainty with less risk. This assurance comes with a higher full price. Conversely, traditional or mainline Protestants adhering to more liberal creeds are risk takers who choose a religious contract with a lower full price and greater risk. The interpretive monopoly of the Roman Catholic and

Evangelical religions promise "heaven" if particular requirements are met and rituals kept and "hell and damnation" if they are not. Auricular confession clears the member to go straight to heaven. The promise of heaven comes with very explicit conditions and requirements. Like the risk-adverse investor, the prototypical traditional Catholic hires a "broker" (Merrill-Lynch) to provide definite assurances (an investment portfolio). Traditional or mainline Protestants and, increasingly, more liberal "cafeteria Catholics," on the other hand, typically in possession of more human capital, seek heavenly salvation and bliss more on their own *through some spiritual or philosophical system.* If "every man is his or her own priest," temporal assurances of heaven are largely self-administered. There is an enhanced risk (variance) but also a higher mean rate of return. Just as those willing to take on more risk in investing (using E*TRADE and other direct investment devices), liberal Protestants will manage (to a greater or lesser extent) their religious "portfolios."[26] Thus we would expect a whole spectrum of religious suppliers giving assurances of salvation with different risk and return tradeoffs. Individual demands, in effect, compare risk-adjusted full price when choosing a religion. That means that the full price of participation—time, ritual, and doctrinal costs plus the monetary costs, discounted by the degree of variance—is the determinant of religious choice by demanders. This analysis applies to cults and small sects as well. As Iannaccone (1992) suggests, ritual is a method of stemming the free rider problem in sects such as the Branch Davidians, but there is yet another reason for ritual. It is to reduce uncertainty of demanders, as we suggest above. Members pay a higher full price for greater assurances, such as the Mormon ladder to heaven.[27]

The analogy of religious choice to risk in financial markets, while apt in many respects, is not perfect. An investor can make finely tuned and continuous choices in adjusting her portfolio in risk-return space. While this is true for financial markets, it certainly does not hold for systems of religious belief. In a modern setting, religious markets in the West generally offer a wide variety of risk-return trade-offs among which individuals can choose, but compared to financial markets, the number of alternatives is more restricted. There is undoubtedly a very wide variety of choices in religious belief, especially when one considers "[non]cafeteria Christians, Jews, and so on," but continuity as in financial choices may not be a perfect analogy to such choices. Clearly, however, an individual will choose—*given all of the elements that determine her risk profile*—to obtain a higher return with less risk. This means that given their preferences, conservative Catholics and Evangelicals will opt for a variety of belief (religion) that carries a higher probability of the "good" afterlife outcome with a higher full price, and traditional Protestants will choose another alternative with a lower full price. This analysis no doubt simplifies the process of religious choice, but it is sufficient to illustrate how risk and full price play out in the choice among religious alternatives. Unlike financial markets, the choice of a religious contract is personal and subjective, and the choice set facing individuals cannot be directly observed.[28]

Risk Aversion and the Historical Introduction of Christianity

A theory that highlights risk profile of demanders also helps explain the "shift" from Roman (pagan?) gods to Christianity. Consider this shift with respect to risk before addressing the switch in detail in chapters 4 and 5. The astonishing fact was the rate of its adoption. Given both Christian and non-Christian sources, Hopkins (1998, 191, fig. 1) calculates a 3.35 percent annual growth rate from 40 to 350 CE. Hopkins's estimates are shows in table 3.1.

Stark provides similar statistical estimates showing that from 250 CE to 350 CE Christians in the population rose from about 2 percent to 56 percent of the Roman Empire (Stark 1997, 7, table 1.1). There are varying explanations for this growth (some of them taken up in later chapters). Stark (1997) argues that the initial adoption of Christianity took place not exclusively or mainly among the "poor" or low-class Romans. Rather, it was the upper and upper-middle classes that led the way. According to Stark, some people are more attuned to the weaknesses of con-

TABLE 3.1. **Growth in Number of Christians, 40 CE to 350 CE**

Year	Number of Converts	Year	Number of Converts
40 CE	1,000	200 CE	210,000
50 CE	1,400	246 CE	1,000,000
100 CE	7,400	250 CE	1,100,000
109 CE	10,000	300 CE	6,000,000
150 CE	40,000	315 CE	10,000,000
178 CE	100,000	350 CE	32,000,000

Source: Hopkins (1998, 191, fig 1).

ventional faiths than others. He notes: "[A]s the rise of modern science caused difficulties for some traditional Christian teachings, this was recognized sooner by more educated people. In similar fashion, as the rise of Greek and Roman science and philosophy caused difficulties for pagan teachings, this too was noticed by the educated [citing deVries 1967]. To state this as a proposition: Religious skepticism is most prevalent among the more privileged" (1997, 37). Others do not provide this emphasis. MacMullen (1984) argues persuasively that the poor and middle classes were converted more by the appeal of and credence in miracles, fear of what happened after death, and the provision of temporal advantages. The audience of the apostle-entrepreneurs "were and should have been scared half to death. Divine power had a terrifying, high-voltage quality that split and blinded. There might be some fate even worst to come, beyond the grave" (1984, 27). Conversely, in Stark's conception, the poor seek more authoritarian religions when religions become "too worldly" (1997, 38). Both analyses—that Christianity's adoption as a low-to-middle-class or as a middle-to-upper-class movement—fit well with our risk-based analysis of religious choice.

We are in full agreement with elements of these analyses of the adoption of Christianity, but we would add that economic notions of risk aversion, self-insurance, and full price also play a helpful part in analyzing this fundamental "gods shift." Higher levels of education, almost always associated with higher incomes, influenced the risk profile of Roman citizens in a predictable manner. Wealthier families might have had access to more information than poorer ones, a networking effect. But there was much more that could have affected risk, especially in poorer segments of Roman society. The instabilities of dictatorship and rule by the "barrack emperors" must have created a great deal of uncertainty that affected the full relative price of a movement to Christianity. The security offered by the "family" of Christian adherents in the face of political and social adversity lowered the full price of Christian adherence as emphasized by MacMullen. Instabilities introduced by the breakdown of the Roman Empire altered the risk profile of Christian adherents in other ways as well. The lack of an effective system of law and property ultimately, under Constantine (reigning 306–337 CE), gave way to the redress from Roman law to the court of a Christian bishop (in 318). The sheer number of Greek and Roman gods—a pantheon that had already competed successfully with Hebraic notions—numbered in the hundreds.[29] Major deities included Jupiter (master of the gods), Mars (war), Minerva (wisdom), Juno (fertility), Venus (love), and thousands of "household gods" such as those of one's ancestors (*lares*). (This system roughly parallels the costly and confusing complexity of Roman Catholic religion in the sixteenth century when Protestantism successfully entered the Christian market.)[30] Ritual and dogma associated with even the main Roman gods became so complex as to become unbelievable. It is important to remember that an individual's risk profile cannot be identified by considering such factors as education and income alone. Two individuals of the same levels of income and education may have very different demands for a type of religion due to different factors entering their risk profile. (Unstable government and economic crises may affect individual's risk profiles in very different ways, for example.)

The rapid spread of Christianity is additionally explainable in the context of network effects whether among the poor, middle, or upper classes. There were clear economies of scale in the provision of Christianity. A common and simple belief structure—one featuring monotheism relative to polytheism—provided religious services at lower cost. The contract between demanders and suppliers was easier to understand. One set of rules prevailed instead of the multiplicity of pagan forms of belief. While even primitive forms of religion (in early anthropological terms) contemplated forms of an afterlife, Christians were offered a clear promise of an afterlife within a common catechism and far simpler ritual. Behavioral norms were established with one set of rules providing assurances of eternal salvation. There were, in the terms of contemporary economics, network externalities involved in the adoption of such normative principles. It is certainly the case that early "heresies" within Christianity existed, many of them within a monotheistic framework.[31] It is equally certain that many competing forms of Christian belief characterized the first three hundred years of Christianity. But that competition was ended in large part in 325 at the Council of Nicaea, called by the emperor Constantine against the so-called Arian heresy (which denied the divinity of Jesus). The rapid adoption of Christianity was in large part the result of network or "superstar" effects (Rosen 1981) whereby one's utility from a belief system was increased when others adopted the same set of beliefs. In short, a changing risk profile coupled with a lower price for Christian religion are powerful factors in explaining the "gods shift" from Roman paganism to Christianity.

Conclusion: Focus on First-Millennium Christianity

There has been perhaps a natural tendency for writers interested in the risk-adjusted demand for religion to focus on the history of Christianity. It is, for one thing, demonstrably, along with Judaism and Hinduism, one the world's longest-running institutions, providing a 2,000-year laboratory wherein a fairly consistent structure of belief prevailed (and continues to prevail) throughout the functioning Western world. Since we are and have been interested in the theoretical personification and evolution of Christianity from the High Middle Ages and onward (Ekelund et al. 1996; Ekelund, Herbert, and Tollison 2006), a historical approach to first-millennium developments is highly appropriate. Our personification of the Roman Catholic Church as a developing firm enables us to use the principles of markets, rational choice, and most especially, industrial organization and a theory of evolving monopoly to analyze its impact and to examine the acquisition of market power. The major device for the acquisition of market power was the development of a vertically integrated firm—one where the *upstream* elements (the Roman papacy and bureaucracy) directed behavior and dictated theology and its interpretation to the *downstream* or "retail" elements of the church (monasteries, parish priests, and so on). That power reached an apogee over the early and High Middle Ages only to be faced with competition since the early sixteenth century. But, to the best of our knowledge, there has been no economic investigation or explanation of how that effectual monopoly was achieved. This book examines the contribution of economic concepts to our understanding of the development of Christianity from its inception in the first and second centuries CE through the final attainment of monopoly power in the tenth and early twelfth centuries. Armed with the economics of industrial organization and monopoly "business strategy," we attempt to show when and how a small cult came to dominate Western culture and governments by 1100 CE, creating and maintaining a belief system that exists up to the present day.

CHAPTER FOUR

Entrepreneurship, Networking, and the Success of Early Christianity

Introduction

One seemingly amazing fact concerning early Christianity was its rapid *rate of adoption* from a tiny sect to dominance over the Roman Empire in a bare three hundred years, as we saw in the previous chapter. This conversion process was primarily based on voluntary and not forced choice, which characterized some conversions over the later first millennium. In other words, in a bare three centuries, a small religious movement developed into a nascent monopoly that began to dominate the empire that once sought to destroy it. Analyses of this remarkable phenomenon have been, almost exclusively, within the perspective of the areas of history and sociology, with sociologist Rodney Stark pioneering the discussion integrating sociology and economics (1997). The economics of religion and the input of economists in analyzing religious phenomena have, of course, spread over the past several decades. However, to the best of our knowledge, economists have not ventured into the study of the *origins* of Christianity. Thus, the central purpose of this chapter is threefold: (1) to initiate an integration of the economic theories of entrepreneurship and networking with sociological and historical analyses of the initial spread of Christianity; (2) to relate these developments to historical Christianity, and (3) to present some (admittedly crude) statistics showing how Saint Paul played an important role in this spread.[1]

Economic Analysis and Early Christianity

We assume the demand for some religion—very broadly defined to include both a belief system and "spirituality"—as axiomatic and determined by the factors discussed in chapter 3.[2] The form of that demand from an economic perspective is entirely dependent on the risk profile of the individual. As with all other goods, "quantity demanded" is a function of full price. A person's risk profile will depend on a number of factors. Specifically, such factors as higher incomes, higher levels of education (clearly correlated), social and political conditions, the level of scientific knowledge, and psychological profiles will determine the form of religion an individual chooses. A "stock" of religious capital built in childhood for some and over time will also have an impact on current religious choice. Demands in the ancient world and in third-world countries in the contemporary world primarily will be centered on Evangelical, ritualistic religions (see, e.g., Gill 1998). Myth and magic are often associated with these religions. Advanced world demands for religious products are composed, but certainly not exclusively, of traditional, more philosophical, and less ritualistic forms of religion.[3] When these demand "shifters" change—risk reassessment due to changes in income, scientific knowledge, education, and so on—so does the form of religion demanded, sometimes leading to schism within particular forms of faith.[4]

Christianity and Afterlife Consumption

The religious environment existing at the time of the arrival of Christ and Christianity must be understood in order to appreciate the *major advantage* of the new religion—a simpler and elaborated monotheism and, most importantly, credible promises or assurances of eternal salvation.[5] Consider Judaism, a monotheistic religion that had successfully competed with pagan religions for more than a millennium. Judaism actually enjoyed a privileged position within the Roman Empire. According to Ferguson (2003, 429), "the Jews were an ancient people with a traditional religion, had been allied with Rome during the Maccabean age, and had rendered important assistance to Roman leaders such as Julius Caesar. Consequently, the Jews had free exercise of their religion and were exempted from worshiping the deities of the Roman state. They could regulate life within their own communities by their law." Thus, Judaism would seem to have been a formidable competitor to the emerging Christian cult, a cult that, of course, had its origins within Judaism.

But there were several problems. The first is that it was extremely difficult to define a Jew. Some were greatly influenced philosophically by Hellenistic culture, while others remained "Palestinian" in orientation. Judaism was a multifaceted phenomenon and, while unified in the eyes of Romans and certainly in the perspective of history, contained a multiplicity of doctrine and theologies. However, Jews were generally accepted, both occupationally and throughout the social classes of Roman society (naturally, until later problems emerged in Jerusalem in the first century), and were left alone to worship their own god without the necessity of obeisance to official pagan forms of worship. The advantages of pagan cults, both public and private, therefore, must have been a lower cost, including the lower cost of approbation by the state, to membership. Complex Jewish rituals, common to all of the Jewish "product offerings," including circumcision and dietary restrictions, could be avoided. Nor was Judaism evangelical in nature or actively trying to expand its members through missionary work.

In terms of Christian competition, Christians also espoused a monotheistic conception of God, which would have put them at a competitive parity with the Jews. But there are other factors to consider. The "costs" of becoming Christian, under the initial teaching of Saint Peter would have been adherence to Jewish laws and practices. Although this requirement changes, as we will see later in this chapter, the same costs would apply to would-be Christians in the early period in the nexus of Palestinian Christianity. But yet another critical advantage of Christian over Jewish belief has been brought forward. According to Hopkins (1998, 216):

> Christianity was different from all religions of the Roman world. Like Judaism, it was (or claimed to be) monotheistic. Like Judaism, it was exclusivist, in the sense that its leaders claimed that believers in the one true god could not, or would not, pay homage to any other god. Unlike Judaism after the de-

struction of the Temple [70 CE], Christianity was dogmatic and hierarchical; dogmatic, in the sense that Christian leaders from early on claimed that their own interpretation of Christian faith was the only true interpretation of the faith, and hierarchical in that leaders claimed legitimacy for the authority of their interpretation from their office as priests or bishops.

It is not that Judaism did not claim that their individual interpretations were the only ones that were "right." It was the case that they came to believe that truth was elusive and consisted in the interactions between competing views of theology. The Jewish sects, in short, agreed to disagree. Not so with the Christians who, as we will see in chapter 5, would not ultimately tolerate diversity of belief. This dogmatic rigidity, created forcefully within the fourth century, made Christianity a consolidated and powerful force for governments as well as a central competitive device against other Christian sects and against all other competitors, including the Jews. Before turning to what we consider the major competitive advantage and cost-lowering, risk-reducing device of Christianity over all competitors (a "filled out" and well-defined afterlife), let us briefly consider pagan competition.

An enormous diversity existed with pagan cults and "public religion," including forms of monotheistic paganism.[6] Like most early temple societies, Roman polytheistic religion was intimately tied to the state. Hellenistic and Roman society always sought a *pax deorum*—a peace as opposed to the anger of the gods, which had ill effects on Roman society. There was a communal concept of worship that was nonexclusive—there was no contradiction in adhering to a multiplicity of gods both in "civic" and personal cults. Polytheistic Greek and Roman gods had already competed successfully with Hebraic notions *that were monotheistic* but did not promise clearly defined or promulgated eternal salvation. But multideity religions created enormous transactions costs for believers— every god had his or her set of rules, mostly related to propitiation, and it must have been difficult to maintain knowledge of them and their rituals and to behave accordingly. It may be the case that little was demanded from adherents from each god in the worship of a "set of gods" vis-à-vis Christianity, but the *net* benefits—a well-defined afterlife included—of Christianity were higher, making adoption of Christianity lower priced. We assert, therefore, that the average costs of Roman religion to adherents or potential adherents (polytheists) were higher than for the new

Christian monotheists when benefits are considered. The Jews blunted their monotheistic advantage with costly rituals.

The assumption that all Roman cults were "disorganized" and "niche firms" (to use Stark's phrase) and that Christianity was concentrated and spread through social networking and generating collective goods for members has been shown to be false in the case of Mithraism (Beck 2006, 238–240), a cult sometimes thought to be related to ancient Zoroastrianism. That cult generated commitments and adherence largely through some of the same means as Christianity. While a good deal of ambiguity surrounds the cult, its iconography appears to center on a cosmic concept of the movement of the sun from solstice to solstice, the analogy being the continuity of preexistence, birth into humanity, and ultimately, the entry of the soul into the afterlife. The point is that the continuous life of the soul as guided by some extraterrestrial god is analogous to the Christian conception.[7] According to Beck (2006), the spread and level of commitment revealed in documents related to Mithraism represent, in all essential elements such as the production of collective goods and a crude concept of an "afterlife" (see next section)— contrary to Stark's analysis—a credible alternative to Christianity and a "full-service" religion. We will see, however, that in at least one crucial respect such pagan cults were not able to compete with the Christian theological message regarding an afterlife.

Ritual and dogma associated with the primary Hellenistic-Roman gods were, as has been suggested, mainly political. Roman leaders often used religion to promote political aims of the state, not unlike the policies of certain contemporary societies.[8] The Roman leader was the original *pontifex maximus*—a title later adopted by the bishops of Rome. In addition to the worship of and offerings to the temple gods, which were presided over by official priests and their bureaucracy, were the augurs— another retinue of official and *politically appointed* priests and "diviners" with lifetime tenure.[9] These groups of spiritually connected priests, augers, and portends constituted interest groups, sometimes wielding enormous power within government throughout most of Roman history. The important connection between gods and the state did not preclude many kinds of tolerance. Problems arose, in general, only when new and/ or competing religions threatened the authority or security of the Roman state in times of political instability, the Jews and Christians (before 150 CE especially) for much of the time, being exceptions.[10]

Differentiating the Product and Higher Net Benefits:
The "Afterlife Difference"

All religions produce multiple products. Social services, temporal solace, medical services, festivals, and all kinds of eleemosynary activities are often included with the sale of religious services. (Contemporary suppliers in megachurches often go much further, providing bowling alleys, clothing stores and the like.) We argue, however, that there was but one essential product of the Christian religion at its inception—*the promise of a well-defined, promulgated afterlife in return for specified beliefs and behavior with mortal assurances of eternal salvation.*[11] While promises of an afterlife were not unique to Christianity, at that time or later, we believe that the *critical emphasis* on it was the fundamental product change that led to its rapid adoption.[12] Images produced by firsthand and later observers of the "second coming" of Christ and of the resurrection of the faithful accompanied burial in the Roman catacombs. Along with a simplified monotheism, Christ's vision of an afterlife—eternal peace and happiness within a beatific communion with God—achievable given fairly specific particular behavior and belief upon earth—was the *price-lowering effect* needed to successfully proselytize Jews, Gentiles, and pagans alike.[13]

Competitors of the earliest and later Christianity, including some Jews and pagans, entertained conceptions of an afterlife, as did most societies and belief systems. And small wonder. The populations of ancient worlds were made up of about 30 percent each of men and women with about 40 percent children of both sexes. Infant mortality was extremely high and, according to Hopkins (1998, 203), "roughly speaking, half of those surviving to the age of fifteen, died by the age of fifty. Sickness and death, and presumably the fear of death, were pervasive. Hence, crudely speaking, the significance and appeal of immortality." But the link between belief, risk-aversion, and religious adherence could only be bridged by particular promises within some religious system. Christianity was not the only sect to provide assurances, but we will argue that it was the only one to do so effectively.

Judaism was divided into several theological groups at the time of Christ and the rise of Christianity. Most important were the Pharisees (upon which much of modern Judaism is built), but there were other groups as well, including the Sadducees and the Essenes (the Dead Sea sect).[14] The Pharisees, unlike the other groups, *did* adhere to a conception of an afterlife in addition to the oral law given to Moses and the written law (Torah), the latter being open to interpretation. The oral tradition was written into the Talmud, which contains no mention of an afterlife.[15] However, the Pharisees, being drawn from the "common people," did believe in an afterlife in which the good and righteous would be rewarded and the guilty punished. Resurrection was anticipated, and it was a physical resurrection in common with Christianity, but the more precise nature of the next world is an empty set filled with folktales (Telushkin 1991).[16] These concepts, while part of Jewish custom (if not writings), failed to keep Christian schism from the Pharisees. They were unspecific in nature, for one thing , and, later, in the early Christian entrepreneurial period, they would have required Gentiles to undergo the costs of conversion to Judaism.

Types of afterlife consumption were highlighted in both early polytheistic temple societies (as it was in some Jewish sects) and in Hellenistic-Roman religions. The Egyptian pantheon of gods was specifically ruled by gods relating to death, contemplating an afterlife that bore clear parallels to existing life. Indeed, an entire society and culture was built upon this edifice. In early Hellenistic-Roman religions a common view was that the dead continue in pursuit of the same activities in which they engaged on earth. In Homeric legend, heroes in life continued to be heroes in death, but all were but a shadow of their former existence, with no future reward or punishment. The views of Plato, according to Ferguson (2003, 249–250), were passed to some Romans and (later) constituted the essence of Dante's exploration of the journey of the soul:

> The celestial world became the home of the virtuous, whose spirits arose through the planetary spheres to the Supreme Being to dwell in luminous bliss, and the netherworld became the abode of the wicked, who were cast down to subterranean darkness in order to suffer eternal chastisement. An intermediate purgatory [later reinvented by the medieval church] provided a posthumous purification for those stained with pardonable transgressions. The bliss of the righteous was commonly depicted under one of three images: repose or rest, a celestial banquet, or the vision of God. The threefold division of the universe and of souls was transmitted by antiquity to the Christian Middle Ages, providing the framework for Dante's *Divine Comedy*.

Among ancient belief systems, only the Zoroastrians believed in the resurrection of the body, with vague indications of the process. Thus, most pagan Roman religions contemplated "otherworldly" gods, but it was not a well-defined and *promulgated* afterlife. A labyrinthine mythology developed around a pantheon of gods with fate and fortune guiding human activities. A clear belief in the "spirits" of the departed and, occasionally an afterlife is affirmed on Roman tombs and grave markers (Warrior 2006, 36–37).[17] And, importantly, a kind of philosophical afterlife was contemplated by many Roman savants. According to Cicero (*On the Laws* 2.22), "The rights of the gods of the dead shall be sacred. Consider dead kinsfolk as gods" (quoted in Warrior 2002, 31). But the Stoic view of Seneca the Younger (*Letters* 54.1–7, quoted in Warrior 2002, 159), who committed suicide rather than endure Nero's insanity, encapsulates the form of atheistic belief among most Romans:

> I myself have long tested death. When, you ask. Before I was born. Death is non-existence. I already know what that is like. What preceded me will succeed me. If there is any suffering in this condition, there must also have been suffering before we came into the light of day. But we felt no discomfort then. I ask you, wouldn't you say that it is the height of folly to think that a lamp was in worse state when it was extinguished than before it was lighted? We mortals are also extinguished and lighted. In the intervening period we suffer, but on either side there is a deep freedom from anxiety (*securitas*).

These existential observations were common among the literate and "philosophical" class of Romans, by Lucretius, for example, but there were exceptions to this concept of immortality. Several cults, including the ancient Rosicrucians, adhered to belief in forms of afterlife. The Mithraists, according to the evidence adduced by Beck (2006, 240–241), sold an "afterlife good" that involved a kind of cosmic soul travel without resurrection. In his response to Stark, who regarded belief in an afterlife as "the ultimate religious good" produced by Christianity, Beck argues that the "Mithras firm undeniably dealt in it, namely, the reward of 'victory over death' or 'eternal life,' which cannot be attained in the present secular order" (2006, 241), but admits that Mithraists were less efficient and ambitious sellers of their collective good.

We doubt this comparison between the pagan "afterlife" and the one promised in Christian religion, although Stark is not strictly correct to claim it unique to Christianity. For example, contrast these obscure, highly philosophical, agnostic, or atheistic views of an afterlife in the Ro-

man tradition with the promises of Jesus Christ, buttressed by a long history of Jewish monotheism. The *essence of the new religion* was that "He
who believes in Me shall never die" (John 11:26) and that "There are
many mansions in my Father's house" (John 14:2). The earthly full price
for salvation (a well-defined afterlife with maximum personal utility) was
respect for the Beatitudes, obeying the Ten Commandments, and following the interpretative admonitions of early apostolic entrepreneurs along
with the ritual that came to be attached to Christian worship (see, e.g.,
John 27–29). Christianity presented *a clear and certain link between human behavior and the specific rewards or punishment for that behavior.*
That "assurances of eternal salvation" is the essence of the Christian religion can hardly be doubted. Consider Psalm 16: 9–11: "Therefore my
heart is glad and my tongue rejoices; my body also will rest secure, because you will not abandon me to the grave, nor will you let your Holy
One see decay. You have made known to me the path of life; you will fill
me with joy in your presence, with eternal pleasures at your right hand."
Or Matthew 25: 32: "All the nations will be gathered before him, and he
will separate the people one from another as a shepherd separates the
sheep from the goats." Some of Christ's last words were to the thief cru-
cified at his side—"Today you will be with me in paradise" (Luke 23:43).

These promises suffuse the message of Christ, offering hope, greater
utility, eternal life with Jesus (and God and the Holy Spirit), and a lower
full price to religious adherents of Christianity.[18] *Credence, underscored
by faith in these promises, including bodily resurrection, was central and
integral to being a Christian.* Furthermore, there were clear economies
of scale in the provision of Christianity. A common and simple belief
structure provided religious services at lower cost. The contract between
demanders and suppliers was easier to understand. One set of simple
rules—far less costly in money or time—prevailed instead of the multiplicity and complicated forms of pagan belief.[19] While even (in early anthropological terms) primitive forms of religion contemplated forms of
an afterlife, Christians were offered a clear *promise* of an afterlife as
the central tenet of religion within a common catechism and far simpler
ritual. Behavioral norms were established with one set of rules providing assurances of eternal salvation. The relative simplicity of one god
and one set of doctrines under the umbrella of ultimate salvation in an
afterlife offered Jews, Gentiles, and Hellenistic-Roman pagans a product at a lower *risk-adjusted* price. Particular demographics underscore

the high risk aversion in such populations (see Hopkins 1998, 203, citing Coale and Demeny 1966). Thus, the risk-adjusted full price of Christianity must have been low for many in the Roman nexus.[20]

Entrepreneurship: Proselytizing the New Religion

The Acts of the Apostles in the New Testament outlines the progress of Christianity from the time of Christ's death and resurrection (33 CE), but it does not explain its rapid spread. Paul's letters (from Acts) are evidence of Christianity's spread during the late 30s and 40s. There is some evidence that Christians were in Rome by the time of Claudius's reign (41–54 CE). According to Suetonius (Claudius 25 quoted in Warrior 2006, 123), Claudius tried to expel the Jews "because the Jews were constantly causing disturbances at the instigation of one Chrestus" (presumably, "Jewish" disciples of Christ). Nero indisputably placed the blame on Christians (probably regarded by Romans as another Jewish sect) for the burning of Rome in 64 CE. (Simon Peter was among those executed.) In short, Christian entrepreneurs were engaging in proselytizing during the period in Rome and in many parts of the Roman world.

Stark identifies a movement that he attributes to a "Christian Difference" (2006, 7). That difference in part relates to particular advantages that Christian monotheism has over Jewish monotheism. Pagan converts to Judaism had not only to become monotheists but to adopt Jewish ethnicity and lifestyle—Mosaic laws regarding diet, and circumcision, among other rituals.[21] Stark believes that this was a limiting factor in conversions from paganism to Jewish monotheism. Christianity, to Stark, was thus more inclusive and credible as a monotheistic creed.[22] Without doubt, the first Christians were mainly Jews and pagan Romans, but the requirements for conversion to Christianity were filled with discord and even acrimony. Paul and Peter carried on a debate over whether individuals had to become Jews in order to become Christians (a costly process). In the end Paul's position—that direct conversion was possible for Gentiles—won the day.

We agree with Stark concerning inclusiveness and credibility but go further to view early Christianity in somewhat more concrete economic terms. Specifically, how and why did the new religion spread? Economic entrepreneurship is ordinarily cast in terms of market exchange of particular goods and services, not in terms of people. Entrepreneurs are individuals who are alive to the potential of *moving resources from less-valued to more-valued uses*, as outlined by economist Israel Kirzner (1973). Kirzner's view of entrepreneurs creating value by shifting resources applies to religious services as well. Christian missionaries—*religious* entrepreneurs—were able, using Christ's teachings and faith in them, to offer a new and unique product to demanders, establishing credibility in the Christian product. Certainly, the religious products prior to Christ were heterogeneous except, of course, for Jewish monotheism.[23] Gods demanded many different types of rituals and participation from the faithful, and priests were effective suppliers, inventing ritualistic and propitiatory forms of observance themselves.[24] Similarly, when Paul, Peter, and the other apostles "preached the Gospel," broadly conceived to comprise *individual interpretation* of Christ's message, they outlined a *new* product offering to demanders. As such, they "discovered" a demand for monotheism *with a well-defined Christian afterlife*.

After Christ's time but before Constantine, the forms of market competition, both Christian and pagan, changed, and products were quite broadly differentiated. But the Christian forms—while certainly not agreeing on a clear doctrinal base—all included both beliefs in Christ and in the afterlife he promised. Official separation of the "heretical" from the "orthodox" did not finally occur until the Council of Nicaea (325 CE), but product differentiation was a clear characteristic of Christian religious competition between the time of the first apostles and the reign of Constantine. In addition, *exclusivity*, in which belief in Christian religion necessarily excluded belief in any and all other gods, was a requirement of being Christian (or Jewish as well). Again, as Hopkins (1998, 218) observes, "the very idea that correct belief identified the true Christian and that incorrect belief pushed the believer who wanted to be a Christian beyond the pale became entrenched as a core defining characteristic of early Christianity."

Entrepreneurial Discount Rates and the Spread of Christianity

The voyages, successes, and failures of the early Christian missionaries cannot be understood apart from the discount rates that applied to these entrepreneurs, who have also been described as "doomsdayers" and "visionaries" (MacMullen 1984, 25–26). Early apostles undoubtedly had a high discount rate in their own minds (and in their preaching), fully expecting Christ to reappear during their own lifetimes. The Evangelist

Mark, whose writings of Christ's words were learned directly from and approved by Peter, was quite clear about the conditions of the promised afterlife of Christ's followers:

> In those days . . . the sun shall be darkened and the moon shall not give her light. And the stars of heaven shall be falling down and the powers that are in heaven shall be moved. And then shall they see the Son of man coming in the clouds, with great power and glory. And then shall he send his angels and shall gather together his elect from the four winds, from the uttermost part of the earth to the uttermost part of heaven. Now of the fig tree learn ye a parable. When the branch thereof is now tender and the leaves are come forth, you know that summer is very near. So you also when you shall see these things come to pass, know ye that it is very nigh, even at the doors. *Amen, I say to you that this generation shall not pass until all these things be done.* Heaven and earth shall pass away: but my word shall not pass away. (Mark 13:24–31, emphasis added)

But when generation after generation—if the word is given its usual meaning—passed, behaviors and preaching were modified accordingly. Certainly, there was an initial intensive urge to proselytize Christianity with all speed because Jesus was returning soon. The apostles and those they converted expected the "interruption" of death to be of short duration. When this did not occur, the product had to be modified so that judgment, reward, and punishment were imminent upon human death. The interpretation of Mark and other Biblical passages had to then pertain to the people living on earth at the time of Jesus's return when there would be a judgment of the dead and a judgment of the living. After generations passed without the return of Jesus, proselytizers had to alter the discount rates of prospective members by altering doctrine, with conditions of an afterlife as an essential part of the product. [25]

Early efforts were aimed at conversions among pagans, Hellenized Jews, Gentiles, and Orthodox Jews. Peter, for example, bridged gaps between pagans and Christians and between Jewish sects and Christian communities. This ecumenical stance may be seen as arising from Judaism. Told by Christ to "feed my sheep" (John 21–7) and to care for the flock, Peter took his mission seriously.[26] Peter, initially headquartered in Jerusalem, was visited by Paul several times and became an active entrepreneur in the conversion of Diaspora Jews (as shown in the Acts of the

Apostles) in Corinth, Greece, parts of Asia Minor, and Antioch. James, the brother of Jesus, took over for Peter in Jerusalem and was ultimately executed by Herod. Clearly, these activities—well documented in the literature—describe how Christianity became an international religion and how entry took place, not only in Rome but elsewhere. Some Jews became Christian; others retained Jewish faith as well as belief in Christ. In the first century in particular, an extremely complex situation arose within the Jewish/Christian community regarding adoption of the "new" religion. The other major (and critical) development was Paul's conversions of Gentiles from (presumably) Latin, Greek, and Egyptian pagan forms of religion and worship. Paul ("apostle to the Gentiles") tried in his preaching and epistles to blur the differences between Judaism and Christ. Paul, according to some sociological interpretations, was deeply involved in adjusting Christianity to social conditions in the wide areas of his preaching. In particular, as noted above, he rejected the necessary observance of Jewish law as a requirement for Christians. Perhaps this was the natural reaction of Paul, who had been an earlier prosecutor of Christians. Moreover, Jesus showed considerable disdain for the rule-following Jewish priests. Circumcision and kosher food did not appeal to the vast number of Gentiles Paul was trying to convert, and he simply abandoned the requirement (Crossley 2006). (Peter, after early reservations and debates, apparently gave his approval of this practice.)[27] Entry strategy was aimed at selling Gentiles and the Jews on the Gospels. It is known that both Peter and Paul were martyred in Rome, providing a rationale for the foundation of the Christian church in Rome.[28] (Naturally, numerous others, including James, Matthew, and John, carried on the task of entrepreneurship both before and after the deaths of Peter and Paul.)

While the many tales and aspects of apostolic entrepreneurship are described elsewhere, several critical aspects of this early form of entrepreneurship have been overlooked. Not all Jews and pagan Gentiles would have accepted all parts of the evangelist's teachings. Slavery, clearly condoned in the early writings, as well as dietary rules and the role of women in the church would have been controversial, as some of them remain today. As we have already noted, despite the belief and preaching of the apostle-entrepreneurs, the imminent return of Jesus Christ did not materialize. For converts the expected "interruption" of physical death was to be of short duration, as noted above.[29] The obvious fact that this did not happen needed to be explained in conjunction with the teachings of Jesus. The teachings of Jesus—as told second- and thirdhand by the apostolic entrepreneurs—had to be "cherry-picked" for proselytizing purposes. This situation gave rise to different teachings and *multiple Christian* sects. *Some kind of unalterable canon of teachings and beliefs had to be established to supply credence to all of Christ's teachings since a central message of Christ*—that there was an afterlife, that members would be judged, and that Christ was going to do that when he returned—did not materialize. Why? Behavior in the present life partly determined one's access to the afterlife (barring a foxhole conversion and the gift of repentance). The discount rate of the apostolic entrepreneurs *had* to change over the first three hundred years of Christianity. Part of this change required written "rules" and instruction to bring the central ingredient of lower costs to Christianity vis-à-vis other sects and religions—the *promise of and elaboration on* an afterlife.

There are alternative interpretations concerning the entrepreneurial, institutional, and organizational structure through which this came about. Some sociologists emphasize the origins of Christian groups as being within the middle to upper classes (Stark) while others emphasize the developments with Jewish converts in communities and house cult-groups. Hopkins (1998, 207–212) argues that early Christian activities took place primarily among house cults (all together composing a "community" in larger cities) where illiteracy dominated. His description of the Christian community toward the end of the second century is instructive since it emphasizes two features that emerged within these communities that forever defined Christianity—the episcopal nature of church organization and the characteristic of Christianity as a "religion of the book," that is, of the written word. He argues that by the end of the second century, literates in the Christian communities were pushing their writings with upper-class pagan classical culture. If Hopkins's assessment is correct, early Christian organization, wherein literate leaders guided the house cult communities, undergirded the *ultimate* "literary" quality of Christianity through a communications network among literate Christian entrepreneurs.[30] Further, it established an elite (certainly by the end of the second century) band of "teacher-entrepreneurs" who were the prototypes for a hierarchical, episcopal church (the cognoscenti vs. the illiterate).

Christian entrepreneurs required credibility-enhancing devices to remind converts and potential converts of the net benefits of the new religion. Thus, all manner of Christian entrepreneurs were faced with the necessity of creating *written elaborations* of Christ and his message. Those written elaborations took on many forms—some which did and many others that did not ultimately become part of the official canon of church teaching at Nicaea. Christian entrepreneurs behaved as agents of change: the product(s) were continually repackaged to suit changing demand segments. Several points are clear. Entrepreneurs had to use final judgment, resurrection promises, and an immediate afterlife at death as central tenets in the emerging literature and in their teachings of the new Christian religion. A written canon emphasizing these promises necessitated the use of hearsay evidence and St. Paul's writings was a necessary accouterment to these oral teachings.[31] Faith-based credence required it.[32]

Network-Consumption Externalities and Credence Issues

Stark, while not emphasizing "product change," clearly recognizes that entrepreneurial activity was one important motive force in the early spread of Christianity. Further, in his emphasis on the early spread of Christianity primarily within Jewish cultures, he does not miss the fact that this spread was based on a kind of networking. But he describes "networks of interpersonal relationships based on kinship, friendship, or commerce" (1997, 135). Elsewhere, Stark argues that *open* Christian networks were central to the astonishing conversion rate between 250 and 350—"each new member expands the size of the network of attachments between the group and potential converts" (1997, 20, 62).

We agree with these sociological expressions of network expansion in the context of early Christianity but would add economic specificity to the concept of networking. Christian entrepreneurship by the apostles and others, particularly in the larger cities and villages, was made possible by entrepreneurial efforts *plus* all forms of network *externalities*. Demand and supply conditions for the product(s) of religion are not the only tools with which to analyze the market for early Christian teachings and religion. Externalities occur when the demands of one individual are affected by the demands and actions of other individuals. *Networking is in the self-interest of each individual who either attaches himself or herself to a network or who recruits individuals into the network.* More formally, the utility of one consumer in consuming a product or service is a function of the utility obtained by other consumers of that product or service.

This concept has been used in a variety of applications in analyzing the spread and durability of technological innovations and demand behavior for products such as the telephone, Facebook, or computer software. *The clear implication of these network externalities is a tendency toward monopoly.* The utility of one's use of any of these technologies is a function of its use by other consumers. Note that the implications of these technologies are that when a superior technology appears, it will spread due to the consumption externalities effect. In the cases described, superior technologies were able to compete successfully with earlier ones. In other cases, a particular technology may create, perhaps over a long period, "natural" concentration.[33] Such natural monopolies do not necessarily exist forever. A superior or advanced technology, if cost-efficient, will ultimately be introduced successfully if markets are generally contestable.[34]

A consumption or "superstar" effect (Rosen 1981), as we noted in chapter 3, can create an extreme consumption externality. This effect means that an individuals' utility increases with increases in the customers or users of some product or service. Our utility and that of others increases when we consume television shows such as Dexter or Meryl Streep movies. For example, I can more easily find people with whom to discuss the murderous adventures of Dexter or the details of Meryl Streep movies when more people demand these products. Naturally, this superstar effect and network externalities do not explain the *initial* demand for religion. In other words, we only observe a demand for religion and the multidimensional products provided by religion, but we do not attempt to explain that initial demand.[35] We simply observe that such demands behave in precisely the same manner specified for other goods and services and, further, that both network and consumption externalities are involved.

The peculiar characteristics of religious goods are related to the consumption externalities described above. Credence goods have been identified as those whose characteristics or qualities cannot be determined before purchase. When qualities of goods cannot be determined prior to purchase, certain assurances must be provided by sellers. In the case of credence goods—such as psychiatric counseling, transmission repair, marriage and family counseling—it is alleged that the quality of services cannot even be determined after purchase. All kinds of quality assurances—

licensing, buyback agreements, and so on—are required in order to provide efficient markets in such goods. But, in reality, the quality of such
goods as psychiatric services can be determined over the long run. Did
they provide the desired effects, or did they not?

Religious goods, as we argued in chapter 3, may be identified as
extreme forms of credence goods (metacredence goods) once afterlife
services are sold as part of the package of qualities because the good's
characteristics cannot be determined before or after purchase. No one
has yet returned to verify the quality of the promises made by religious
suppliers concerning the nature of an afterlife. But while this is the case,
temporal assurances may work to provide assurances of quality. There
are many kinds of assurances: the quality of social services, the degree of
ritual, the pomp and circumstance of church organizations, and church
size are all examples, and there are others (see below).[36] But the number of believers is also a form of credence building for demanders. Thus
consumption externalities—the so-called superstar effect—are directly
related to the provision of credence in the religious good. The probability that one with a Christian belief will encounter another with the
same belief rises with the size of the network. (This does not mean that
no two Christians or believers of any kind will have *identical demands*
for "assurances" or identical beliefs about the supernatural. There is a
low probability of this situation since individuals differ on so many margins, including attitudes toward risk). Networks thus also help provide
credence. The greater the number of believers in some particular form
of religion, the greater the credence in the doctrinal propositions associated with that religion.

Then there are so-called supernatural assurances, and their manifestations were thought to be of critical importance in the early Christian
era—miracles and Christians going willingly to their deaths in Roman
persecutions. These two aspects of metacredence must be included in
the effects on conversions by entrepreneurs. Apostle-entrepreneurs often claimed that their Christ (working through them) had divine power
over the world, evidenced by miracles. Tales, for example, of Christ's
apparition to the apostle Thomas after his death and resurrection was
one example, of course. MacMullen (1984, 27), quoting non-Christian
sources on apostolic activity, notes that the poor and ignorant, the un-
sophisticated and the uneducated were prepared to believe anything
the entrepreneurs told them. Stories of the vagaries of life, controlled
by an unseen god, were a powerful tool to scare listeners and prospec-

tive Christians. Through belief, the sick could be cured, and according to MacMullen (1984, 40), "[o]f all worships, the Christian best and most particularly advertised its miracles by driving out the spirits and laying on of hands. Reports would spread without need of preaching." Disciple-entrepreneurs claimed the power to drive out "demons" and cure sickness, a power given them by Jesus, and in John (14:12) he admonished his followers that "I tell you the truth, anyone who has faith in me, can do the same miracles I have done, and even greater things than these will you do." In a dangerous, ignorant, and punishing world filled with suffering, such claims must have provided a great measure of credence to potential believers.

But of all the credence provisions for early Christian converts, open persecution by the Roman state, especially in the mid-third and early fourth centuries, must have had a pivotal impact (Stark 1997), affording missionary-entrepreneurs a "handle" with which to sell the product by making clear the link between behavior and rewards. Generally, Christians were persecuted if they declined to worship or pay money to the Roman pantheon of gods. Those who refused were or could be put to death. The willingness to die for their faith provided a heady dose of credence for members and potential members of the faith. Importantly, since resurrection through belief in Jesus Christ and his teachings (as interpreted by a plethora of apostle-entrepreneurs) was thought to be imminent, personal discount rates supported martyrdom. But these stories, spread by Christian apostle-entrepreneurs from the earliest days as a credence-producing element, were highly exaggerated, according to a number of sources. Roman law militated against large-scale persecutions. Christians created persecution as a means of creating an identity, according to Hopkins (1998, 196–197). It was only in the third century (roughly 250–252, 257–260 CE) and later under Diocletian (around 303 CE) that the most severe persecutions took place, and, simultaneously, over the third century the Christian population grew from 200,000 to over 6 million. (Indeed, miracles or reports thereof may have had a "mass conversion" effect over the third- and early fourth-century period.) Despite the sometimes apocryphal nature of the magnitude of Christian persecution, the willingness of some to die for the faith (or the proclamation of willingness) apparently had an enormous credence effect on the sale of Christianity by apostle-entrepreneurs. Martyrs and those willing to be tortured and die for the faith had the impact of demonstrating that risk and uncertainty of becoming Christian were low.

This is exactly what the "superstar effect" tells us. Martyrs and those espousing particular ideologies are, in substance, advertisements for a cause and elevate the "club effect" of joining a movement. Thus, martyrs must be counted, along with afterlife assurance and entrepreneurship, as elements in the success of early Christianity.[37]

Beyond credence considerations, we are in broad agreement with sociologists who maintain that the spread of the new religion was an urban phenomenon with appeal to certain middle- and working-class people (Stark 1997) and to the poor as well (MacMullen 1984, 37). Greco-Roman cities were small in both area and population. But one key to understanding the rapid spread of Christianity is the astonishingly high level of population density in these cities. According to Stambaugh (1988, 90), "If we assume a population of about a million, we must conclude that Rome in the early principate was one of the most densely populated cities the world has ever known—as crowded, probably, as modern Bombay or Calcutta." Stark calculated population per square mile for Greco-Roman cities against modern statistics for selected cities. A sample of his calculations is contained in table 4.1. These data, generally corroborated by Stambaugh and others, clearly reveal that the transactions costs of "networking" in Greco-Roman cities were low. And population density was accompanied by multifamily dwellings with groups cordoned off by ethnicity.

The original Christian entrepreneurs set out from Jerusalem and headed for the Jewish diasporas of the Hellenized world. These Jews, used to receiving teachers from Jerusalem, would have been more open to the new ideas of Christianity. It represented cultural continuity within a familiar conventional religion—Judaism. Put in economic terms, the marginal costs were low relative to the marginal benefits (well-defined

TABLE 4.1. **Population Density in Contemporary and Greco-Roman Cities**

Geographical Area	Population per Square Mile
Nanshi area, Shanghai	147,187
Greco-Roman cities	128,200
City area, Calcutta	108,005
Hong Kong	73,627
Mexico City	30,263
Tokyo	18,401
Washington, DC	9,882
Los Angeles County, CA	2,183

Source: Stark (1997: 149).

afterlife, possible social welfare benefits, and so on) of adoption of the new religion. But we would argue that networking would have worked for the Christian entrepreneurs who addressed the *non*-Jewish population as well (Gentiles and "pagans") because it was in the self-interest of non-Christians to adopt the new religion and to *proselytize it* as well. Gentiles, if we assume that they enjoyed lesser social cohesion and welfare-giving attributes than the Jews, would experience *greater* benefit than Jews from becoming Christian (the net value of the new network exceeded that of Judaism). The price to Gentiles of a monotheistic religion with a well-defined afterlife (in addition to "social and economic benefits") would be even lower relative to those in the Jewish Diaspora.

The Adoption of Christianity: The Role of Saint Paul

Rodney Stark (1997, 129–145) developed a formal model of the adoption of Christianity in the first and (to the best of our knowledge) only quantitative-statistical approach to the subject. He pioneered a code for the timing of the first Christian church in major cities and offers additional evidence for an economic hypothesis of networking in the quest to date the degree of Christianization in the Greco-Roman world. From five different sociological, archeological, and anthropological sources, Stark calculates an index of cities possessing local Christian churches by the century marks 100 and 180 CE.[38] Stark's analysis gauges the "receptiveness" to Christianization, and there are, as he notes, many reasons for this result. In particular, Stark defines a number of variables that might affect the adoption of Christianity (that is, the number of Christian churches extant between 100 CE and 180 CE, as defined above): *population* estimates in twenty-two (nonrandomly selected) cities in the Greco-Roman world; *synagogues in cities* by 100 CE, synagogues being a proxy for Jewish population in cities; *miles from Jerusalem*, being a proxy for ease of Christian conversion; *miles from Rome*, being another proxy for ease of Christian conversion; *amount of "Romanization,"* which was a ratio of distance to Jerusalem to distance to Rome; and finally, *Gnostics*, which is a three-level categorical variable for the existence of known Gnostic groups in a city before 200 CE and 400 CE.

Stark's model of early Christianity includes the following expected direction of the variables. For reasons established in the literature (including a crude concept of networking), one would expect an inverse relation between population and Christianization. Likewise, distance from Rome, the number of synagogues by 100 CE, and the number of Gnostics (a form of Christian religion that, Stark argues, was an offshoot of *Christian* rather than Jewish religion) would also be expected to have a positive relation with earlier Christianization. Negative relations would be expected on simple distance from Jerusalem and from Rome for other apparent reasons.

Stark finds vindication for all of these expectations in his correlations and in two simple regressions, which contain two independent variables each. One shows significant relations between earlier Christianization and Synagogues (positive) and Romanization (negative). The other shows significant relations between Gnosticism and Synagogues (positive) and Romanization (negative).

Stark argues that "everyone agrees that Jews were the primary sources of converts until well into the second century," but that "there simply is no good way to calculate the probable size of the Jewish population in these cities" (1997, 138). Hence he uses number of synagogues in approximately 100 CE as a proxy for Jewish population. Stark also recognizes that Christianity did best in Greek cities until Roman antagonisms tended to reduce Christian influence. We agree that the Jewish Diaspora provided ripe pickings for the early Christian entrepreneurs— who might well have chosen cities on the basis of personal reasons (and relationships) and demographic considerations not based on the number of Jews. Christian entrepreneurs would have employed cost/benefit analysis in their travels. But we believe that a more complete model of early Christianization would include the significant emphasis of the Apostle Paul (and others) on conversions of the Gentiles and presumably "pagans" who worshiped Greco-Roman gods or no gods (Fox 1986).

Toward an Expanded Model

Stark's formal models of the influences of the above variables utilizing his data set can be fully replicated, and we have done so. We believe, however, that an improved analysis of early Christianity may be obtained using Stark's fundamental methodology. That improved analysis of early Christianity, which we outline below, consists of the explicit recognition of (a) the role of apostolic entrepreneurship—here represented specifically by Saint Paul; (b) a further consideration of networking and city size; and (c) an improved statistical technique. Consider each issue in turn.

First, the networking described by Stark within Jewish communities of the region undoubtedly had a positive impact on conversions. But there is reason to believe that Gentiles and pagans, facing a far lower relative price and even higher benefits (in the form of social welfare interactions as well as a lower full price due to monotheism and a well-defined afterlife) would not be immune to Christian entrepreneurship. We examined Paul's travels to the cities Stark identifies and his epistles to them as a proxy for the proselytizing of Gentiles in the region. Paul, of course, directed his efforts to Jewish communities as well, but given all reports had great success with the non-Jewish demanders as the "Apostle to the Gentiles." The journeys of Saint Paul are listed as follows.

FIRST JOURNEY: Antioch, Seleucia, Cyprus, Salamis, Paphos, Perge, Antioch in Pisidia, Konya (Iconium), Derbe, Lystra, Antalya, Antioch (returns to beginning of his journey).

SECOND JOURNEY: Cilicia, Derbe, Lystra, Phrygia, Galatia, Mysia (Alexandra Troas), Samothrace, Macedonia (including Neapolis, Philippi, Amphipolis, Apollonia, Thessalonica and Beroea), Athens, Corinth, Cenchreae, Ephesus, Syria, Caesarea, Jerusalem, Antioch.

THIRD JOURNEY: Galatia, Phrygia, Ephesus, Macedonia, Corinth, Cenchreae, Macedonia (again), Troas, Assos, Mytilene, Chios, Samos, Miletus, Cos, Rhodes, Patara, Tyre, Ptolomais, Caesarea, Jerusalem.[39]

Clearly, Paul's travels were vast and varied, but it is noteworthy that he had visited fully half of the cities that Stark designates as having a Christian church by the year 100 CE.[40] Four of these cities were visited twice. This fact, together with the fact that the vast majority—fully 59 percent of Paul's accepted epistles (excluding Hebrews)—were directed to the citizens of the cities with a Christian church by 100 CE, leads us to suspect that Paul's entrepreneurial abilities were brought to bear on the Christianization of the empire in its early days, apart from his proselytizing through synagogues.

Second, consider the issues of city size and location. Stark (1997, 131–132) includes a (nonrandom) sample of twenty-two cities listed in descending order of size and also calculates the distance of these cities (according to accepted travel routes) from Jerusalem and Rome. Clearly, city size is a factor in some metric. The adoption of Christian religion by date was *directly* related to city size according to Stark and earlier investigators. But note the sociological analysis of the impact of city size.

> Is there any reason to suppose that city size would have influenced Christianization? . . . Moreover, there is a solid theoretical basis for such a hypothesis in the sociological literature. In his well-known subcultural theory of urbanism, Claude S. Fischer offered this proposition: "The more urban the place, the higher the rates of unconventionality" (1975: 1328). Fischer's thesis is that the larger the population in absolute numbers, the easier it is to assemble a "critical mass" needed to form a deviant subculture. Here he specifically includes deviant religious movements. During the period in question Christianity obviously qualifies as a deviant religious movement in that it clearly was at variance with prevailing religious norms. Therefore, Fischer's theory of urbanism predicts that Christians would have assembled the critical mass needed to form a church sooner, the larger the city. (Stark 1997, 134)

We do not question the essence of this sociological argument if it supplemented with an economic concept of networking in the following way: City size is only one factor in explaining the conversion rate. Population *density* and the *intensity of entrepreneurial activity*, the creative factor in networking, are other factors that must be included. The reason for the deviance in the movement was the lower full price created by clear and outlined promises of an afterlife and Christ's resurrection. It would be highly unlikely that the ratio of "unconventionality" to total population would be the same or even approximately the same in all large cities (compare, e.g., those ratios in Boston and San Francisco or Des Moines and Boulder) or cities of any size. Economic networking, in other words, would not require high levels of deviance, but would exist on the basis of concentration of population and the intensity of proselytizing entrepreneurship. Given these factors, a negative relation between population and the degree of Christianization would not be completely unexpected.

Similarly, location may be a factor, but only one factor, in the success of entrepreneurship. By arguing that distance from Rome or Jerusalem (or their ratio) impacted the spread of Christianity, Stark is focusing only on cost, and then, on only one aspect of it. Ostensibly, the more Romanized a city—the closer to Rome and the more distant from Jerusalem—

the more dangerous or "costly" the activity of Christians. This view, however, must be supplemented by the possible benefits to Christians. The more concentrated the population of any city, the higher the probability of getting "caught" if Christian activity was outlawed or made punishable by Roman governments, but the greater the benefits of Christian networking. Gentile population in a city, moreover, may have some positive benefits to entrepreneurs if they were (in some sense) easier to convert because their conversion would have brought them larger benefits than conversions by Jews. Further, the distance from Jerusalem variable as defined by Stark would be highly correlated with the number of synagogues by the year 100 CE. The Hebrew population spread out from Jerusalem to the more "reachable" cities long before the appearance of Jesus Christ. We would fully expect synagogues in cities to proxy "miles from Jerusalem." The impact of including both variables in a regression would likely be to introduce some bias in one or the other variables.

Paul and the Adoption of Christianity

We offer a reformulated model of Christianization in a technical appendix at the end of this book. This model includes the travels of Paul; also, it redefines the Christianization variable in continuous terms by adding all of Stark's sources together. The rest of the model is based on Stark as defined above. A number of extremely important pitfalls must be issued in interpreting Stark's and our results. First, and obviously, both estimations used a very limited number of observations (22). This small number, constrained by the availability of data, can lead to many kinds of statistical difficulties. The unique data set relies on estimations of a number of variables, for example, of population and city size. The inclusion of the journeys of Saint Paul likewise has statistical problems. "Rational choice" suggests that Paul might have picked cities with the highest population or the nearest cities from Jerusalem or perhaps some other metric. Or he might have used some other reason or reasons for his visits (perhaps he had friends who were good cooks in Antioch). We cannot know how his choices were made.

But to our knowledge, no one denies the importance of Paul in the spread of the Christian religion. Given all of these caveats outlined above, we find that Paul's visits are a *statistically significant* and positive determinant of Christianization. In fact, the statistical results we obtained can be read as showing that Paul's visits were more important than the Jewish Diaspora and that Paul may well have been competing with the synagogues on some margins. These effects continue to hold sway when particular statistical problems are accounted for in our statistical model. In short, Paul was a major driver of Christian expansion, perhaps more so than Judaism. Of course, anyone who has read the New Testament knows this already, and our analysis simply adds some quantitative weight to this reading.[41] Again, our statistical test is not definitive but illustrative: the analysis is intended simply to provide some empirical evidence on apostolic entrepreneurship, and it is clear that Saint Paul had an enormous effect on the spread of Christian religion.

A critical caveat must be noted concerning Saint Paul's entrepreneurship. As we have stated, we do not argue that Paul was animated by simple economic gain. Rather, he was driven by his faith and his calling from Christ to expand and develop the new religion. This does not mean that economics cannot be used to assess Paul's entrepreneurship. Given Paul's goals, economics simply asserts that he would have pursued them effectively. This is the spirit in which we analyze his writings and travels. Paul's genius lay in his ability to interpret Christianity in a way that made the new religion competitive with Judaism and Roman pagan beliefs and in his organizational skills in establishing outposts of the new religion throughout the areas in which he travelled. And, of course, Paul's travels were not without peril. He and his colleagues were hounded and prosecuted by Jewish and Roman competitors, jailed, stoned, and remanded to Rome to face the emperor's judgment (after a harrowing sea journey). So while we analyze Paul's work from an economic perspective, we do not lose sight of the fact that his purposes were by no means strictly economic. We do maintain, however, that his methods can be seen as an application of the economics of entrepreneurship. In short, Paul was an immensely successful entrepreneur who helped develop a new product in the marketplace for religion and marketed it brilliantly both door-to-door (travels) and through mail order (epistles). Faith drove Paul; economics drove his methods.

Conclusion

Total utility among individuals increased as Christian networking spread. Extensive poverty, the lack of a social welfare network, internecine political struggles, and probable early death also must have contributed to

the success of Christian entrepreneurs. Christianity enhanced social cohesiveness. "Networking" among Christian families and groups and,
we believe, offering the ultimate cost-lowering feature relative to other
religious organizations—a promise of and elaboration upon a happy
afterlife—all played a role in the success of the new religion.[42] Other factors created success. Stark emphasized the role of Christians in plagues
and the role of women in addition to the spread of apostolic preaching
(1997, 95–128). But others have challenged aspects of Stark's view (Hopkins 1998; Klutz 1998; Castelli 1998). While citizens other than Christians also engaged in welfare activities, the survival rate of Christians
was likely higher in plagues where Christians took care of their families and others—risking their own lives to promote survival. There was
a Darwinian metric at work.[43] The appeal to women was also a critical
ingredient in success, which Stark suggests (1997, 95). Generally, there
was a shortage of women in the Roman population. In a Beckerian
sense, at least, this made women more valuable than men. Women, more
than men, sought a cohesive family unit. The adoption of Christian religion helped achieve this goal since, in Christ's teachings, as propounded
by the apostolic entrepreneurs, adultery was a grievous wrong. Thus, two
factors—a high-risk component created by the "shocks" of plagues and
Darwinian survival that followed from Christian behavior, together with
the disproportionate input of women in Christian cohesion—helped lead
to the successful introduction of Christianity.

The present analysis, both theoretical and historical, of the initial (and spectacular) conversion of Jews and pagans to Christianity is
complementary to standard treatments, but goes further in an explanation of economic motivations. The spread of Christianity by rank-
and-file missionaries through synagogues is consistent with the spread
by professional missionaries such as Paul. It is an example of the network or superstar effects described above. The utility of a network is far
greater than the sum of individual utilities in isolation. There is no contradiction or even opposition in the fact that Christianity was spread by
professional preachers and within family and clan networks. It was accomplished in this fashion. We simply add the (empirical) influence of
Paul and his work with the Gentiles and others to the explanation. Christianity brought religion "to the people" as well as to the temple. Thus the
early spread of Christianity was accomplished by the interplay between
entrepreneurial activities and network effects, aided, we have argued, by

the incredibly effective teachings of Saint Paul on Gentiles as well as through the more traditional means of synagogues.

It is often said that without Saint Paul, Christianity would not have spread so rapidly or, perhaps, not become the dominant and growing force in the middle to late Roman Empire that it did. There appears, from the above analysis, to be some truth to this proposition. But a haunting and critical question remains: why were the Romans ultimately, that is, by the early fourth century, so hospitable to a religion that in earlier periods (and admittedly in cyclical fashion) they were so eager to erase.

CHAPTER FIVE

Constantine and Rome's Acceptance of Christianity

Introduction

The simplified history of early Christianity provides the following sequence: Despite Roman persecution and crucifixion of early Christians in the empire, the number of Christians grew at a high rate. This growth, despite cyclical and violent retributions from Roman authorities, culminated in the legitimization of the religion by Emperor Constantine (313), the Council of Nicaea (325), and in the ultimate dominance of the religion over European civilization in a vertically integrated organization up to the Protestant Reformation. In later lore, much of it apocryphal, Constantine (285?–327 CE) is made the champion of Christianity—one who was allegedly struck with a vision of Christ in battle leading him to adopt the religion that the Roman Empire had tried to contain over the first three centuries CE. Constantine, moreover and at least apocryphally, established the organizational structure of the "Holy See" in Rome with papal primacy over the secular as well. Early Christian historians such as Eusebius and theologians such as Augustine as well as later writers (mostly with slim evidence) set these views in concrete.

Some facts are clear. Constantine *did* "legitimize" Christian religion in 313 CE (Lenski 2006b). Persecutions *did* occur in cycles over the first three hundred years. We have analyzed the supplementary economics of these movements, in particular, the roles of entrepreneurship and economic networking in chapter 4, and found other reasons for the spread of Christianity. But serious questions remain concerning the nature of Rome's "supply-side" response to Christianity. Relative tolerance of the religion, along with Judaism, had been given—again in cycles—by the Roman state. If Christianity was actually subversive to the state, a belief that brought on cyclical persecutions, the state would have had the resources to stamp it out completely or at least to suppress the religion far more than it did. Constantine, moreover, was a violent man of great power who would have had little trouble in renewing persecution, especially against some of the assorted varieties of Christian belief that existed in his lifetime. He did not do so. While we do not take any position on his "battlefield conversion" to Christianity, there may be other more concrete and tractable reasons for his actions and the acceptance of Christianity by Rome.

This chapter provides an economic theory illustrated with historical discussion underlying the adoption of Christianity by the late Roman Empire and its critical relation to the state's ultimate drive to cartelize that religion. Our economic explanations are seated in transactions and agency cost reductions for the growing Roman acceptance of Christianity and its doctrines, which culminated in Constantine's legitimization of the religion in the Edict of Milan in 313. Transactions and agency cost reductions mean that the establishment of Christianity and its principles and practices released policing and other resources to the Roman state for other uses. These might include, for example, fighting frontier wars and barbarian incursions. Throughout, we analyze the movement and motivations to solidify the proto-orthodox version of Christianity (as encapsulated in the Nicene Creed at the Council of Nicaea) and to *cartelize* the new religion in doctrine and organizational structure under Constantine. While the actual motives of Constantine in legitimizing Christianity would be difficult or impossible to discern, we analyze his actions within major political and theological controversies of the day. Finally, we briefly comment on the cartelization and ultimate triumph of both Eastern and Western Christianity after Constantine, leading to the eventual medieval monopoly of *Western* Christian religion that flourished up to the sixteenth century.

A Theory of the Adoption and Cartelization of Christianity by Rome

If morality is defined as a set of logically coherent, mutually consistent internal constraints on behavioral choices, then a large number of distinct ethical systems are possible, presently or in the distant past.[1] Alternative sets of moral rules are potentially available to rational individuals. However, some conceivable moral rules contribute to social efficiency, while others may have the opposite effect. These features of religion—pagan, Jewish, Moslem, or Christian—apply in all places and at all times.

When religious competition exists, we expect that consumers of religion will be provided with the precise mix of services they consider best (satisfaction-maximizing), subject to relevant constraints—usually a combination of money costs and rituals. This mix and the strictures associated with it will be determined by the factors affecting demands.[2] (Such a model is approximately the reality in many nations today, including the United States.) The services of religion include the moral code associated with the religious belief.[3] Religious firms will have a comparative advantage in the provision of sets of moral rules because the theological basis of such firms imparts credibility to the moral structure.[4] A consumer has reason to rely on the quality of the given set of moral restrictions because he or she believes, given the credibility of the religion supplier, that they have received divine sanction. This lowers the cost of marketing sets of moral rules to consumers and also lowers the cost of generating compliance. The same divine entity that guarantees quality provides for enforcement against moral transgressions (e.g., access to an afterlife).

If religious doctrines achieve market success purely as a function of their ability to compete freely for adherents, the religions that survive will be those providing the most acceptable moral requirements to demanders. If we assume that all potential church members are members of the species *Homo economicus*, then the best moral rules (from their individual perspectives) will be those that require them to do exactly what they would otherwise most prefer to do, other things equal. This does not necessarily imply that the list of rules will be empty; in fact, it might be consistent with immensely detailed and severe moral strictures. Rather, it suggests that however many nominal moral requirements there may be, they will collectively imply that the individual's behavior will be subject to those constraints that he or she prefers. All of the religious competition with Christianity and Christianity itself fits this profile.

People will, given their demand profile, gravitate to religions that promote codes of morality producing the least impact on those particular individuals' actual behavior on the basis of costs and benefits; individuals will tend to adopt systems of moral rules most consistent with their preexisting individual preference orderings.[5] As outlined in earlier chapters, this means that individuals will demand a particular set of moral rules and rituals based upon risk profile—itself a function of demand determinants such as relative real price of other systems, incomes, education, and the state of scientific knowledge.

The moral order—considered as the effect of, but separate from, the moral beliefs of individuals—is a public good, which technically means that consumption is nonrivalrous. This suggests that, once produced, it is available to all at zero cost. Moral order was a public good in Rome, as it is in all contemporary societies. Rational wealth-maximizing persons will act to protect the value of their reputations for being moral individuals, but will tend to free ride and behave opportunistically, accepting the benefits of moral order without paying for them when they expect such malfeasance will remain undetected and unsanctioned. To a rational self-interested individual, behavioral (moral) restrictions are simply constraints. Naturally, some individuals will be unaffected by some external restrictions. The costs of behavioral restrictions are a subjective phenomenon and may have no observable manifestation. But, in general, a rational individual will prefer fewer effective behavioral moral restrictions.

Competition in the market for religious services, such as that existing between Christian sects and other religious alternatives prior to Constantine, improves the efficiency of those markets in providing religious goods to consumers. These private goods include the insurance benefits (implicit and explicit) associated with church membership, the club gains, socializing, reputational advantages (Jane goes to church, so Jane is perceived to be more trustworthy by potential traders as a result), and other effects. Such private goods will be available in larger quantities and at lower prices than would be the case if the religious market is monopolized.

But because consumers of different religions do not, other things equal, demand utility-reducing moral constraints to be imposed on themselves, moral order as a public good tends to be *underprovided* in a competitive market for religious services as existed prior to the time of Constantine.[6] Competing sects—pagan and Christian religious forms in the first centuries after Christ—competed by improving service (and reducing price) to consumers—including producing and marketing more attractive (i.e., more liberal) moral restrictions. This process will tend to produce religious rule structures that are more congenial to those individual consumers. Again, this does not mean that there will be no restrictions on behavior or ritual, but only those restrictions desired by adherents.

Individuals often voluntarily join sects that nominally restrict their behavior in various ways. But a given nominal restriction may only reflect the preexisting dislikes of the individual adherent. Many people simply do not have libertine preferences, but instead place high value on goals such as security and orderliness; they may also have preferences influenced (in the long run) by their economic circumstances (such as income). For example, many of the medieval heresies in Western Europe—that is, black market providers of illegal alternative religious doctrines—rejected material wealth, glorified poverty, and advocated extreme sexual abstinence. While early Christianity attracted adherents of most classes, many were poor. Requiring the (already) poor to reject material wealth is hardly an onerous restriction, and many medieval heresies inspired their adherents to reduce the sinful material wealth of the rich by relieving such sinners of their property—another requirement likely to be highly attractive to many poor believers. Similarly, a rule requiring sexual abstinence was potentially a welfare-enhancing *relaxation* of a social norm of producing children, at least from the standpoint of women, to whom pregnancy and childbirth often had fatal consequences.

Markets and Moral Order

An organized church or pagan belief system can be thought of as a firm or firms that markets a metacredence good. Consumers cannot sample the promised life after death and use that experience to evaluate the reliability of the church's advertised claims. Consumer acceptance of the church's product depends on their trust in the church's reliability. A firm marketing such an unusual product must carefully protect its brand-name capital by refraining from activities that might be taken as indi-

rect evidence of insincerity or dishonesty.[7] Otherwise, the demand for
the services produced might disintegrate altogether.

Therefore, profit-maximizing firms marketing a pure credence good
will avoid activities that might be construed as evidence of opportunistic motives. Elaborate justifications will be developed for payments from
consumers to the firm. The very profit-maximizing goal will be disguised
for fear of causing consumers to question the validity of the intangible,
nonobservable goods available for purchase.

Assume that one religious firm has achieved a pure monopoly in the
sense that competing entrants into the market for religious services are
subject to harsh coercive penalties. The monopoly church then behaves
like a typical monopolist, setting price by equating marginal cost with
marginal revenue in order to extract monopoly rent from consumers.

Historically, among other motives, churches have tended to extract
rent (obtain net revenue) by structuring doctrines in such a way as to require individuals to pay fines "for the good of their souls" to the church.
While this feature was not a part of the early days of the Christian
church, it became more prevalent toward the latter part of the first millennium and certainly in the High Middle Ages.[8] The church in question may describe the resulting revenues as destined for various "good
works," such as aid to the poor, the glorification of God, Christian or pagan, or any goal other than the comfort and consumption church or temple officials. While the monopoly church might have a number of revenue sources, other things equal, the greater the stringency of moral rules
imposed on individual behavior, the greater will be the opportunities for
revenue (that is, fines imposed on sin or in propitiation of the "gods"),
and therefore the larger the rent that can be extracted. In a competitive
market for religion, sects will face the loss of members to other sects if
they implement policies that impose burdens on their present congregation, other things equal. Even some nominally strict requirements
may actually impose a zero or negligible burden on particular individuals. However, if one organization holds a legal monopoly in the market for religion, this process is constrained. Consumers are prevented
from shopping for the least-cost set of moral requirements. The welfare
of individual consumers may suffer in the short run, but the effective re-
strictiveness of moral rules will tend to increase. This constraint, in turn,
may enhance economic efficiency if the monopolist has an incentive to
produce efficient moral rules.

Although religious sects often provide some collective goods to their members, the most basic services they ostensibly provide are purely private goods. These services involve the intercession on the believer's behalf with the divine power. For example, the principal service the Christian church purports to provide to its members is "assurances of eternal salvation," not bingo games or insurance benefits. Salvation is necessarily a purely private good, in which others play no role. (The official doctrine of the Roman Catholic Church has long held that salvation was strictly a function of faith on the part of the individual, and good works only play a role insofar as they represent an expression of that faith.) In pagan religions existing in Rome over the first three centuries after Christ, the gods were believed to reward their faithful servants with good fortune during life. But whether it takes the form of expected reward in an afterlife or a more tangible reward in the here and now, the favor of the deity or deities is an ordinary private good, albeit with some extraordinary characteristics. A monopoly church may provide a socially efficient bundle of moral rules as a by-product of its attempts to maximize rent extraction from consumers of religious services.

Monopoly, Rent Seeking, and the Provision of Moral Order

Under some circumstances, a rent-maximizing religious monopoly may tend to benefit from promoting certain kinds of moral rules even though those rules do damage to the overall economy. Such a monopolist may maximize its return in the short run by supplying moral rules that represent public "bads" in this sense. The medieval church's rules and proscriptions relating to interest-taking or extreme cases of endogamy (degrees of relationship) regulation might be other examples. Another example may be certain religious monopolies that find trading in a market economy for profit sinful. This argument would seem to suggest that monopoly religion might tend to *oversupply* moral rules of an inefficient type.

This short-run model, however, neglects the monopoly religion's long-run incentive to maximize profit, possibly along with other motives. If a monopoly religion benefits directly from economic growth, it will have an incentive to provide moral rules that promote economic efficiency. These direct benefits would take the form of tithes, bequests, and other contributions from believers, which would tend to grow with the wealth of those contributors. Given this assumption, monopoly religious organizations will have a vested interest in economic efficiency, which implies that the provision of economically efficient moral rules will be a wealth-maximizing strategy from the perspective of the rent-extracting monopoly religion, such as that which existed in the High Middle Ages.[9] Competing sects would create schism, which reduces the production of the public good (consistent moral order) by a monopoly church.

Internal and External Constraints on Behavior

Thus, the market form of any religious system, competitive through purely monopoly, carries with it both efficiency and welfare characteristics. *External* forms of constraints regarding moral rules, such as laws against theft, murder, and so on, constrain the individual to socially desirable behavior. Why, for example, when costs of criminal acts or unlawful behavior are relatively low compared to benefits, is there not more criminal behavior? Basically, there are three explanations for why this is so—two "external" and one "internal." There is an *external* law enforcement against such criminal acts, for example, the machinery of justice in society, recognized by Adam Smith and by many writers before him. Smith's interesting addition in the *Theory of Moral Sentiments* (1759) to the explanation of moral enforcement was the understanding that there is an additional *external* reason for the control of opportunistic behavior—a clear market for reputational human capital. Those who build such capital—principally through religious participation—have advantages in markets and in market exchange. This form of external incentive for "moral behavior" reigns in opportunistic behavior and contributes to social welfare and to the efficiency of society.

As discussed above, there is yet another self-enforcing function, one that is performed principally by religion. Religion provides an *internal structure* of the individual's preferences that creates self-monitoring against opportunistic behavior. The efficient supply and organization of such religion is composed of a monopoly market structure (e.g., cartelization). As Smith argued, individuals have incentives to protect their reputational capital as individuals trustworthy in exchange, but individuals also benefit from a personal moral constitution, which allows them to minimize the cost of day-to-day decisions. It is important to note, however, that moral choices that are efficient from the perspective of society may not be efficient or welfare-enhancing from the standpoint of the choosing individual. Theft may be efficient for the thief, but not from society's viewpoint. Diverse moral rules—personalized for the individual—may be utility-maximizing, but a multiplicity of such rules is not efficient for society or for the interactions of individuals within a society. Some rules may, but others may not, contribute to social efficiency. In the early days of Christianity, the Gnostics (who did adhere in various ways to Jesus Christ) believed in a dualistic philosophy by which all things of this world (goods, exchange, sex) were evil created by an evil deity.[10] The "other" world of "the good" was to be aimed for. This kind of "Christianity" would not have been efficient from the perspective of the health or growth of the economy. Thus, the provision of moral rules by religion may be regarded as the efficient provision of a public good. From one perspective, the gains from efficient provision of moral rules through monopoly may offset the costs associated with individuals having their choice set constrained by that monopoly.[11] Efficiency gains *that freed resources for other activities* (imperial rent-seeking adventures, protecting the frontier) may therefore explain why the Roman state legitimized and then cartelized the Christian religion under a single banner of orthodoxy. For church fathers, the ability to collect rents along with other motives (e.g., membership maximization) was a strong motive for cartelization. How exactly, did these two events—adoption by the state of Christianity and cartelization of the religion under the aegis of the state—take place in the Roman setting?

Roman Acceptance of Christianity: Economic Factors

The appeal of Christianity to Roman demanders is believable even if the statistics of its adoption are somewhat exaggerated. The essence of the new religion was that "He who believes in Me shall not fear death" (also see, e.g., John 27–29). The earthly *full price* for salvation, a well-defined afterlife with maximum personal utility and explicit directions for its attainment, was far lower than for the "spiritual" forms of Roman religion and paganism. These promises suffuse the message of Christ as spread by apostolic entrepreneurs such as Peter and Paul. Furthermore, there were clear economies of scale in the provision of Christianity. A common and simple belief structure provided religious services at lower cost. The contract between demanders and suppliers was easier to understand. One set of simple rules—far less costly in money or time spent in ritual—prevailed instead of the multiplicity and complicated forms of

pagan belief. While even primitive forms of religion (in early anthropological terms) contemplated forms of an afterlife, Christians were offered a clear *promise* of a happy afterlife within a common catechism
and far simpler ritual. *Behavioral norms were established with one set
of rules providing assurances of eternal salvation.* But the relative simplicity of one god and one set of doctrines under the umbrella of ultimate salvation in an afterlife offered Jews, Gentiles, and pagans a higher
quality product at a lower price. Lower full price, together with (as emphasized by Stark 1996, 95–128) an enhanced role for women and risk
avoidance (social insurance) in the face of the many calamities of the
era—invasions, plagues, and political repressions—helped propel the
new religion forward on the demand side.[12]

Supply-Side Factors in the Acceptance of Christianity

The lower full price and success of Christianity explains much of the
growth of the new religion over the first three centuries CE. We believe, however, that there were important supply-side factors as well in
explaining its success. Specifically, in addition to the economic factors
affecting demand, we argue that adherence by growing portions of the
Roman population to Christian principles lowered certain costs to Roman authorities. For reasons given above, Christianity lowered costs for
the Romans on a cost/benefit basis emanating from the supply side by
promoting behavior that reduced agency and policing costs and led to
greater economic growth.[13]

   Consider an analogy to individual states within the United States.
Each state or state locale exhibits different degrees of organized religious
membership and participation. It is possible to devise a rigorous statistical format in which these measures of religiosity are included in models
of various social pathologies along with other characteristics. The relationships between religion and the pathologies are negative in predicted
signs of the variables. Greater religious characteristics would correlate
with reduced pathologies.[14] Religion, in effect, "crowds out" crime and
other unsocial behavior. Participation in Christian religions saves enforcement resources. The Ten Commandments and other adjurations of
Christian belief are clearly related to economic behavior—to such matters as unwed mothers, orphans, violations of implicit and explicit contracts, social order, and so on. To the extent that Christianity was successful in promoting adherence to such rules, agency costs are generally

reduced as a result. The state is required to spend less on law and contract enforcement, freeing up resources for other purposes. The acceptance of Christianity by Constantine and later Roman rulers is therefore no mystery. Christianity was a good bargain for Rome from the perspective of state leaders. Christian principles led to such economic factors as an increased tax base and to reduced costs of internal police enforcement. These economic features that are inherent in Christian behavior and principles freed up resources to fight ever-encroaching external enemies of the empire.

Crime in Roman Society: Indirect Evidence

Crime within society is also a predictable result of imperial and expansionist policies. Naturally, crime statistics from the Christian era through Constantine do not exist. Important evidence, some of it very recently adduced, paints a fairly clear picture of the state of Roman society from the end of the Roman Republic (27 BCE) into the so-called Principate and Early Roman Empire (27 BCE–200 CE) and afterward. The stability of societies—relating to crime, social unrest, theft, and so on—is intimately related to income and in particular to income distribution. With respect to infrastructure, gross domestic profit, and economic well-being, it was not until the early modern period that societies achieved Roman levels of the first century CE.[15] Further, a recent study (Milanovic, Lindert, and Williamson 2007) examines income distribution in a number of ancient and postindustrial developed and poor societies including Rome approximately for the year 14 CE. While the authors find income distribution to be similar in ancient and poor modern societies, Rome appears to be something of an exception. In a study of eleven income classes at this time in Rome, Milanovic et al. calculate a Gini coefficient[16] of about 40 and argue that "the top percentile was very rich in the Roman Empire (16.1 percent of total income), but the cut-off point was very high too: 12.4 times the mean. This suggests a Roman income distribution with a long tail of rich people such that the 2nd–5th percentiles were also quite rich" (2007, 22). At this time average per capita income is calculated by Milanovic et al. at 380 in standardized units with a subsistence minimum of 180 and with farmers and farm workers (85.4 percent of the people in the empire) making 234, clearly above subsistence. Even the poorest workers, in other words, were fairly well off, and this does not include the important "free" distribution of food and other in kind subsidies (e.g., example, water) in the Roman cities. Peter Temin (2006, 137) concludes, with good anecdotal evidence, that "ancient Rome managed to achieve this high standard of living through the combined operation of moderately stable political conditions and markets for goods, labor and capital, which allowed specialization and efficiency."

This state of affairs, as history affirms, did not last, and neither did economic growth or a distribution of income resembling that in the Republic and early empire. Probably during the second century but most assuredly by the third, the character of Rome's society changed radically. Economic growth lagged as a command economy, personified by conquest and imperialism, supplanted a market system. Rule by autocratic emperors, drawn heavily from the military, created internal revolts. Internal weaknesses invited foreign invasions. In economic terms, Rome in the second and third centuries became a rent-seeking society as it evolved from early to late empire (DeLorme, Isom, and Kamerschen 2005). Most heavily taxed were the average peasant farmers who (ultimately) had to pay taxes that reflected the productivity of their land.[17] These regressive taxes displaced the poor, who opted for religion as an alternative. Christianity made such rent seeking by the state from the poor and from the upper classes much easier. The rent transfer was used for sumptuary expenditures of the ruling class and to wage wars by the state.

Additional general evidence from the third and early fourth century is instructive. A drumbeat of conflicts at the frontiers of the Roman Empire punctuated the latter half of the third century CE. Plague struck Italy, the Goths threatened on the Danube frontier, and the Persians threatened on the eastern frontier, all engendering numerous upheavals of the populace.[18] Official and unofficial attitudes toward Christians waxed and waned over the period. Valerian, becoming emperor in 253, began persecuting Christian clergy and members of the upper classes in 257 and 258 in an attempt to unify traditional Roman religion. After the capture of Valerian by the Persians, his son Gallienus established a peace with the Christians that lasted some forty years, although the empire split into three parts and other multiples thereafter (Bleckmann 2006, 36), exacerbating the confusion.

Emperors, primarily with military backgrounds, began to shun Rome as the seat of government due to the incessant chaos. Closest to Constantine's time in Christian persecutions was Diocletian (c. 244–313), a Roman-based military man who created a military tetrarchy in 293 and attempted to eliminate Christianity in 303 by requiring all to sacrifice to the traditional gods under penalty of death.[19] Persecutions, most strongly felt in the East and North Africa, were accompanied by further chaotic and terrifying problems brought on by Diocletian's attempts to reform the currency. Shortages and hoarding of "normal chaotic times" created by drought and wars were exacerbated by Diocletian's invocation of price and wage controls. In 301, Diocletian doubled the face value of all coins, creating havoc and ruin among creditors, establishing legal values for gold, silver, and bronze units. A cascade of inflation ensued whereupon Diocletian issued his price ceilings with the well-known consequences. Gold and commodity inflation thus created a massive redistribution of wealth from poor to rich. The chaos and upheavals, social and economic, led to rampant crime in the third and early fourth centuries. According to one contemporary source, "the poor were driven by their afflictions into various criminal enterprises, and losing sight of all respect for law, all feelings of loyalty, they entrusted their revenge to crime" (*De rebus bellicis*, 368, cited in Depeyrot 2006, 239).[20] Unquestionably, the turmoil within the Roman world, especially after Diocletian's economic "reforms," created agency costs for the government.[21] Internal policing and enforcement costs surrounded the empire in the third and early fourth centuries. Moral and ethical principles espoused by traditional Roman religion and championed during the Republic and early empire failed to stem the tide of violence and crime across the empire (and particularly in Rome). These high and rising costs were mitigated to some extent by the widespread adoption of Christianity in its various forms and precepts. As incomes, economic well-being, and security all declined—and as rent seeking by those at the top of income distribution proceeded apace—domestic peace was mightily threatened. Christianity became far more attractive to rulers as it reduced policing and agency costs in a society where enforcement resources were scarce and the opportunity cost in using them to fight civil unrest was extremely high.[22]

The Critical Role of Constantine and the March to Cartelization

Agency cost reductions for the Romans were accompanied by the drive of the new religion to ultimate cartelization and dominance over large portions of the former empire. This process involved movement from legitimacy (under the emperor Constantine in 313) to a cartel (developed

under Constantine at the Council of Nicaea in 325), to official state religion (in 380 CE under Emperor Theodosius), and ultimately (during
the late Dark Ages and under the Carolingian dynasty [Maclean 2003]
and later), to the dominance of Roman Catholicism throughout Europe.
But over the first three or four hundred years of its existence and indeed through the achievement of medieval monopoly, some fringe competition existed. Moreover, cartelization was important for theoretical
reasons, as discussed above. A monopolized church would have yielded
more agency cost savings to the Romans than a system of myriad Christian sects competing with one another.

But how was cartelization achieved? Certain particular factors are
conducive (or antithetical) to cartelization (Stigler 1964). Generally, the
smaller the number of sellers, the easier it is to cartelize a market. The
large number of groups calling themselves "Christians" or with Christian
affiliation over the early development of Christianity militated against
effective collusion. Some Christians believed that Christ was divine and
not human, some that he was exclusively human, and others that he was
both (the position finally adopted). Other sects emphasized dualism or
mild or extreme points of view (e.g., the Gnostic groups who viewed the
physical world as evil created by an evil deity). Thus, given the fact that
there were so many alternative written versions of Christianity and great
uncertainty as to when Christ would return, it is hardly surprising that
collusion was too costly to achieve over the first three hundred years of
Christianity's existence.

Collusion and cartelization are also facilitated by the production of
a homogeneous product. Heterogeneity would allow nonprice competition. As we have already stated, the numerous varieties of Christianity
itself entail high collusion costs. In the event, however, that groups got
together and established a homogeneous dogma, it could pay one group
to differentiate its product, however slightly, in order to gain additional
adherents.[23] So, without some kind of enforceable sanctioned body of
dogma and interpretation, cartelization of the early church before 313
would not have been possible.

Cartelization is also made easier where industries are growing and
progressive. In the year 250 CE, based on a population of 60 million persons in the Roman Empire, only an estimated 1.9 percent was Christian,
but over the next one hundred years, that percentage grew to 56.5 percent of the imperial population (Stark 1997, 7, table 1.1). Further, in Hopkins (1998, 191, fig. 1), the Christian population's approximated growth

was from 6,000,000 in 300 CE to 10,000,000 in 315 CE. This means that in the years just prior to Constantine the ease with which cartelization could take place was rising. A rising "majority" of believers in (what became) the traditional orthodoxy enshrined in the Nicene Creed and in the accepted and "proper" books of the Bible (dictated by the Eastern bishop Athanasius) helped create one of the preconditions of cartelization—a growing "industry." This, coupled with the fact that there were many "small buyers"—individuals and families—of Christian products, helped lead to ultimate cartelization. (Large buyers of the product would have encouraged cheating on the cartel price [i.e., a modified doctrine] if cartelization would have been feasible in the early period of Christianity).

Thus, the growing number of Christians as a proportion of the population, along with its effect of lowering agency costs to the Roman government(s), constituted a "perfect storm" for the legitimization of Christianity and the ultimate cartel it formed. A private collusive arrangement among Christian groups would have undoubtedly broken down for the reasons given above. What was needed was legitimization first and, most importantly, legal or other enforcement of the cartelized Christians with a *homogeneous product*.

Cartelization benefited the Romans as well as the Christian movement, as we have argued. Further, an alliance based on a common set of principles permitted, at least eventually, a political and religious component to collect rents. The focus of the initial Christian moves to legitimacy and cartelization occurred during the rule of Constantine (306–337 CE). At the outset, we do not dismiss the fact that Constantine might well have adopted Christianity—or ensured its legitimacy—because he was simply a good political agent of the will of the people. If Stark's data are correct (1997, 7, table 1.1), between 300 CE and 350 CE Christian numbers grew from 10.5 to 56.5 percent of the total population, and virtually all sources report very high growth over this period. Thus, the "tipping point" of legitimization may well have occurred before or after the emperor's reign. But the triumph of Christianity, commonly and with good reason attributed to the emperor Constantine, was the product of some of the forces discussed above. Christian morality ("Thou shall not steal") and the establishment of a Christian ethical system reduced crime and enforcement costs, making government control cheaper and more effective. These reduced costs would be greater with a government-sanctioned monopoly provision of religion. Although Christianity was not declared the official state religion of the empire until 380 (by Emperor Theodosius), the adoption of the religion by Constantine was the linchpin of Christianity's legitimacy. Constantine, who claimed to have had a battlefield apparition-conversion in 312 (defeating his core-gent Maxentius at the Battle of the Milvian Bridge in Rome), united the western and eastern parts of the empire and created at least a regional homogenization of Christianity three centuries after Jesus Christ. As we will see, these events were not unrelated. But in order to unify the em-pire successfully, Constantine had to address religious differences within the various Christian sects. That required the establishment of a theo-logical Christian cartel. Cartels of any kind are easier to form when the numbers of alternatives are smaller. This means that it is easier to reach a cartel consensus when homogeneous products are sold. When prod-uct differentiation is allowed, competition for market share ensues. Con-stantine's problem, then, was to attain political unity by *homogenizing* the major theological and politically related strands of Christianity at the time. His political and theological motives were of course intertwined.

Political Motives

Political turmoil punctuated the reign of Constantine. After the abdi-cation of Diocletian in 305, joint control of the empire was divided be-tween Maxentius (in Rome) and Constantine in the year 306. After battles at the frontier (chiefly with the Franks) and much political and military posturing, Constantine defeated Maxentius, a battle that was won, according to Constantine's belief, through the intercession of a "di-vine power." He then shared control of the empire with Licinius (who married Constantine's half-sister Constantia in the traditional path to unity) until Constantine took total control of both western and east-ern empires through military operations and political machinations in 324–325 by defeating Licinius militarily. Importantly, for our purposes, both Constantine and Licinius recognized the necessity for religious unity, passing the so-called Edict of Milan in 313. The edict is in ef-fect a declaration of the legitimacy of the Christian religion laced with promises of the return of property seized under the reign of Diocletian. Further, it rejected the kind of coercion of belief that motivated Dio-cletian's persecution of Christians (Drake 2006, 121). The edict, or "im-perial ordinance," read in part, that "we decided to establish rules by which respect and reverence for the Deity would be secured, i.e., to give the Christians and all others liberty to follow whatever form of worship they chose, so that whatsoever divine and heavenly powers exist might be enabled to show favor to us and to all who live under our authority" (quoted in Eusebius 1984, 402).

This initial step, fully supported by Constantine, was (if we are correct) an attempt to bring uniformity to religious observance and the inculcation of Christian principles, which would reduce all manner of "bad behavior" within the populace and the costs associated with it.[24] But the interface between political and theological issues was crucial throughout Constantine's reign and the entire fourth century. In particular, the multiplicity of Christian religious sects and beliefs, especially in the eastern parts of the empire, were a barrier to political unification between Rome and the East (Byzantium).

Theological Homogeneity

The solidification of a common Christianity under Constantine was a major factor in the political unification within the eastern part of the empire and between the western and eastern branches of power as well. (Theologically, the unification of eastern and western branches of Catholicism remains incomplete.) Early spread of Christianity was accomplished by the interplay between entrepreneurial activities and network effects as discussed in chapter 4. Forms of Christianity were extremely diverse, ranging from extreme Gnosticism (Grant 1966; Pagels 1989) to multiple variations on what would become "traditional" Christian belief. After persecutions in the early period, a period of relative toleration of most forms of Christianity by the imperial government occurred. Prior to Constantine, a long "peace" materialized for Christians between the reigns of Valerian and Diocletian. Indeed, persecutions varied widely from locale to locale, being more severe in Africa (and Spain) than in the many western parts of the empire. More importantly, there were *many* forms of a belief system called "Christianity" (and of competing paganism) over the first three hundred years throughout the empire. In addition, the term "Christianity" took on many meanings as multiple sects adopted new (and alternative) forms of the new religion.[25]

Two sects in particular had a direct impact on Constantine: Donatism and Arianism. Donatism emerged during persecutions in North Africa (Frend 1952), where a local bishop (Felix) was accused of being a traitor to the cause by turning over "sacred documents" (written forms of Christian belief) to the Romans. Two factions developed, and internecine warfare within the church broke out with supporters of Felix siding with his ability to perform the sacraments such as Holy Orders (ordination of priests and bishops at that time). A second group argued that Felix's "mortal sin" made him incapable of performing valid sacraments, making all of his clerical descendants invalid. This cause, dividing North Africans and political and violent in nature, came to be taken up by a bishop Donatus (providing a name for the controversy). Adding fuel to the controversy, the issue of marriage—which had been a purely civil matter under the Romans—was taken over by the Christian church under Constantine with important implications for the transfer of legal property rights. If marriages were deemed invalid (the Donatist position in North Africa), property inheritance was also invalid. Although Constantine was originally ambivalent about the situation, political and religious pogroms (Christian against Christian) endangered the political unity he was trying to achieve, and he opposed the sect, arresting its leaders and warring against them until 321.[26]

Theological Issues

A second major series of issues were theological, and some of these differences continue today. Clearly, these alternatives to (what became) orthodox Christianity in the fourth century were also plagued by the issue of the loci of interpretation of Christ's message. Alternative interpretations of Christ's mission on earth differed from the beginning. Disciples had different interpretations of particular events in the life of Jesus. But even if all accepted the traditional New Testament as "the" doctrine of Christ from the beginning (Gospels of Matthew, Mark, Luke, and John), interpretational issues would arise. Some *interpretation* is still required. But who had the authority to interpret scripture? As numerous writers have emphasized, things were even more complicated. The writings of traditional Gospels, thought to have taken place between 117 and 138 CE, varied between individuals who were eyewitnesses to Jesus Christ and his resurrection and their scriptural descendants. *Different* doctrinal forms were being promulgated among Jewish converts and pagan converts. Scriptural scholar Bart Ehrman (2005, 11–12) emphasizes the role of copyists—transcriptions of transcriptions of transcriptions by

scribes—in providing alternative and contradictory expressions of scripture. Noting that there is no extant autograph edition of the New Testament, the text was

> written by different human authors at different times and in different places
> to address different needs. Many of these authors no doubt felt they were in-
> spired by God to say what they did, but they had their own perspectives, their
> own beliefs, their own views, their own needs, their own desires, their own
> understandings, their own theologies; and these perspectives, beliefs, views,
> needs, desires, understandings, and theologies informed everything they said.
> . . . Among other things, this meant that Mark did not say the same thing that
> Luke said because he didn't mean the same thing as Luke. John is different
> from Matthew—not the same. Paul is different from Acts. And James is dif-
> ferent from Paul. . . . The Bible, at the end of the day, is a very human book.

Clearly, the early writers had the Old Testament to draw on—the Ten
Commandments were and are very much a part of Christianity.[27] But
even here, interpretation is not always clear. How far does "Thou shall
not kill" go in meaning? There is a literal interpretation and many
(many) others. Who interprets and where they find the authority to interpret are important elements in the story of religion. These issues and
those related to organization are the core problems of early Christianity. For three hundred years, the canon of Christianity and the interpretation of the meaning of Christ and his message took center stage among
competitive Christian and non-Christian beliefs. In brief, the early Christian church was, for three centuries, in the same position as modern nonestablishment Christianity.

Consider the situation at the time of Constantine. Extreme positions
of the Gnostics aside—those that posited a dualism between the evil
of all things worldly and the completely separate "good" of Christ and
God—there were major theological differences between those who would
establish the orthodox view of Christianity. Was Christ both human
and divine? Was Jesus Christ coequal with God, or was He less "eternal?" Was monotheism threatened by the concept of the Trinity? How
could there be three persons in one god? Most importantly, perhaps, for
early, later, and contemporary Christianity: how were the words of the
scriptures to be interpreted—literally or as metaphor? These and a multiplicity of theological issues plagued the early centuries of Christianity before and after Constantine. One issue was a key to Constantine's

"integration" of Christianity—the issue of the equality of Jesus Christ to God the Father. The movement was an Eastern controversy called Arianism.

Arianism, named for an Egyptian priest Arius, was the view, promulgated around 320, that Christ, being the Son of the Father, could not be coequal but had to be an inferior deity. This view gained an enormous amount of currency in the Eastern Church (it was accepted by the great church historian Eusebius, for example), and it was the cause of a major split in the Eastern Church. Athanasius of Alexandria opposed this theological position, and Constantine was embroiled in the controversy as the differences threatened the unification of his empire. The Council of Nicaea (in Asia Minor) was called by Constantine in 325 to settle the controversy, which in reality continued for some centuries.

These were not the only variants of early Christianity, and entry into the Christian market was relatively simple. Nuances of doctrine or Christian belief were rampant prior to the fourth century and the Council of Nicaea. Unless steps are taken to cartelize and monopolize Christianity as a whole, history, both ancient and modern, teaches that competitive networks of Christ-centered variants of Christianity will proliferate. In other words, networks do not lead to permanent natural monopolies; they lead to *competition* at the network level. Any monopoly power will be transitory, and schism and product differentiation will characterize the market for religion, just as hundreds of variants of Christian religion exist today. Religious monopoly may be "natural" in the sense that there can be only one true way to heaven; that is, there is a natural inclination to aspire to be a religious monopoly. But the plain fact of the matter is that individuals and groups will compete to provide that one true way. This means that long lasting monopoly power in the market for religion will be "unnatural" and promoted by monopolistic practices related to cartel/monopoly formation and enforcement such as that established at Nicaea in 325 by Constantine. Such monopoly is not the inevitable outcome of market forces but rather results from efforts by market suppliers to reduce competition in the marketplace for Christianity.

The Council of Nicaea, which established the fundamental beliefs of orthodox Christianity for all time, if not settling interpretive issues, was called by Constantine ostensibly to attempt to resolve an acrimonious theological debate that had critical political overtones. Indeed, all of Constantine's actions relating to Nicaea and later actions as regards "theology" had several overarching practical goals: to resolve the major

conflict dividing the eastern parts of the empire; to help unite the Roman (Western) and Eastern Christian Churches and empire; and to use
a united Christian religion and its implication of political unification as
a weapon against the single most important enemy of the empire—the
Persians.

In 324 Constantine celebrated the foundation of Constantinople as the
"New Rome," a move that one observer cites as providing "easy access
to the east without turning its back on the west" (Fowden 2006, 381). He
then convened the Nicaean Council the following year with the intention
of including all Christian bishops, although the vast majority came from
the eastern empire, including a Persian bishop. The Armenian Aristakes
and the Lazican (west Georgian) Stratophilus were among the prelates
in attendance. Actually, Constantine invited *all* of the bishops of the
Christian church and their retinues to the council—numbering approximately 1,800 individuals from East and West. Most authorities, including
Eusebius, believe that about three hundred bishops attended with some
multiple numbers of attendees to account for the bishop's entourages.[28]
Among attendees, most of them from the Eastern Church with only five
from the west, were bishops whose titles would later be patriarchs—
Alexander of Alexandria, Eustathius of Antioch, and Macarius of Jerusalem. (Constantinople, later to become one of the two major divisions
of the church, was not yet established.) The Roman bishop [Pope Sylvester I, 314–336] did not attend due to age and ill heath but was represented by two prelates. Among the critical actions taken there were the
condemnation of the Arian belief , the date and time of the celebration
of Easter (divorcing Christianity from the Jewish time of the celebration of Passover) and the passage of twenty canons, several of which are
quite interesting. One of the canons provided for two provincial synods
to be held annually, and another recognized the exceptional authority of
the patriarchs (bishops) of Alexandria and Rome in their respective regions.[29] The council, made up of less than one-fifth of sitting Christian
bishops, did not recognize the primacy of the bishops (or pope) of Rome
over the entire church, but rather clearly stated that the episcopal form
of the church—where rule was "localized" by region and where church
governance was collegial with inputs from the faithful in each region—
was to be the organizational structure of the Christianity.

Constantine presented himself as a divinely appointed unifier but
with a far broader intention. According to Fowden (2006, 282),

Constantine considered his flock to be those outside the church regardless of political boundaries. The groundwork for this universalism was to be laid in the form of mission, alliance, and warfare. We should not be misled into thinking that for Constantine it was sufficient merely to discern the universality of Christianity. Discernment was a prelude to the unification of all peoples into one political empire. Although political restraints limited his lawgiving to "all those under Roman government," Constantine's ecumenical council and the cultivation of holy sites were international in scope.

In the thirtieth anniversary of his reign, Constantine called another assemblage of Christian prelates and laity gathered at Jerusalem, again the vast majority from the East including Persia, to dedicate the church over Christ's tomb (founded earlier by Constantine's mother). Fowden reports that "Constantine's plans for a campaign against the Persians worked in concert with these dedications and celebrations" (2006, 282). Thus, whatever Constantine's theological intentions (or beliefs), his central goal in calling the Council of Nicaea was to unify the empire and to create a cartel of (approximate) conformity among Christians who would support him, help lower internal agency costs, and suppress pagans, sometimes for profit as we will see.

Evidence for these overall propositions is indirect but compelling. While conventional wisdom often maintains that the Nicaean Council and Nicene Creed meant a complete condemnation of Arianism, the evidence is that Constantine and his successor Constantius ultimately oversaw Arius's recall (by the bishop of Constantinople) only in 337. Ultimately, after some time Arias and his view died out, but Constantine's (relative) tolerance in theological matters meant that an uneasy peace between opposing theologies would be tolerated with respect to somewhat esoteric Arian beliefs and their differences from orthodox Christianity. Constantine came down hard, however, on the Donatists and pagans who were a clear and present danger to political unity. This represents the power of the state being used to enforce the decisions of the church *cum* cartel. Thus Constantine's motives in establishing a quasi-homogenous set of religious beliefs were fundamentally political as well as for economic aggrandizement. While Christians had once been on the receiving end of property confiscations, one authority notes that "Constantine himself after his conversion organized a similar transfer of wealth from pagan temples and Donatist schismatics to the state and

the church. And Constantine's sons continued the policies of their father by despoiling temples, a policy with which Christian authors, in a
paradoxical twist, fully agreed: 'Take away, yes, calmly take away, Most
Holy Emperors, the adornments of the temples. Let the fire of the mint
or the blaze of the smelters melt them down, and confiscate all the vo-
tive offerings to your own use and ownership'" (Brown 1989; Depeyrot 2006, 244). In this, Constantine would be followed by such leaders
as Henry VIII, who confiscated the assets of the monasteries and the
Roman Church in England in the sixteenth century. Not only was the
population taxed by Constantine, but the funds flowed into state cof-
fers and then were handed over to the church. Constantine, at the same
time, paid people to become Christian, and Christians became eligible
for high government positions, land doles, and so on. Constantine was simultaneously destroying pagan temples, killing eunuchs, using "judicial
savagery" to end pagan cults, and "encouraging" elites to make donations to the Christian church.[30]

While we have emphasized the mélange of "Christian" theologies
that developed in the face of the fact that Christ did not return quickly
in human time, there was an organizational crisis as well. Ehrman describes the early Christian communities as "charismatic communities,"
believing that each member has been given a spiritual "gift" to assist
the community (teaching, almsgiving, healing, prophecy, and so on).
But, "as the expectation of an imminent end of the world began to fade,
it became clear that there needed to be a more rigid church structure,
especially if the church was to be around for the long haul . . ." (2005,
25–26). Churches began appointing leaders and establishing rules about
how baptisms and celebration of the Eucharist and other rites should be
"properly" performed, and "church orders" relating to these things and
to the order of leadership became more and more common in the second and third centuries. Later these accompanied the establishment of
theological Christian orthodoxy. The organization of the church was like
most competitive industries—it was congregation-based. It was "flat" in
an economic sense. When cartelized, a hierarchy was mandatory, and
so a vertical structure emerged. It would take centuries for this vertical structure to develop more completely and manifest itself in efficient
rules such as "laws of succession." (*How* the church accomplished this
vertical integration is a principal issue of the remainder of this book.)
Such laws have yet to become ubiquitous, as the opposing beliefs of the
Eastern rites of the Roman Catholic Church reveal.

Nicaea was thus one if not *the* central moment for Christianity in terms of product definition. The fact that Christ had not returned "quickly" meant that some *official and exclusive code of beliefs and an organizational structure* had to be firmly established.[31] Intense competition and fragmentation of the religion would occur otherwise, perhaps resulting in a multiplicity of Christian "paganisms."[32] But the Council of Nicaea and its establishment of Orthodoxy through the definition of the New Testament and the Nicaean Creed, in addition to a theological rallying point for Christians, was a political move as well. While theological and interpretational points such as that raised by Arias were (and continue to be) debatable, the ground rules for the underlying political structure of Christian interpretations vis-à-vis the state were established.[33] Donatism and paganism, two threats to the unification of the eastern and western branches of Christianity, were outlawed at Nicaea. It is in this sense that political control was made easier since no cartel—Christian or otherwise—is possible where product differentiation is meaningful. The Gospels included were those most generally accepted within the church, east and west. In addition to all of the benefits that accrued to Constantine from this pivotal event, these homogenizing elements gave the church cartel a handle to fight all ensuing doctrinal challenges right up to the medieval monopoly of Roman Catholicism and beyond.

The critical and most important point was that Constantine and all secular leaders that followed him reaped the benefits (and later the costs) of theological homogeneity under the Christian banner. The council, in effect, created externalities favorable to the state. First, there were the immediate benefits: Constantine and his immediate successors financed the institution of Christianity and other projects by taxing pagans, atheists, and followers of nonorthodox (e.g., most other non-Nicaea believers) Christianity. But in the long run secular government acquired a massive civil tool. It gave the orthodox-defending secular ruler a pretext to battle and conquer all those who did not espouse orthodoxy. It was an "us against them" mentality that developed. Christianity was, in other words, exclusivist, and this exclusivity was defended for political as well as religious reasons by civil governments. Deviants must be expelled or expunged, and there was a high risk to schismatics or to those who espoused other belief systems.[34]

Exclusivity had enormous benefits at least as long as church and state were "in agreement" over policy. In sum, the Edict of Milan and the Council of Nicaea, both sponsored by Constantine, had deep implications for the course of politics and religion over the ensuing centuries. As always, there were winners and losers. Constantine, who organized the council and, by extension, the consiliar form of church government along the lines of the Roman Senate, was the big winner, as were his successors in the East for some centuries. Product definitions gave state and the orthodox Christian church a potent tool to suppress competition by adopting uniformity of doctrine. Unified Christian religion created externalities for the state by reducing agency and enforcement costs. It also enriched the orthodox Christian church with power and booty from pagan and other Christian sects. Pagans and nonorthodox competitive Christians were the big losers over both the short and long runs. Christian theologies and interpretations other than the one chosen—in all likelihood the most popular and politically adaptive—were ultimately all but eliminated. Heretics, now clearly defined, became all but extinct or were driven underground in regions dominated by Christians. The reign of Constantine and his support for *one* Christianity constituted, without question, a turning point in Western history.

We have portrayed Constantine and the Nicaean solidification of product definition as pivotal in creating a nascent hegemony over Christianity. These observations must be tempered with some caveats. First, the initial major moves toward the monopoly came not from *within* the church but from Roman emperors Constantine and Theodosius, who were, after all, resident in Constantinople, not in Rome, although the reach of their authority certainly extended there. There would (ultimately) be a separation of church and state for *Roman* Catholicism that did not extend to the independent patriarchs in the East. The Roman Church would always have an institutional rival in the state, a situation that was not produced in the Eastern Orthodox brand of Christianity. Second, Nicaean product definition did not completely succeed in eliminating other Christian beliefs such as Arianism (the later German invaders were largely Arian).[35] Third, and perhaps most importantly, Nicaea and the empire's support of Christianity did not at all provide Roman Christianity with a monopoly at the time. Of the five patriarchates of the early church, three were eliminated by Arab conquests of the seventh century and Constantinople was not (and is not) eliminated by Roman bishops.[36] As we will see, Rome declared itself primal in the mid-eleventh century. We do not maintain that there was some unilateral self-direction then in creating a Roman monopoly over vast parts of Europe. Many other factors were in play. We do note, however, that the

foundations of that monopoly occurred with a firmly defined product at
the council called by Constantine.

Conclusion

Given the context of this discussion, one can hardly avoid a comment on
the relative "rise" of Christianity and the "fall" of the Roman Empire.
There is no dearth of candidates about possible linkages now as there
has not been for hundreds of years. Clearly, a government out of control
with imperial and expansionary military policies was a factor. The tax
policies on the working poor—mainly farmers and low-grade workers—
forced labor off the land yielding lower productivity. Rent seeking by ancient *rentiers* and politicians further concentrated wealth in the hands
of individuals who used it for sumptuary consumptions rather than productive investments. High on the list of reasons and a major cause of increased taxation was the incursion of Goths, Vandals, and invaders from
outside the Roman frontier. A weakened and unstable empire, so the argument goes, was unable to resist precipitous decline. A Marxist line of
argument emphasizes the inability of the upper classes to inculcate education and higher values into the lower classes. The argument culmi-
nates in the dominance of lower-class values (Rostovtzeff 1926, 539–541
et passim). Likely and dramatic changes in the distribution of income
accompanied these institutional changes. The economic, political, and
social all contributed to the emergence of the so-called Dark Ages, or the
early medieval period in the fifth century—a period of alleged stagna-
tion within a feudal context that lasted for at least several centuries.

The identification of cause and effect is all but impossible. This chapter has focused on the role of Christianity in the sweep of Roman history
over the period up to Constantine. There appears to be a highly significant negative relation between the decline of the empire and the rise of
Christianity.[37] But Christianity was not, as has sometimes been argued,
a cause or "the" cause of the decline of the Roman Empire. Rather, we
have argued that due to particular economic factors—the reduction in
agency and enforcement costs on the part of Roman state—Christianity
became an acceptable alternative (or initially a supplement to) the Roman gods and ritual. Those who did not adopt Nicaean Christianity,
legitimized and then sponsored by the state, were outcasts at best and
persecuted at worst. The emphasis of inclusiveness, forgiveness and the

condemnation of economic transgressions toward the state helped lead Constantine to legitimize the religion. But for Constantine the adoption of Christianity was actually "all about the state." Christians were essentially deferent to the secular role of government in the early period ("render to Caesar"), if not later over the first millennium. Constantine was able to perceive the critical role that Christianity could play in the economic and social unification of the empire, and he and his successors attempted to use the religion in an attempted resurgence of the empire. It is interesting that the roles of government and religion reversed themselves between the fifth and tenth centuries when Christianity ultimately claimed dominance over secular governments. At first, the state legitimized Christianity. Later, the state(s) required Christianity for legitimacy, the latter being a tool and an entree for a vertically integrated organization of the church.

Christianity, with its emphasis on providing social welfare and on nonviolence, was a boon to the Roman state. Crime and societal divisions, so common from the second century onward, required costly resources to be spent. Christianity led to a reduction in the need for internal policing, freeing up resources for other uses (such as fighting invasions). Hostile treatment of Christians by the Roman state is often exaggerated. In reality, it ranged from tolerance to hostility depending on whether Christians were regarded as a threat to the polity. We argue that, certainly into the third and fourth centuries, Christians also produced positive economic and social benefits in the form of reduced agency costs to the state.

Constantine was, without doubt, the key figure of the fourth century and in the ultimate domination of Christianity. For political and economic reasons, and possibly for religious ones as well, Constantine sought to establish a homogeneous product through the Council at Nicaea. This version of orthodoxy became the standard around which a religious and *political cartel* could be built. Theological issues were and are not yet not solved by the products of the council, but the (approximate) product homogenization helped Constantine and his successors build an empire, sometimes united, sometimes bifurcated, around the Christian religion.[38] That religion ultimately became a close approximation of a monopoly over belief in the early Middle Ages. And, importantly, the monopoly structure possibly increased the provision of external effects and lower agency costs by the church.

Christianity refined monotheism making it more attractive as a belief system with the critical assistance of self-interested political individuals such as Constantine and certain church fathers, finally becoming the dominant force in Western governments and civilizations until the sixteenth century. The road to a medieval monopoly was accompanied by internecine struggles within and onslaughts on the Roman Empire and other polities as the latter declined (McCormick 2001). Further, the Council of Nicaea was a poor predictor of subsequent developments regarding Christian church structure. While it, in effect, established precedent for general ecumenical councils or synods of bishops as the (at the time) leading body of Christianity, the role of defining belief systems and doctrinal orthodoxy was, after many skirmishes and battles between East and West, preempted by *one* bishop. As the empire became Balkanized, the power of the Roman Catholic Church ascended as a "legitimizer" of civil governments, characterized by the coronation by the pope of Charlemagne on Christmas day in 800 CE. That struggle, circa 476–1100 CE, to arrive at the medieval monopoly of the *Roman* Catholic Church remains to be assessed.

CHAPTER SIX

The Drive to Church Monopoly: Constantine to Charlemagne

Introduction

Our investigation up to this point has centered on the application of modern economics to the historical origins of Christianity and to its ultimate acceptance by Constantine and the remnants of imperial Rome. These developments were essential to the future of both church and state. Chapters 6 and 7 outline the *organizational revolution* that enabled the Roman Church to become a virtual multinational monopoly by the end of the twelfth century. Economic concepts of networking and entrepreneurship were brought to bear on the sociohistorical arguments for the initial rapid development of Christianity in earlier chapters. We now focus on the manner through which the church created an organizational revolution in order to control doctrine throughout the church and to control behavior of downstream agents that "sold" the product— a Christian *interpretation* of the Old and New Testament concerning salvation and an afterlife on what might be broadly called "assurance services' for members.

Important backdrop frames these critical centuries. The Roman government accepted the growing Christian movement which, among other effects, helped keep internal peace and freed up resources to help fight invading tribes. Most critically, the orthodox product of Christianity was established by the Edict of Milan and at the Council of Nicaea with the support of Constantine. Both the council and Constantine's subventions are the foundation for the development of Christian monopoly in the ensuing centuries. A single orthodoxy—defended by the state—was established that gave moral authority to that segment of the church against *newly defined* heresies and heretics. Likewise, it gave civil government a hammer to impose costs on enemies of the Roman state *in the name of religious orthodoxy*. But mutual advantage to Christian religion and the Roman state could not last forever. An orthodox Roman Christian monopoly took centuries to form in spite of glorious beginnings under Constantine. Legitimization was a critical step on the road to monopoly, but the declarations of Theodosius were only a beginning of the hegemony acquired by the *Roman* Christian church between the end of the fourth century and the beginning of the ninth century with the coronation of Charlemagne (Boussard 1968). Toward the end of the first millennium a virtual monopoly over religion and a close-knit oligopoly of Christian and a variety of secular powers gathered critical mass across most of Europe.

How did Christianity attain this position in economic terms? We argue that three key economic factors go far in the explanation of how monopoly was advanced from the springboard of fourth-century developments. First, the church continued to promulgate the product definition of "Christian" established at Nicaea together with assertions of *Roman* papal primacy. Secondly, economic *reciprocity* emerged between civil entities and the church within the political and jurisdictional melee that replaced the Roman Empire. Both civil governments and the church used this orthodoxy to suppress competition and interlopers in civil and religious markets. Finally, and critically, the continuing entrepreneurial activity of the church spread Christianity across Europe creating an emerging *vertical integration* within the church even as the primacy of the Roman bishop remained in dispute. The church evolved a vertically integrated monopoly firm over this period (fourth through ninth centuries) and solidified it in the ninth through twelfth centuries (chap. 7), an invention with multinational influence that gave it great advantages over civil governments. Despite contentious battles with civil authorities over the "rights to appoint and tax," its vertically integrated monopoly enabled the church ultimately to win these critical battles with civil governments (e.g., the Investiture Controversy). A multinational presence to-

gether with a superior ability to collect taxes at downstream levels gave
the church singular advantages over individual states. The integrated
church monopoly had greater control over local agents and provided services demanded by consumers as well. But the story of these centuries is
one of the techniques used by the church to achieve this position by the
twelfth century, and simple economic theory goes far in supporting an
understanding of this process.

Economic Theory and Christianity in the
Fourth–Twelfth Centuries

A vast skein of historical events, many of them cataclysmic in a geopolitical sense, formed the backdrop for the ascendance of Christian religion
between Constantine and the establishment of the Holy Roman Empire
in the year 800 CE with the crowning of Charlemagne. The decline of
the Roman Empire and its reestablishment in the East (Byzantium) was
not a discrete or sudden event but was a gradual evolution. Germanic
and other tribes did not so much conquer Italy and the western empire
as assimilate into the cultural, political and religious milieu. Broad historical events accompanied these developments. After Constantine, the
western and eastern parts of empire were shared until 476 when the center of the old Roman Empire became Byzantium with Constantinople as
its centerpiece and capital, with remnants lasting until the High Middle
Ages. Western developments that mightily affected and were affected by
Christianity began with the development of the Frankish kingdom under
Pepin and Charlemagne, setting the stage for a new *Holy* Roman Empire. The power of the church was commercial as well as spiritual. Before the year 900 CE, the church owned or controlled one-third of the
cultivatable land of Europe, including 31 percent of such land in Italy,
35 percent in Germany and 44 percent in northern France (Herlihy
1961). (Naturally, these commercial riches brought the church in conflict
with the powers and tax revenues of civil institutions.)

   The Christian church achieved dominance of varying degrees as a religion and as a foundation for secular governments against the massive
and diverse tapestry of events forming the basis for Western civilization.
Fundamentally, this was achieved by *noncoercive, voluntary agreements*
between religious and secular institutions wherein the *Roman* Catholic

Church achieved virtual monopoly over religious practice in the eleventh and twelfth centuries. This monopoly was the product of a unique solution to problems that inured to the ever-growing firm. In a nutshell: How was the firm to organize, maintain doctrinal orthodoxy and repatriate revenues to the top, the *upstream* church, when the source of its main product was in the hands of local priests, monasteries and missionaries, the *downstream* church, and were widely and organizationally dispersed across a whole Continent and beyond? The answer was the application of an organizational form of the firm: vertical integration.[1] Thus, the path to victory and dominance in the early Middle Ages may be analyzed with the tools of modern economics, in particular, with the principles of industrial organization and public choice. The path to monopoly included the following critical economic elements: maintenance of the purity and integrity of the product of the firm established at Nicaea; an economic "reciprocity" which provided benefits for both the church and civil governments; and, critically, the implementation of the vertically integrated firm. Consider a theoretically stylized discussion of these three key elements.

Product Integrity and Economic Reciprocity

Effective (or mostly effective) entry control into the monopoly market of the Roman Christian church required a clear definition of the product that was being sold. This meant that the identity of the entire structure of the faith had to be defined to create an orthodoxy against which heresy, including nonorthodox forms of Christianity, could be condemned. Importantly, this definition was fairly complete by the time of Constantine and the Council of Nicaea and other councils of the church, but, in addition, the Roman Christian church had to make and enforce claims on the *interpretation* of the holy scriptures and other essential elements of the faith (e.g., the New Testament or the Ten Commandments). Recall, however, that the primacy of the bishop of Rome over the entire church was not a part of the Council of Nicaea. But after the fourth century, the centralized church (patriarchs, church councils, the Roman pope and his entourage—the Curia) had to maintain "purity" of fourth-century doctrine to forestall entry by other still-active rival Christian sects and to establish a bastion of interpreted dogma to defend against other monotheistic religions and paganism as well. As we will see, political leaders and entities were used to accomplish these suppressions, as was the force of excommunications and punitive tools.

A form of reciprocity was also used by church and state. The church, with growing legions of followers that now included the Christianized barbarians, provided support and increasingly vital credence to secular governmental units. In return, the church received protection from punishment and competitors from secular governments. An interest group theory goes far in describing these reciprocal arrangements between secular power and religious authority. More importantly, it is critical that active duopolistic (two-party) competition for the rights to revenues played a pivotal role in church-secular relations and consolidations.

These principles may usefully be expressed in terms of demand and supply. Consider the nature of what was supplied to secular governments. The church, especially as the Roman Empire's control over its territories deteriorated, became a *primary supplier* of social and civil services. Its monasteries became the "protectors" of the learning of the ancient world and Roman cultural traditions. It took over educational and health service functions as well. It supplied a theological-philosophical product—a philosophy of love and peace in this world as taught by Jesus Christ in a monotheistic framework and, crucially, the strong promise of an afterlife, which was a key (if not *the* key) product of Christianity. The success of the Christian message meant that in order to gain widespread support, civil governments had to accept Christianity.

On the other side of the equation, why would civil governments *demand* Christianity and the Christian church apparatus? Clearly, as we argued in the previous chapter, there are agency costs associated with social and political upheaval that are reduced by the Christian philosophy of love and peace. But there are other important factors explaining the demand for Christian services on the part of civil and political authorities. Christian practices and culture provided a set of rules that amounted, especially after the emperor Justinian in the seventh century, to "laws" that where translated into more formal canon and civil laws. Another critical factor was the credence and legitimacy that the church was able to provide civil governments and rulers. (For example, it was not for nothing that Constantine and later, Clovis I of the Franks, submitted to battlefield conversions to the Christian faith.) Christian social services, which substituted for civil expenditures on health, education, and welfare, were other powerful reasons for civil governments to demand the services supplied by the Christian church(s).

The Organizational Solution: Vertical Integration

The Christian church in the post-fourth-century period has been described in many ways. Its historical evolution, its spread, and the spatial
and sociological aspects of the church have been given brilliant and ex-
haustive treatment over the centuries. But one component of the church
has not been plumbed—the adoption of an evolving form of church economic organization. The problem facing the young church by 400 CE
may be stated in simple terms. Products or services in this case are often developed at the highest or "upstream" levels of a firm. Microsoft
or Google define and develop the products they sell at the highest levels
of firm management. These firms often create divisions—financial, technological, human resource—at the top levels to define and develop the
product. The ultimate products (computers, software) or services (religious assurances of eternal salvation and promises of an afterlife) are
"sold" at lower divisions of the firm. The rational firm manager will look
at the so-called make or buy option. That is, depending on the costs and
market conditions, the upstream firm may decide to franchise (a Kentucky Fried Chicken or Wendy's restaurant)—the "buy" option—or it
will sell the product itself to downstream consumers (a vertically integrated firm). The latter sells the product *itself* in the "forward" market—
the "make" option (Holiday Inn hotels). A firm attempting to create a
monopoly will often behave in this fashion, and the Christian church,
circa fourth to twelfth centuries, was in principle no different than contemporary firms that are vertically organized in this manner. However
organized, each firm, including Christianity, faces different kinds of
problems in the upstream-downstream sale of products or services in the
marketplace.

Consider figure 6.1, which presents a stylized account of Christian
church organization over the long period we are considering in chapters 6
and 7. In the early period, before Roman Church dominance, the upstream church consisted of patriarchs (Roman, Byzantine, Syrian, Alexandrine, and others), archbishops, and church councils (consortia of
bishops). These individuals, generally through the aforementioned councils, made policy and biblical interpretative decisions that affected the
entire church. Much later, after the bishop of Rome achieved priority
in these matters, conciliar decisions along with policy decisions by the
pope (bishop of Rome) and the Curia, were the upstream arm of the
church. The doctrinal monopoly established at Nicaea (and amended

Vertical Integration of the Church

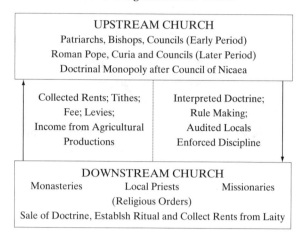

FIGURE 6.1. Economic Organization of the Monopoly Church, Fourth to Twelfth Centuries

at Chalcedon in 451 CE) was interpreted, embellished with policy implications, and defended against all threats by the (now) Roman establishment. It is also important to note that as the geographic spread of Christianity increased through the first millennium, additional offices representing the papacy—archbishops (later cardinals), papal nuncios (apostolic diplomatic representatives), and other high-ranking church officials—were dispatched from Rome to oversee church operations in far-flung nations.

The product was "sold" at the downstream level in local parishes by priests attached to dioceses that were administered by bishops, by missionaries and itinerant prelates and through monasteries, sometimes attached to particular bishops and sometimes not. It was at this "retail" level of the church that conversions were made, church doctrine was preached, and revenues were collected. In figure 1, moreover, two arrows show the flow of revenues and services that this vertically organized firm transacted between upstream and downstream levels of the church. Although most of the revenues collected at the retail level stayed at that level, the upstream church collected rents in the form of tithes, land rents, bequests, special collections for the papacy (e.g., "Peter's Pence"), and a portion of the income from monasteries' agricultural production. The two major forms of donation were bequests and tithes. Bishops and monasteries were huge landowners in particular and were ripe sources

of rents in return for protected exclusive properties and territorial restrictions provided by the upstream church. Further, monies were collected by bishops and papal representatives for "visitations" (audits?)
of the monasteries.[2] Initially, after the primacy of the bishop of Rome
had been effectively established against the other patriarchs, the collection of revenues was centralized in the office of the *camera*, an office initially part of the papal household but one that became more centralized
as church revenues grew. Eventually, annual cameral receipts exceeded
those of any European government.[3]

In return, the upstream church maintained the definition and interpretation of the product (assurances of eternal salvation) and established
the human conditions upon which a happy afterlife could be attained.[4]
Because salvation is a metacredence good (the quality of the goods is
unknown either before or after the purchase), the quality of the good
had to be authenticated by the upstream church thereby validating and
solidifying the spatial monopoly powers of the downstream bishoprics or
monasteries.

The church evolved toward complete vertical integration with "transfer prices"—prices at which resources moved between upstream and
downstream segments of the firm—equal to marginal costs. Monopoly
profits were maximized by contractual arrangements within the firm
and upstream and downstream units shared profits (Blair and Kaserman 1983). The fact that the church was a vertically integrated monopoly (with monopoly provision of the product at the upstream level) did
not mean that all problems of repatriating rents and contractual issues were solved. In an early medieval setting between the fourth and
twelfth centuries, information and transportation costs were high. Furthermore, it was the practice in some locales for bishops and/or civil authorities to appoint the heads of monasteries. The upper levels of the
church were therefore unable completely to avoid the opportunistic behavior that arose downstream by bishops, civil governments, and monastery heads and local priests as well. Competition at the local level
would have driven down monopoly profits, and the upstream church created, for monasteries at least, exclusive territories within which local
operations took place. "Unorthodox" doctrine taught at the local levels would damage the integrity of the product. Diverted revenues such
as taxes on monasteries by local or other lords would reduce monopoly
rents flowing upstream. Controls had to be instituted by the upstream
church.

The church in fact instituted a number of downstream controls—in effect contractual controls—with the goal being wealth maximization and complete vertical integration. The church fought at every possible instance, as we will see in chapter 7, civil appointment of abbots and clerics (the Investiture Controversy) and the civil taxation thereof. The church used "tying arrangements" to extract lump-sum payments from bishops and monasteries. Later in the mid-eleventh-century Cistercian monasteries typically paid a sales revenue royalty of up to 5 percent of annual gross income to the bishop for annual "visitations"—the only way the upstream church could practically keep track of the localized activities of monks and priests (Snape 1926, 97–98).[5] This generated income for the pope and/or the patriarchs of the church. Transaction costs would have included such policing of downstream agents and would have included "auditing" and harsh penalties for malfeasance. These penalties would have been, among other sanctions, excommunication of religious and civil persons engaged in opportunistic behavior. That meant complete separation from the church and assurances of eternal salvation. Thus, much of the downstream policing was self-policing. Cheating on the church, after all, was a most serious sin.

The church, however, despite the aforementioned problems, was a loosely integrated monopoly that became more efficient and "tighter" through the era of our concern. It, unlike civil government, had a product or products to exchange for contributions that were, by and large, voluntary. Civil governments, including local feudal lords, were principally rent extractors providing few services in exchange for taxes. In addition, the church was a more efficient tax collector than civil government. Taxes are easier to collect when they are seen as an "exchange," lessening problems of evasion and the hiding of assets. Moreover, the agents of the church would have been bound by the dictates of honesty more so than tax farmers who were "downstream" agents of government. For such reasons, the church was able to displace civil authority economically and politically over this time period, that is, the church was a lower cost producer in the relevant markets.

Thus, maintenance of product definition and quality, reciprocity with civil governments, which amounted to protection for credence, and most of all, the development of a vertically integrated church led to the church monopoly of the High Middle Ages. That process took time, but these elements of economic theory give us insight into how that happened between the fourth and twelfth centuries. Of necessity, our approach to these central themes is broad-stroked. We are primarily interested in the *process* through which the *Roman* Church achieved a monopoly position in dealing with competition within its own ranks (the Arian controversy and dealings with pagans) and in its dealing with secular governments, both Western and Eastern at all levels of influence. It is useful throughout our discussion to think of the Roman Church as having established a "business plan" much like a modern corporation. That plan included reactions to conflict and competition that would leave the church with greater political, religious, and economic power in all of its dealings with the post-Roman civilization. The "mission statement" of the plan was to create a virtual and *vertical* monopoly over religion and a substantial (if not dominant) interest in secular governments over all of its geographic reach.

Expressed in the terms of economics, the church's "business plan" included the following:

1. Defense and continuous promulgation of the principles of the Council of Nicaea, which definitively established the product for the Western Church.
2. The provision of credence and legitimacy to successive emperors and other secular governments and their leaders.
3. Maintenance of the assertion that the bishop of Rome was the *primal* as well as titular head of the church, with supreme power over bishops and prelates throughout the West *and* the East in all matters, including the appointment of bishops and the interpretation of the product.
4. Conversion of barbarians and infidels of all types and the use of missionaries and monasteries to convert tribes in all lands to *Nicene* Christianity.
5. Maintenance of traditional or orthodox authority of *Roman* Christianity by the suppression of heresy, either through doctrinal pronouncements or through the enlistment of secular leaders and governments to attack heretics.
6. Adoption and use of a novel method of economic organization—the vertically integrated monopoly firm, which included upstream and downstream elements of interaction and control—church elements that remain in place today.

While civil regimes changed throughout the Dark Ages, with power moving from West to East and back again through various political blocs in Europe and alternative barbarian regimes pushing at the border, the urge to monopoly was the principal goal of the church. It became, with allowances for variations in theologies, a supranational institution. While economists ordinarily analyze institutions and markets in the terms of competition, monopoly was the clear goal of a major segment of the Christian religion—the Roman Catholic Church. That is the manner through which we interpret the trajectory of the Roman Church from its beginnings through the Protestant Reformation in the early sixteenth century. As Schumpeter (1981 [1911]) would have predicted, the Roman Church met competition and competitors with a process of creative destruction in terms of product definition, product innovation, and entrepreneurship. The problem, once monopoly was achieved, is that there was little or no meaningful competition in the marketplace for religion, at least until the beginning of the sixteenth century. The story of how monopoly was finally achieved—over the roughly one thousand years from Jesus Christ through the twelfth century—achieves great importance after Constantine in the fourth century.

Caveats concerning the time line of these developments toward vertical integration must be made. The Eastern Church was early on the seat of the Roman Church. The orthodox language of Chalcedon (451) was accepted in the East, in part because it did not come from Alexandria or Antioch. Nicaea, moreover, did not put an end to competitive theologies—Arianism and other (now) "heresies" continued, some of them introduced and espoused by "invaders," but the orthodoxy of Nicaea and Chalcedon ultimately created the solid product that the Roman Church and the state needed to ultimately claim singular authority in Western Christendom. It is also important to remember that the existence and structure of the Roman monopoly was a product of events as well as desire on the part of top-down suppliers (ultimately the bishops of Rome). The elimination of patriarchies by the Arabs in the seventh century—events not controlled by Rome—and the "divorce" from Constantinople, plus the missionary efforts of the Latin church all ultimately combined to give the church a monopoly over much of Western Europe.[6]

Constantine through Justinian and Gregory I: Centuries of Competition and Consolidation

The church was a unifying force in political affairs after its acceptance by Constantine and other "Roman" governments afterward. Just how did the church support the coercive powers of the state and how did the state in turn provide legitimacy for the church and help quell its internal and external enemies? We argue here that this phenomenon was an ever-evolving process of shifting power blocs and allegiances throughout the early years of the church in the West, and, after centralized power moved to the east in the fourth and fifth centuries, the reciprocity between religion and secular governments continued in Western Europe as the Frankish empire evolved into the leading political power in the West. As populations moved and evolved, the church made optimizing policies and moves for both temporal power and protection. It was a matter of credence and security. Christianity became the unifying force of the late Roman Empire as it moved to the east and Byzantium. Later, within the European West, it became the major unifying force of the Frankish kingdoms that became the "Holy Roman Empire." It was in the interests of both church and empire that competitors to Nicene Christianity be suppressed.

The fourth century was the capstone of the monopoly development of Roman Christianity as the initiator of these goals. The seminal figure of Constantine (his religious exploits were depicted hagiographically in retrospect) was the key to the Western domination by the church.[7] The fourth century saw both the establishment of Christianity as the religion of the Roman state and a growing wealth of the church as Constantine and later emperors expropriated the wealth of competing Christian and pagan sects.

Roman Dominance

At the root of these fourth-century developments was the necessity of maintaining Christian belief among citizens, invading barbarians, and political leaders. That is, adherents and converts to the orthodox Christian religion had to continue to believe in the Christian principles set down at Nicaea and to reject the polytheistic sects from Rome and elsewhere. The exact nature of Christian organization and belief was not to be resolved at this time of course. Over the fourth century, churches and bishoprics coalesced around several great sees—those of Rome, Antioch, and Alexandria and, in the following centuries, Constantinople. The Council of Nicaea explicitly recognized rites of the prelates of Rome, Alexandria, and Antioch. As figure 6.1 shows, these patriarchs were the upstream church in the period before Roman dominance. Further, the political units in these cities tended to assert their prerogatives over the church in these regions. Again, the bases of conflict between Roman authority and secular governments were not only political in nature. Many among the Eastern Christians followed Arius (see chap. 5), and the theological dispute was over the primacy or equality of God the Son versus God the Father and over the Trinity generally.[8] Thus in the early period the principles of Nicaea were promulgated to the downstream church, but doctrinal interpretations varied between Roman and Eastern patriarchs.

Prelates over the fourth century, one that witnessed a rapid growth in the wealth of the Roman Church, continued to assert Roman dominance over the entire church, an assertion that was later to be rebuked.[9] Control over church wealth was in dispute in the late fourth century when the (Western) emperor Gratian (375–383), at the request of the Roman bishop Damasus, extended two new powers to the Roman see: "(1) He made the pope master of the process for trying all accused metropolitans (a territorial title equivalent to archbishop) throughout the West. (2) He provided for appeals to the pope for bishops tried by local synods" (Hinson 1995, 271). These dicta only applied in the West, however, and despite the best efforts of Roman pontiffs, such assertions of authority depended upon the ability to enforce them.[10] As imperial Roman power waned in the late fourth and fifth centuries and imperial secular power shifted to the East and Constantinople, support for the primacy of a Roman papacy declined. It declined, that is, until the church turned to the Franks and the Merovingian and Carolingian empires in France and other parts of Europe for support in the late fifth century (continuing until the ninth). Indeed, it was the conversion of Clovis I (496) that relieved the Roman papacy from Eastern imperial control. Before turning to these developments, however, consider the impact of the oft-cited reason for the decline of Rome—the barbarian invasions.

The Barbarians and the Course of Christian Religion

The decline of the Roman Empire, beginning in the third and continuing into later centuries, has often been blamed on barbarian invasions. These so-called barbarians were (with the exception of the Huns) also settlers. The Visigoths from Spain, the Vandals of North Africa, the Franks from Gaul (the most successful of the barbarian invaders), the Arian Ostrogoths in Italy, fringe competitors for power, were all part of the ostensible decline of Roman imperial power. In truth, however, most of the "barbarians" came to stay. They were assimilated into Roman society but were unable to match the kind of economic and cultural development that characterized the Roman period and legacy. More importantly for our purposes, the church began to fill the role of providing secular stability for the invaders and had great success at converting them and assimilating them into the fold of Catholic Christianity in its then-several variants. The role of Catholic Christianity is critical in this regard. Disintegration of Roman civil government and authority left a vacuum that was filled by Christian belief and organization, which, of course, mimed that of the Roman imperial structure. Pagan invaders had the military might to conquer Rome and its settlements but not the acumen to actually govern. Cannon (1960, 20–21) shrewdly observed,

> In every principality where they ruled they were a minority of the population, the majority of which was Roman and Catholic. The conquerors needed the superior culture of the conquered to be able to endure. Only the kingdoms of the Franks in Gaul and the Visigoths in Spain survived among those of the invaders at the close of the sixth century. Both were vigorously Catholic.

The Roman Church, and also the tenets of Christianity, by being the only cohesive and "civilizing" institution remaining, reduced the "agency" costs of social peace for the invading barbarian tribes just as it had for Roman society in the earlier period (as discussed in chap. 5).

A caveat is clearly in order concerning both pagans and these "barbarian tribes" that were converted to Christianity at the time. Nicaean Christianity, imposed by Constantine, grew as the Roman Empire declined, but for many centuries to follow there were dissenters from Catholic orthodoxy. In other words, between the fourth and eighth centuries and even later, despite forced and voluntary conversions, there existed a co-mingling of creed and pagan practice. Many barbarians were wont to give up practices regarding immortality and ancestor and hero worship. But as the Romans themselves were affected by those conquered, so were the Christians. Christians adopted many of the cultural practices and folkways of pagans and barbarians including death cults, shrine locales, and the use of bells and candles. Bishops were unable to persuade their congregations to give up such practices, and they became part of Christian worship. As MacMullen (1997, 154) concludes, "Foremost was the cult offered to the immortal in humans, the ever living

spark or spirit of the dead," a cult that flowed into "the cult of the spe-
cially honored heroes of the Christian history: the martyrs." The cult
of martyrs, as mentioned earlier, began even earlier as well and was responsible for credence building in third- and fourth-century Christianity. The "immortality cults" of the pagans reinforced this development,
however. Further, the Christian practice of "protection" from evil spirits
also emerged from pagan practice after conversion (e.g., the use of holy
water). In sum, Christianity won the battle against the barbarians and
the pagans, but it is clear that the confrontation, again in the words of
MacMullen (1997, 159), "did not and could not conclude in any sort of a
total eclipse or displacement of the past. The triumph of the church was
one not of obliteration but of widening embrace and assimilation."

Imperial and Christian Competition in the East

In the East (Constantinople and Africa), there was (and is) more of a
marriage of church and state. At times the church was supported by this
configuration and not at others. The Eastern patriarchs sometimes performed the role of agents of the emperor rather than as representatives
of the church. The official date for the fall of Rome is usually given as
476, although secular authorities ruled the political and religious aspects
of the empire from the East. Assertions of *Roman* papal authority were
met with resistance from the beginning of the geographic split between
Rome and Byzantium, although Constantine purportedly acknowledged
the primacy of the Roman bishop in the fourth century. It was alleged, in
a creative forgery written in the eighth century, that Constantine established the imperial (political authority) of the papacy, giving the pope in
Rome authority over secular monarchs (the power to crown and so on).
As noted earlier, the interpretation was sometimes based on the baptism
of Constantine in the Lateran Basilica in Rome—which became a gift of
Constantine to the pope and (supposedly) an acknowledgment by him
that religious and political power belonged to the pope. (Constantine allegedly offered the pope his crown but the pope refused it.) Most writers
(Lieu 2006, 301, 305) recognize these allegations as apocryphal. Nonetheless, the Roman papacy had to look to Eastern emperors for support
after the "fall of Rome."

During the fifth and sixth centuries, doctrinal disputes within Eastern Christianity threatened to destroy the unity of the eastern part of
Christian religion. Here is where the firmly established product defini-

tion of the Council of Nicaea came into play. In order to establish monopoly, the Roman half of the church defended the letter and spirit of
that council. Most importantly, the dispute illustrates the growing rift between Rome and the East and between church and state from a Roman
perspective, and the first major schism between West and East. These
disputes revolved around the nature of Christ. The Monophysite teaching (repudiated by the Council of Chalcedon in 451) taught that Christ
was of two distinct natures—human and divine—but that he became
only divine after birth. The Chalcedonian teaching was that through in-
carnation, Christ was one individual with two separate and distinct natures, human and divine. Yet a third school, Nestorianism, separated the
human and divine completely "by saying that Jesus of Nazareth was a
complete human being in whom dwelt the Second Person of the Trinity
as a man dwells in a house" (Cannon 1960, 27), a position taken by the
Syrian Catholic Church.

The Byzantine emperor Zeno (474–491) issued the Edict of Union (the
Henotikon) under his authority—a statement that vaguely homogenized
the positions, which became acceptable to major Eastern sees—Constantinople, Alexandria, Antioch, and Jerusalem. The bishop of Rome (Felix III, 483–492) was not amused and made all bishops adhering to the
Henotikon anathema (a form of excommunication). Felix was angered
because theological issues were conflated with state directives although
it did not presumably offend official church teaching. Acacius, the patriarch of Constantinople (471–489), returned the favor and excommunicated Felix in a formal ceremony in 484. A schism between Western and
Eastern Churches ensued for the following thirty-seven years.

And so it went between the western Roman Church and the eastern branches (including Syrian, Palestinian, and African). While this
early rift between the eastern and western spheres of Christianity was
healed, the Roman Church had to navigate strategically throughout
the fifth and sixth centuries in order to achieve quasi-monopoly dominance over Western religion. Despite a manifold growth in wealth of the
Roman-affiliated church throughout Europe over the late fourth, fifth,
and sixth centuries, the Roman bishop had to manipulate numerous
circumstances in order to maintain the claim that the seat of Christian
religion lay in his control. It is worth repeating what these central problems were: (a) a sharp diminution in Roman civil authority due to the
barbarian invasions; (b) assertions from the Eastern Church (and emperors) that there was virtual equality among patriarchs; and (c) require-

ments of theological protection from Eastern emperors and other political interests from heresy and from invasions into the Roman sphere of
influences (the Lombards in southern Italy, for example). The Roman
patriarch managed to navigate these issues so that, by the eighth century, Roman dominance (in the West) was for all practical purposes accomplished. Consider some of the highlights of this strategy.

Justinian and His Code

The sixth century was a benchmark in the development of Roman
Church monopoly due to the actions of Lavius Petrus Sabbatius Iustini-
anus (484–565), who was known as Justinian I (Eastern Roman emperor
from 527 until his death in 565). His infamous wife Theodora ruled with
Justinian, and some argue that she actually was the source of many of
his policies. Nonetheless, he is regarded as the most powerful and important Eastern emperor for a number of good reasons. First, Justinian
attempted a complete restoration of the old Roman Empire. North Africa, Sicily, Italy (including Rome), and the territories of Illyricum and
Dalmatia were again brought under the umbrella of the empire. In the
end, however, Justinian was only partially successful in the restoration
of the old Roman Empire, and enemies at the borders of the empire
could not permanently be kept at bay (especially the Persians and the
Lombards).

The interests of the Roman (Western) Church were tied to these
events and, in particular, to the policies of the Eastern emperor Justinian. Unity in both East and West was given to the Christian church, but
the church had to submit to Justinian's control. In particular, the problem was theological. The above-noted schism between the Roman bishop
and the Eastern emperor (along with the Eastern bishops and other prelates) was over the doctrine of Monophysitism, a view held by a number
of Eastern bishops, thinkers, and clergy. *Again the issue was product
definition*—an issue that riddled disputes within the church and among
political entities during this period. Earlier Roman bishops were re-
pulsed by their own orders to Eastern emperors to condemn the "heresy." Justinian, a great politician, sought a compromise that would please
Rome and assuage some of the Eastern prelates, issuing a document, the
"Three Chapters," which in effect added condemnations issued by the
Council of Chalcedon regarding several (deceased) Nestorians. This created great tension in Rome since it infringed on the asserted prerogatives

of the Roman bishop—at this time a weak bishop (Vigilius), who owed his position to Justinian and Theodora. Justinian, asserting his own ecclesiastical authority, convened a council in Constantinople in order to add his "Three Chapters" to the heretical proscriptions of the Council of Chalcedon. Vigilius was brought bodily to Constantinople and resisted (along with other Western bishops). Justinian held the council (553) anyway, which included 160 Eastern bishops (all the patriarchs but that of Rome) and many North Africans. Vigilius was cowered into ratification of the new proscriptions of the council. The problem with Roman interests was not the "matter" of the council—it was the presumption of Eastern authority over the theological teachings of the Christian church and the implicit denial that the bishop of Rome was the actual and not the figurative head of Christianity. It was also the fear that Justinian was a bit too cozy with the heretical Monophysites, although he had openly condemned them early in his reign (a charge which later proved to have some substance).

Despite these differences, Justinian did more than any other emperor to solidify Christianity as the major religion of the East and West. An organizational genius, Justinian developed the Codex Justinianus (529, with a revision in 534). In these and in ensuing works, Justinian did nothing less than (a) revise and systematize earlier Roman law—a harmonization of all the laws of the Roman Empire, and (b) conform the Christian religion to civil law (although, curiously, marriage remained a civil matter). Justinian's great achievement formed (and still forms) the basis for much of Western civil law and Roman Catholic canon law. He *created institutional uniformity as a code of behavior*. It explicitly defined what Christian behavior is and what it is not. And while the Christian religion was "validated" by Constantine and Theodosius in the fourth century, the great leap forward was accomplished by Justinian. It was built into the code as much as were regulations of persons, property, crime, and slavery. Justinian completed what Constantine had begun. According to Cannon (1960, 31),

> The antipathy of the emperor to what he took to be heresy within Catholicism was intensified into intolerance and hatred of any religion or any system of ideas other than Christianity. This was in keeping . . . with his world view: God ruled over everything, and the divine economy of creation ought to be imitated in the structure and operation of the empire. Church and state were one, and the *imperator* was *pontifex maximus* as well. Justinian was the

personification of Caesaropapism, and he acted in all religious matters with a confidence in his own infallibility comparable to that of any pope. Consequently, by royal fiat, he closed the pagan academies of philosophy in Athens, destroyed the few remaining temples of Egypt, and persecuted the Samaritans in Palestine.

Justinian was not merely a "paper tiger" in these regards. The record reveals virulent reprisals against any enemies of Christianity that the emperor could find, and he was known to execute Christian heretics. However, a golden age of Byzantine art and culture remains associated with Justinian, his masterpiece being the construction of Saint Sophia in Constantinople. Literature also flowered under Justinian, and there was open debate between those espousing "orthodoxy" (including the Roman Catholic interpretation of Christ's nature) and dissident voices that espoused the beliefs of the Monophysites. It is the latter belief (that Jesus was of a single nature) that had attracted Justinian's consort (Theodora), and one that Justinian himself adopted toward the end of his life. He remains a questionable hero in the annals of *Roman* Catholic Christianity.

There appears to be great irony in the treatment of Justinian by the Roman Church. No secular leader of his period did more to promote and protect Christianity. His code and the organization and conduct of the church were powerful underpinnings for medieval Christianity. His so-called fatal flaw was twofold, however: (a) he did not submit completely to the Roman bishop, and (b) he (apparently) adopted a theological variant of Christian belief about the nature of Christ that was at odds with the commonly accepted view of Western (but not of Eastern) Christians—that Christ was one person with two natures, fully human and fully divine. These two matters stood in the way of the Roman Catholic Church's drive to monopoly. Whatever Justinian's official status at the time, however, he was later treated as a saint when his code was rediscovered in the eleventh century (Dante puts Justinian in heaven!).

Pope Gregory I "the Great"

After the death of Justinian, the eastern empire lost both territory to its enemies and the ability to assist the causes attached to the Roman Church, and power and authority devolved to the patriarch of Constantinople rather than to the succeeding emperors. There were three

Roman bishops between the death of Justinian and the elevation of
Gregory I (540–604 CE; pope, 590–604). But it was left to Gregory to
protect Roman Christianity and to further the causes of Roman theological supremacy—maintenance of product definition for the downstream
church—in any way he could. Included in this quest were new statements
in which he proclaimed that he was directly responsible to God for his
ministry. And, in maintaining primacy of his interpretation of the Christian faith, including the scriptures and the substance of the faith, Gregory set the stage for the following thousand years of Roman Catholic belief and power.

Earlier Roman pontiffs had made claims of authority over Christendom, but Gregory I was emphatic. The *Catholic Encyclopedia* characterized Gregory's stance in his epistles on these matters:

> There cannot be the smallest doubt that Gregory claimed for the Apostolic
> See, and for himself as pope, a primacy not of honor, but of supreme authority
> over the Church Universal. In Epistle 13.50, he speaks of "the Apostolic See,
> which is the head of all Churches," and in Epistle 5.154, he says: "I, albeit un-
> worthy, have been set up in command of the Church." As successor of Saint
> Peter, the pope had received from God a primacy over all Churches (Epis-
> tle 2.46; 3.30; 5.37; 7.37). His approval was what gave force to the decrees of
> councils or synods (Epistle 9.156), and his authority could annul them (Epis-
> tles 5.39, 5.41, 5.44). To him appeals might be made even against other patri-
> archs, and by him bishops were judged and corrected if need [be]. (Epistles
> 2.50; 3.52; 3.63; 9.26; 9.27).[11]

These positions were all-encompassing. Gregory, at least in principle,
could give no quarter to the use of the title "ecumenical bishop" that
was assumed by the patriarch of Constantinople at a synod in 588. Gregory protested any and all assumptions by the patriarch of Constantinople and/or the Eastern emperor that the bishop of Rome was just another patriarch, albeit one of honor, but not one deserving of primacy.
And Gregory was up against stiff opposition in these views. According to Pirenne (1956, 61–62), "In the various kingdoms the bishops appointed by the kings paid him deference at the most: their relations with
the Papacy went no farther. The Pope himself was regarded by the Patriarchs of Alexandria, Antioch, Jerusalem and Constantinople as an
equal merely. The Emperor of Byzantium, indeed, reserved to himself
the right to ratify the nomination of the Pope, no less than the nomina-

tion of the Patriarchs, or, after Justinian, to have it ratified in his name by the Exarch of Ravenna."[12]

The claims of primacy by Gregory were not honored by the Eastern emperor (or his political representative in Ravenna, the exarch), but Gregory had other strategies to enhance the power of the Roman papacy. First, in the matter of theology, although he believed it "settled" (ostensibly by the Councils of Nicaea and Chalcedon), Gregory established a "fire and brimstone" brand of Christianity firmly fixed on heavenly rewards and punishment in Hell—moral choices and consequences that followed from Christian dogma and *his interpretations* of it. Gregory, according to Pirenne, was "enormously effective in helping to give mediaeval religiosity that gloomy and agonized cast, that preoccupation with terror, that obsession with eternal torments, which found their immortal expression in the *Divine Comedy*" (Pirenne 1956, 62–63). This was in contrast with earlier Christian practice and with Augustine's conception of the Christian message—love, forgiveness, and hope—but it was Gregory's conception that permeated the medieval church.[13] This interpretation was eventually supplied to the downstream church (see fig. 6.1), which sold this version of Christianity to the laity.

Gregory, Temporal Power, and Anglo-Saxon Allies for Rome

More importantly for the immediate power of the Roman papacy, Gregory set about recovering and enhancing the property of the Roman pontiff. Once more, Justinian and the Byzantine branch of the church must be credited with helping the Roman or Western part become a major property owner. Here we have an example of *economic reciprocity* whereby a more or less well-defined Christianity supported the secular governments, and the latter, in turn, provided economic benefits to the church. Early Christians around Rome congregated in "halls" of the rich and in churches as well. By bequest these significant properties became part of Roman Church holdings, as did the huge Lateran Palace (which remains the bishop of Rome's home church), thanks to the emperor Constantine. The same was true of other properties in the numerous regions of Italy. Although these properties were "relinquished" when the barbarians took control of the Italian peninsula, many were retrieved by the armies of Justinian. Importantly, the Papal States as a sovereign political body was first established in the Byzantine reconquest of Italy. Even after the Lombards entered the peninsula from the north—and, importantly, they were held off from attacking the church through negotiations instituted by Gregory I with the cooperation of the Eastern emperor—lands along the eastern part of the peninsula south of Ravenna and close to Rome formerly under the control of Byzantium fell under the control of the pope. Not only did the papacy control the land, they used the land as sources of revenue. The Papal States, ruled by and helping to finance the church, thus originated in the seventh century. According to Pirenne (1956, 63), "The Papacy found itself in possession of a regular income and abundant resources. It had become the first financial power of its time." Thus, the reciprocity of legitimizing civil government in the East (which also claimed religious authority)—along with the moral hammer of "orthodoxy" versus heresy—paid off for the church in terms of growing wealth and power.

The important issue for our investigation is that as property owners with the support of the Christian populace, the Roman Church, with an increasingly powerful local leader—the *Roman* pope—gained a counterweight against Byzantine power and authority. The Roman Church focused the Lombards' attention on the northern areas of Byzantine control while keeping them at bay in the Roman areas. Further, the counterweight against Eastern influence was to bring in elite Roman families as part of the Western liturgical apparatus.

There was, however, a second strategy used by Gregory to dilute the power of Byzantium over the Roman papacy and its claims. It was to more concretely establish the lines of Christian authority, including monasteries, which *vertically integrated* the Christian church. (This integration held fast during the Middle Ages and exists, virtually unchanged today in the West, with the addition of the pope and Curia as primal figures in the church's hierarchy.) Figure 6.1 provides a schematic of the lines of authority (and disputes) that existed between Christian patriarchs and the lower echelons of the Christian church. Depending on the number of Christians and major cities in a given region, metropolitans (archbishops representing major metropolitan cities and sees) were placed in particular geographically dispersed areas of the church. Bishops held authority in areas that were subdivisions of a province. Answering to the bishops were all nonepiscopal orders such as priests and orders below the level of priest. (Priests were allowed to marry at this time but were not encouraged to do so.) Importantly, and as shown in figure 6.1, monasteries were brought under the direct control of the patriarch of Rome.

Gregory—the first monk-pope—used monasteries and missionaries in two ways to enhance the power of the Roman papacy. By Gregory's time there were monasteries all over Europe. First, Gregory brought European monasteries under the direct authority of the Roman papacy and energized them as downstream elements of Roman Catholicism. Indeed, he was a key player in strengthening the vertical integration of the Roman Church through the establishment of and control over monasteries. In particular, Gregory focused on the life and works of Saint Benedict (480–547), who had designed (with the famous "Rule of Saint Benedict," expressed in Latin) a form or platen for an aesthetic religious monasticism that included "vertical integration" with the upstream areas of the church. Second, Gregory was responsible for creating Latin as the single language of the church so that all church business had to be conducted in that language. This in effect created yet another "monopoly element" for the Roman papacy. Eastern rites used the local language in communications.[14] Gregory was able to establish Latin in new areas, namely, into England. Third, and most important, perhaps, he used monks to evangelize the Anglo-Saxons in England in a bid to expand the Christian monopoly at the downstream level. Christianity was extant in Britain before Constantine, who did not employ conversion efforts and resources there. British bishops existed in the third and fourth centuries (mainly "underground") under Roman rule (Johnson 1982, 46). When the Saxons replaced the Romans in the 420s, Christians had to battle old Celtic cults emerging from Ireland. In this transition there was a gradual assimilation of Christians into the culture. Gregory sent a mission led by Augustine in 597 on a preplanned conversion scheme with a strategy of establishing episcopal sees in London and York. Augustine established functioning monasteries in previously established towns and became the archbishop of Canterbury in 599. Conversions by missionary efforts were so profound that some Anglo-Saxon kings renounced their thrones to lead monastic lives (Collins 1991, 189) in the eighth and ninth centuries. But Gregory was the central impetus in the conversion efforts.[15] This transformation began with the arrival of Saint Augustine and with the entrepreneurial efforts of missionaries and monastic interests. Using "meditative" methods and having studied the customs, language, and religion of the inhabitants, Gregory's monks won the confidence and, most importantly, the allegiance to Rome that likely helped to provide an *effective counterweight* to the asserted Eastern authority over the Roman patriarch and, at the same time, extend the "franchise" of the increasingly vertically integrated Roman monopoly.

The new Christians of the north viewed the pope as the vicar of Christ and as the representative of Christ on earth. An extremely clever Gregory I (and later patriarchs of Rome) created a state of incompatibility between the authority that the Eastern emperor and his agent, the exarch of Ravenna, claimed to have over the Roman bishop and the beliefs of Italian and northern European Christians concerning the primacy of the patriarch of Rome (later known as the pope). These were crucial steps in the monopolization of Roman Christianity. It meant that an upstream church was developing in Rome with a pope and his entourage, the Curia, at the apex. The downstream church sold the product—in franchise fashion—to consumers. Such tying arrangements, where rents flowed upward and credence-creating doctrines and rituals concerning the attainment of the final product flowed downward, is the essence of the vertical integrated organization developed by the church.

The increasingly vertically integrated church in Western Europe, later extended to all areas of Roman Catholic domination, would be faced with opportunistic behavior from the lower levels of Christian authority in this "episcopal system." Such behavior, as in the organization of the Roman Empire, had to be contained through monitoring behavior and penalties and (in the church's case) through self-enforcement in order that the aims of the central organization be met. In the case of the Roman Church, sanctions such as excommunication, anathema, and interdict developed in order to control untoward behavior at the lower (retail) levels of the church along with "visitations" from upper level church officials.[16] Ultimately, the multinational Roman Catholic system was superior to secular expansions for that reason.

The role and functioning of the monasteries were especially important as regards church integration and credence. The development of monasteries from about the fifth century onward was both defensive and offensive. Naturally, the establishment of monasteries and their satellites spread Christianity and increased membership. Geographically dispersed monasteries helped spread the Christian faith, but they also served a defensive role. Specifically they acted as a bulwark against corruption of local prelates and (often) as conduits between papal interests and local civil authorities. This issue naturally relates to the natural tension between elements of a vertically integrated firm. The upstream church (Roman establishment and bishops) had an interest in controlling downstream corruption and opportunistic behavior. Geographically dispersed monasteries were an important element in that equation.

The idea is for the upstream church to have central control and auditing but, at the same time, to provide incentives for the local arms of the church to be effective promoters and custodians of church doctrines as propounded by Rome. Although problems in the vertical arrangement arose, monasteries and local (parish) divisions of the church were generally an effective method of promoting these goals.

A Digression on Doctrinal Disputes

Modern eyes sometimes view the kind of theological disputes that appear to be central to early and early medieval Christianity as a debate over minutiae. But they were central to providing a single undifferentiated definition of the product sold at retail. The great Monophysitic controversy between Byzantine and Roman Church interests or the Nestorian heresy would appear to be picayune reasons for war or torture. But disputes of this nature occurred over the period 400–600 and throughout the Middle Ages. The debate was over the nature of Christ. The Nestorians believed that Christ was one person, of two "essences" and of two natures. Monophysites believed that Christ was one person, of one essence and of one nature (divine from birth), and the orthodox Roman Catholic view was that Christ was one person, of one essence—human and divine united—but of two natures (fully human and fully divine). Naturally, some important consequences flow from such distinctions. For example, if, as the Monophysites argued, Christ was divine from birth in "nature," how could he have suffered on the cross?

Economically, however, the Roman Catholic view had to become the predominant theology as a well and unalterably defined product. Differentiated products create further moves to differentiate, and, in order to create a church monopoly in Rome, a single monopolized belief in the nature of Christ and in the ability of the pope to exclusively provide that belief was imperative. There was, in short, a necessity to be able to define "the product." Quality variation and product development are familiar methods of nonprice competition by oligopolists. Oligopolists will alter products to increase their demand curves and to make demand more inelastic in consumers' minds. One might imagine the Christian church over the early medieval period as a group of oligopoly sellers, rather than "true" Christians and "heretics." In order to maintain a monopoly, the monopolist must be willing to alter the product sold or to be able to suppress competing products. The Roman Church en-

gaged in the latter at least from the fifth century, going to war against
heretics and heresies—declared so by the patriarch of Rome. Product
definition—including the exclusive right to *interpret* scripture, council
doctrines, and church dogma from any source—was a necessary (but not
sufficient) characteristic of Roman Church power on the road to high
medieval monopoly.

The Frankish Kingdoms, Charlemagne, and the
Rescue of the Roman Papacy

The Merovingian and Carolingian dynasties of the Franks in Western
Europe were key to the ongoing quest of the Roman Church for the monopolization of religion. The Merovingians (approximately between the
mid-fifth through the mid-eighth centuries) were the most successful
of the barbarian invaders. Clovis I (465–511), with Paris as his capital,
united the Franks north of the Loire River and was the earliest barbarian
convert to Roman Catholicism. Like Constantine, Clovis became Christian due in part to the reasoning of his wife Clotilda that he would have
a great victory over a major enemy if he converted. Clovis undoubtedly
also recognized, like Constantine, the very practical reciprocal benefits
that could be attained from the growing Christianization of lands under
his control, that is, full support from the Christians. Clovis was baptized
by Archbishop Remi at Rheims on Christmas Day, 496. Clovis remained
a bloodthirsty tyrant but the church prospered. A lengthy description
by Cannon (1960, 18–19) places the status of the Roman Church in clear
perspective:

> [T]he Catholic church became the most powerful Frankish institution. Soci-
> ety on all its levels seemed to take pride in it. The king had to give his per-
> mission before a person could become a clergy, while the process of selection
> was rigorous. Bishops were elected in theory by the clergy of their diocese;
> though in practice the king said first who were eligible. They had heavy re-
> sponsibility since in addition to their sacerdotal functions they administered
> the property of the church and in many places superseded civil magistrates
> in dispensing justice under law. All clergymen were answerable only to ec-
> clesiastical agencies and immune to civil jurisprudence. The church grew
> wealthy through ample donations from kings and nobles anxious to compen-
> sate for their sins. In addition to these donations and the customary gratuities

and fees, it collected a tithe on all income in the kingdom. The highest form of both piety and learning was in the monasteries. Out of this rough people came the vision and strength to forge an empire under the religious tutelage of the Catholic Church.

Thus, the penetration of the barbarian Franks provided a foothold for Roman Catholicism throughout the Western European continent. The Franks gained as well, with Christians supporting their regimes and with the Christian "imperative" to separate Frankish supporters from all others. Conversions were largely accomplished by monk-missionaries founding monasteries as they progressed though the regions of France. There were costs to the church in terms of challenges to the Roman Catholic chain of command and authority divided between secular and religious interests. These costs involved disputes over the authority to appoint and administer priests and monks throughout the Frankish kingdom. As the power structure and chain of command within the Roman Church developed, the Frankish monarchs created a supportive aristocracy by awarding episcopal seats to favorites, donating huge parcels of land to monasteries, relieving them from taxation, and maintaining control over the aristocracy. Inevitable disputes between secular and religious authority were made more complex by the instability of hereditable monarchy. Stable units of Frankish lands (then called Austrasia, Neustria, Burgundy, and Aquitania in southern France and independent at the time) were established under Clottaire II (613 CE), but competition at the fringes of the Frankish kingdom continued. The incursions ultimately proved daunting for the Merovingians. Dagobert I, Clotaire's son, who died in 639, was the last strong monarch in his line. As inter-Merovingian feuds between "kings" of the various regions of the Frankish kingdom and incursions from "outsiders" progressed, the historical record of church and state became complex and muddied (Fouracre 1996). The church always had an extremely powerful weapon, however. Legitimization of a civil regime for Christians was a heady credence-building factor in acceptance of particular civil governments.

One of the most important figures in the long Frankish dynasty in terms of the preservation of Roman Christianity and its quest for monopoly over religious belief entered this milieu. Charles "the Hammer" Martel (688–741) filled the vacuum created by the decline in the Merovingian kings. He was named mayor of the palace (fundamentally, a "strongman" or warlord) and became the de facto ruler of the Franks.

Once more the Roman Church was aided by a man who reinvented warfare by developing heavy cavalry (later with stirrups), and founded an
entirely new dynasty—the Carolingian empire (named after Charles). In
bloody combat Martel saved Western Christianity from the Muslim invaders from Spain. (For this latter feat at the Battle of Tours, sometimes
called Poitiers since it took place between Tours and Poitiers, Martel is
often regarded as the savior and defender of Western civilization itself.)
But we are here concerned with Martel's relation and importance to the
Roman Church and the kind of economic reciprocity his rule created
with the church.

In many respects the emergence of Martel from the declining Merovingian empire was a key factor in Roman Catholicism's progress toward
monopoly. This ruler actually rejected the offer from the pope of the title
Roman consul in 739.[17] Battles between the regions of the Merovingian
kingdom (specifically between Austrasia and Neustria) were put down
early in his career, and Charles was later able to consolidate the entire
Frankish kingdom as it had existed under the Merovingians with additional lands to boot. Within the parameters of this achievement, Charles
was able to protect Christianity from the Muslims, but he also managed to forge an alliance between the Roman bishop (the pope) and the
Frankish kingdom, giving strong support and power to Rome to resist
the assertions of the Eastern emperors. This alliance added credibility
to the Roman bishop's assertion that he was the actual primate—greater
in power than his fellow bishops—over the entire Christian church. Further, Martel supported the evangelization of areas of Europe that had
not adopted Christianity. As early as 723 Martel supported the missionary efforts of Saint Boniface in the Germanic regions and later erected
four dioceses in Bavaria with Boniface as archbishop of all Germany
east of the Rhine.

A great deal of controversy exists in the accounts, largely hagiographic church writings, of Martel and his relationship with the church.
The campaign he waged against the Muslims and pay for his army was
apparently partly financed with properties confiscated from the church.
This act may or may not have gotten him excommunicated, a fact that is
disputed by some writers (Fouracre 2000). Further, there is a great deal
of debate over the importance of Martel's victory over the Muslims who
had overrun southern France (Aquitaine) and who might have captured
all of France. Some argue that the Muslim fight at Tours was only a skir-
mish in a much larger campaign that had been waged earlier, whereas

others see it as the turning point of Western civilization and the success of Christianity (Nicolle and Turner 2008). Roman Christianity, whatever the interpretation of Martel, was mightily propelled forward by his actions. Late in his life Martel was apparently forgiven by the Roman papacy. (Forgiveness, of course, ensured continued Frankish military and political protection of the papacy in Rome.) Pope Gregory III implored him to engage in defensive battles in 739 and repeatedly requested his assistance. Indeed, the case of Martel's relationship with the Roman papacy provides insight into the kind of reciprocity that existed between church and state throughout the Dark Ages. The church was apparently willing to overlook the sins, transgressions, and confiscations of rulers, thereby trading credence for protection, in order to further its interests and monopoly. The church, moreover, sought protection from the most powerful ruler (or rulers) no matter how ruthless or bloody they were in achieving and maintaining power.

Pippin and Charlemagne

Roman papal position and strategy was clear as Christianity's influence spread over Europe. Frankish control over Europe and support of the Roman papacy gave any papal claimant a wedge against the assertions of the Eastern emperor—who still had at least nominal claims against the lands of the old Roman Empire including France. Further, and crucial to the health and spread of Christianity, enemies and competitors such as the Muslims and the Lombards had to be kept at bay. It was clearly in the interest of the bishop of Rome to build a power base to defend the primacy of the Roman Church over all Christendom—including exclusive rights to interpretation of scriptures and church laws such as had been established at synods and councils by the year 600. These principles were applied immediately by the Roman Church to the descendants of Charles Martel, Pippin (or Pepin) the Short (714–768), and Charlemagne.

Martel divided his realm among his sons, among them Pippin the Short, who, after a series of events, emerged as the de facto leader of the Frankish kingdom. While these Carolingians had been termed "mayors of the palace" in the various kingdoms of Francia, it became apparent that the "kings" of these particular subdivisions were merely puppets. Pippin used the Roman Pope Zacharias (741–752) to be invested with royal authority and proclaimed king of the Franks. Later, Pope

Stephen III anointed Pippin at Saint Denis Basilica (where his father Martel is entombed). The church added the title *patricius Romanorum* (patrician of the Romans), supporting Pippin's credibility and panache. In return, Pippin almost immediately went to war against the Lombards and their king Aistulf, who had seized lands, including Ravenna, claimed by the Eastern emperor and who had designs on adding Rome to Lombardy's possessions. After an initial rebuff by Peppin (who returned to France), the Lombards renewed harassment of Rome. Pope Stephen sent out a desperate call for Pippin to defend Rome, claiming the apostle Peter himself would guarantee salvation if the Franks came to the aid of the pope. Pippin responded to Stephen's call and crossed the Alps to repatriate lands and cities.[18] Ravenna and what later became the "Papal States" were at this time ceded to the papacy—property that the Lombard king had seized from the church.[19] Cannon (1960, 55) describes this critical result: "The new commonwealth radically changed the office of the papacy. Because of it, the pope became something more than a spiritual pastor of souls. He was a temporal prince as well. Unfortunately, more often than not his temporal responsibilities took precedence over his spiritual duties. The bishops of Rome frequently lost all interest in theology. They left intellectual problems to the East. They were kept too busy being politicians."

Thus, even before the great contribution of Pippin's son Charlemagne to the stability and dominance of a *Roman* Christianity, the Roman papacy had taken a giant leap toward monopoly. By sanctioning and giving credence to Pippin's claims to kingship and royalty over a Carolingian empire (a reason not noted above by Cannon for Pippin's gifts to the pope), the Roman papacy created an ally who would subdue enemies of the Roman Church and provide it with property and wealth, strengthening the pope's claims to primacy among Christians. This was clearly an *economic and political reciprocity.* Fundamental doctrinal issues—the content of Catholic Christianity such as scriptures, belief in the Ten Commandments, fundamental sacraments, and the dimensions of worship— were settled relatively early. But primacy in *interpretation* and *policy* were perhaps more fundamental issues. Importantly for the Roman Church, property restoration, validation of authority, primacy in interpreting church rules and regulations, and total control over church property were all of a piece. The Franks provided a continuing support for the superstructure of papal monopoly in the person of Peppin's more famous son, Charlemagne.

Charlemagne (Charles the Great, 747–814 CE), one of the period's and Western history's best-known figures, turned the kingdom of the Franks into an empire. Now known as the "father of Europe," Charlemagne gave Western Europe an *identity*—providing (ultimately) the basis for the French state and the German state as emanating from monarchies. Most importantly for our purposes, Charlemagne's lineage from Clovis onward provided a background and support for Roman papal monopoly.

Charlemagne, as most of his Frankish predecessors, unflinchingly supported the Roman papacy, and he did this in a number of important ways. First, in 772 the Lombards tried to retake the Papal lands and gain the support of the Eastern emperor (now Rome's competitor in the market for the provision of Christianity). In response to admonitions from Pope Hadrian I, Charles crushed them and ultimately received the Lombard's "Iron Crown." Second, Charlemagne, after three decades of war and many battles, subdued the Saxons and forced them to convert from Germanic polytheism to Roman Christianity. In the process he enlarged the Frankish empire and was able to provide a bulwark for the Roman papacy against the Eastern emperor and his pretensions to religious authority. The Saxon leader, Widukind, had escaped to Denmark in an earlier Saxon campaign. Charlemagne returned to Saxony in 782 and instituted a legal code that placed dire restrictions on the remaining Germanic pagans, stirring a renewal of the religious wars involving the Germanic pagans and a return of Widukind with renewed attacks on Christian churches and installations. Charlemagne again prevailed and at Verden in lower Saxony ordered the mass beheading of more than 4,500 Saxons who had returned to paganism after initial conversions to Christianity. (Later, Widukind converted, wisely perhaps, to Christianity.) This act and the bloody warfare that surrounded his reign, acts that presage the persecution, punishment, and murder of heretics by the Roman Church and its civil allies throughout the Middle Ages and beyond, did not prevent the church later from canonizing Charles.

The most significant event solidifying the relation between church and state that occurred over Charlemagne's reign, however, was his "coronation" in the year 800. Charlemagne, king of the Franks, received the imperial crown at the altar of Saint Peter's in Rome by Pope Leo III on Christmas Day 800 CE. This "marriage" of church and state created the Holy Roman Empire and presented Charlemagne as the supreme leader of the entire Western world as well as the protector of the Roman Church. But, with the pope placing the crown on Charles's head, the pope signaled to all that his "civil" position depended on the papacy (which was ordained by God). There were to be many disputes and contrary claims between church and state(s) in the coming centuries, but the events of that Christmas Day was a high point for the Roman papacy. (Actually, Charles was in Rome to rescue the pope, Leo III, from the Romans).[20] Charlemagne used Christianity as a catalyst to suffuse his reign with art and culture, including education and the arts.

The church by this time was the largest property owner in Europe. Donations, tithes, gifts, and donations in partial restitution of sins and the growth of monasteries as production and tax-collecting units made this so. With wealth came abuse, however, and Charles set down all kinds of rules to assure that receipts were relegated to the poor or for pious, intended purposes. Bad behavior in congregations of priests and in monasteries was conscribed by Charles also, but the widespread adoption of the austere Rule established by Saint Benedict (750–821) furthered this goal from within religious organizations. The emperor called a council (the Council of Aachen) in 802 to determine how a program of education would be fashioned. It was to be taught to those within Roman Catholic institutions—cathedrals and monasteries. Thus the church was integral to the Carolingian Renaissance in almost every respect and one of its chief beneficiaries.

Importantly, however, especially for the future of church-state relations, the "emperor" insisted upon interventions in the appointment of bishops. While nominally elected by the clergy and people of a diocese, Charlemagne and his kingly successors across Europe insisted in supplying recommendations for clerical posts (which were almost always honored) and/or veto power.[21] In this manner, involving the so-called Investiture Controversy, which was of so much importance in the medieval period, bishops, abbots, or other clerics had divided allegiances—to both civil and religious authorities. In this manner, Charlemagne, while unquestionably an unexcelled supporter of the Roman Christian papacy, wielded enormous temporal power that affected the church in both positive and negative manners.

The success of the Frankish empire under Charlemagne was, in large measure, contingent upon the prevention of opportunistic behavior on the part of leaders in the subdivisions of the empire. Possessions and allegiances of the empire had to be policed. Charles, from the beginning, appointed three of his sons—in their youth governed by trusted regents—to the various kingdoms in Europe. His son Carloman (renamed Pippin) was made king of Italy (taking the Lombard crown), Charles the Younger received Austrasia, Neustria, Saxony, Burgundy, and Thuringia, and his youngest son Louis was crowned king of Aquitaine. Pippin died in 810 and Charles in 811, and Louis was made co-emperor and co-king of the Franks before Charlemagne's death. Upon his father's death, Louis (778–840) was crowned Holy Roman emperor in 814. Charlemagne's "empire" did not last (see chap. 7), but its spirit of culture did. Most importantly, his actions and those of his predecessors were critical to the success of the Roman Catholic monopoly in the Middle Ages.

Conclusion: The Roman Church circa the Early Ninth Century

The Roman Church was on a trajectory toward a vertically integrated medieval monopoly by the time of Gregory I (early seventh century). By the ninth century, the church was finally in position to exert its authority and control over larger and larger governmental entities in the West (and in the East as well). Indeed, the underlying foundations for Western Christianity were solid by the beginning of the ninth century.

The present chapter has outlined, in economic terms, how the Roman Church was able to achieve this position: through theological concretizing of the product, through economic reciprocity with civil governments (trading credence for protection), and by developing a unique form of economic organization that established vertical integration between the upstream and downstream churches. Christian missionaries as entrepreneurs had remarkable success in converting the barbarian tribes that came to settle various parts of the Roman Empire. In particular, the church filled a central cultural and institutional gap in the fourth, fifth, and sixth centuries and beyond by being the only institution to substitute for the order with which Romans had suffused their empire. In doing so it began to establish a vertically organized church centered on the power of the bishop of Rome. (The eastern empire was unable to contain the invasions of Italy and other parts of Western Europe.) Fundamentally the Roman Christian church did for the barbarians what they had done for the earlier Roman Empire—provided stability and reduced agency and policing costs as pagans and barbarians were converted to Christianity and its precepts. There were of course, continuing disputes over small points of doctrine (minor "product issues" remained) and the mega-issue of the primacy of the see of Rome. These disputes with the *eastern* empire were often acrimonious—presaging the great schism between East and West in the eleventh century—but the Roman Church and, indeed, the survival of Christianity depended in the fourth, fifth, and sixth centuries on the protections of the Eastern emperor, who also considered himself a "church leader." The emperor Justinian is rightly regarded as a bulwark for the firm cultural and legal establishment of Christianity as the dominant religion of East and West over this period. Whatever these contributions, however, Justinian supported a marriage of church and state with the emperor (and patriarch of Constantinople) as infallible in decision making as the bishop of Rome. Thus, the dilemma of Rome was to obtain the protection of Byzantine monarchs, along with their assistance in putting down competitors to Christianity, while at the same time maintaining a monopoly over all religious decision making and doctrinal interpretation in the assertion of the primacy of the chair of Peter.

The Roman Church sought and obtained other allies when the Byzantine Empire began to lose territory and the power to protect the western branch of Christianity (about the time of Justinian). The business strategy of the Roman papacy at this point was clear. Proselytize pagans, barbarians, and whole societies that could come to the aid of a vertically integrating Roman Church and who would recognize its primacy. In this quest, the church had both very temporal services and assurances of legitimacy for civil governments to supply (in addition, of course, to a monotheistic religion with assurances of eternal salvation). Barbarians, including the Saxons of northern Europe (and the British Isles) and, in particular, the Franks had many reasons to demand these services, which included a "Roman" cultural and institutional framework for society in the form of an educational and legal system within which civil governments could function. Most importantly for Western Christianity and civilization, the emergence of the Frankish kingdom under Pepin III and his son Charlemagne provided an opportunity for the church to *assert* control over secular authority even as it sought protection from these regimes. The contretemps between secular and religious authority would go on for centuries. The so-called Investiture Controversy— over whether secular or religious authority would control appointment of local and regional bishops and heads of monasteries—also punctuated church-state relations over the early, middle, and late Middle Ages.

Approbation of civil regimes by the Roman Church was a key factor in obtaining cooperation from such entities. This reciprocity, moreover, built the necessary connections between church and state at the highest levels, which facilitated the upstream church's dealings with downstream matters. While, as we have stated, problems concerning taxation and appointment of local prelates would continue for centuries, the required ascent by the church of the legitimacy (credence) of governing regimes gave the Roman Church a critical tool with which to solidify and direct a vertically integrated monopoly.

The "business plan" of the Roman Church to achieve monopoly was thus well advanced by the time of Charlemagne. The church's attachment to and conversion of the Frankish kingdoms (both Merovingian and Carolingian) allowed the church to navigate with its interests intact through all manner of challenges over the centuries from Constantine through Charlemagne. Christianity became supranational and was superimposed upon the European identity established by Charles Martel and Charles I. The latter enforced a whole set of regulations and rituals to aid the church, of course, and by the time of Charlemagne, the church was moreover the largest property owner in Europe with the bishop of Rome—the pope—as a temporal as well as a spiritual leader. Tax collections and revenues to the church were funneled to Rome and to the geographically dispersed bishoprics and monasteries loyal to Rome in a form of economic organization known today as the vertically integrated firm. The church, in return for civil services to and protection of the Roman papacy and its properties, gave its legitimacy and credence to individuals who were little less than bloody tyrants. Pagans of all types were forced to Christianize or be put to the sword under Charlemagne, apparently with the approval of the Roman Church. This practice became the rule rather than the exception in the later Middle Ages. But, whatever the costs or the propriety, the Roman Catholic Church became the principal institution, international in scope, in European society by 800 CE.

The Carolingian empire would soon collapse under the maladministration of Charlemagne's son Louis the Pious (Scott 1964, 50–52). European monarchies would be faced with onslaughts from Arabs, Magyars from the East, and Viking raids, which also had profound effects on the Roman Church—sometimes called a "second Dark Ages." But that period was brief, and the church would continue to expand its influence over society with various entrepreneurial-missionary activities and in its dealings with the rise and fall of civil governments over the next 250 years. It would have to contend with competition from the "other"

eastern branch of Christianity and deal with contentious civil governments, their alignments, and their allegiances. But in the end, the development of an integrated church organization gave the church superiority over secular powers in the continuing conflicts with civil governments
and authorities at all levels, as we shall see in chapter 7. But by 800 CE,
the Roman Church had managed to secure market dominance, if not total religious control, over downstream religious practice, ritual, and activities, across the European continent and in the British Isles as well.

CHAPTER SEVEN

Roman Christian Monopoly in the Early Medieval Period

Introduction: The Bumpy Road to Monopoly

The quest for Roman monopoly was greatly propelled by church association with the Frankish rulers. From Merovingian times, the church found converts to Roman Orthodox Christianity among the Franks, converting leaders such as Clovis and Charles Martel to become protectors of the Roman papacy, its property, and most centrally, its claim to priority, authority, and monopoly over all Christendom.[1] In a fundamental sense, the road to monopoly of the Western Church was almost complete by the year 800 and the crowning of Charlemagne. Church influence reached across Europe, independent of particular monarchs but with Frankish defense for its assertions of dominance against claims of Eastern patriarchs.

By the time of Charlemagne, the Roman Church had made enormous strides toward dominance, both in assertions of the primacy of the Roman bishop and in the vertical integration between upstream and downstream segments of the church. (The reader may wish to refer back to fig. 6.1 on these matters.) In particular, the church had a clearly defined product in the form of the establishment of the New Testament (together with the Old Testament), emerging homogenization of ritual, a single declaration of faith (the Apostles' or Nicene Creed), and the promise of an afterlife. Heaven and hell had emerged as final destinations, depending on increasingly and specifically defined behavior in the present life. The church devised tools, quite early on and certainly by the time of Pope Gregory I in the sixth century, to punish behavior that it deemed unacceptable. The inculcation of belief that hell was a punishment for behavior forbidden by the Roman Church created a form of self-policing on the part of believers who were reminded at every possible point that hell was the consequence of disobeying Roman dicta. Indeed, the preaching of hellfire and damnation in an afterlife for particular infractions identified by the church is critical to the self-policing of consumers by most Christian religions. Declarations of excommunication (total separation from the body of Christ), anathema, and interdict were utilized by the Roman (and Eastern) churches to keep miscreants in line. Roman bishops—popes—were quite willing to apply cost-benefit analysis to violence against heretics, turning the other way when Charlemagne massacred thousands of Saxon pagans (i.e., non-Christians) who would not convert to Roman Christianity.[2] Church tolerance of such murderous behavior on the pretext that it was "for their own good" grew throughout the Middle Ages with torture and with "holy wars" being the rule rather than the exception.

Before the Roman Church could reach the levels of power achieved in the High Middle Ages, there were fundamentally three critical problems to be solved. In what we regard as descending order of importance, the issues were:

(1) COMPETITION, CONFLICT AND CONCORDANCE WITH CIVIL GOVERNMENTS. As we will see, there were (at least for the church) two "dark ages" in terms of successful associations with civil governments. The decline of the Carolingian empire coincided with renewed barbarian invasions across Europe and in England. Competition continued at the fringe from pagan tribes, that is, those with different belief systems. Viking raids, in particular, created havoc in Europe, and the continuing Arab-Moslem threats remained. These factors, along with degeneration in the standards of the papacy, created important problems for the Roman Church in maintaining its sphere of control, both spiritual and temporal. A protracted battle between temporal and religious authority punctuates this period, which ended in the powerful papacy of the central Middle Ages, where its vertically integrated monopoly reigned over spiritual matters and, in many areas, over the temporal as well. The so-called Investiture Controversy was fought by the papacy for control over the power to appoint prelates and over church holdings, wealth, and

property. Later in this chapter we discuss how church strategy was used to navigate these civil difficulties.

(2) CONTINUATION OF THE CLAIMS AND DEFINITION OF ROMAN PAPAL DOMINANCE WITHIN THE VERTICAL INTEGRATION OF A HIERARCHICAL CHURCH. Civil governments changed and evolved over the period 800–1150. For example, the locus of power shifted from the Frankish world to Germany. These changes and extremely unclear rules relating to succession, together with impious behavior by Roman popes, created difficulties in the maintenance of the asserted monopoly of Christian organization. Specifically, a self-inflicted challenge to the credence of the *upstream* church developed within the papal structure over the period, along with the emergence of multiple papal claimants, presaging later medieval developments. Refinement of the structure of papal elections was part of the reform that solidified, at least for a time, the top-down organization of Roman Christian monopoly.

(3) COMPETITION WITHIN THE CHRISTIAN CHURCH FOR ABSOLUTE AUTHORITY OVER WESTERN EUROPEAN CHRISTIANS. The Eastern Orthodox Church remained divided from Roman Christianity on a number of issues, particularly the issue of church organization. Eastern Christians, while recognizing the bishop of Rome as having a special place of honor and as "first among equals," clearly adopted a looser form of organization with a collegial structure of the episcopate. The pope, in other words, was respected as having a special "primacy of honor" but not as having a "primacy of authority." But over the ninth, tenth, and eleventh centuries, two primarily theological issues (of a larger number) divided the western and eastern branches of the Christian church. One concerned the exact content of the Nicene Creed and the ordering of the Father, Son and Holy Ghost in it, and a second related to the question of the worship of icons or "images" relating to the Christian religion. We will argue that Christian division between East and West, although fought on these and other theological divisions, was actually over the question of the asserted monopoly of the Western Church and the primacy of the pope.

While it may appear that theological and institutional issues are two separate means of explaining church phenomena, this is far from the case. Theological disputes between East and West, while not over unimportant religious issues, were also an underpinning or pretext for a fundamental institutional conflict. The Roman branch of the church sought and was achieving an organizational structure of a vertically integrated monopoly with the pope as primate. Eastern belief was centered on a conciliar and solidly episcopal form of upstream organization—at odds with the Roman view. As such, theological squabbles were fundamentally a stalking horse for the much larger issue of Christian church organization.

After Charlemagne: Breakdowns, Conflict, and Invasions

Three great empires controlled the West in the year 800 CE. The Islamic or Moslem civilization was the product of the religious teachings of Mohammed, whose religion contained significant elements of Judaism and Hebraic thought as well as the teachings of Jesus, a prophet of Allah, the one true god. The religion stressed the integration of church, state, and military authority and instituted jihads or "holy wars" against infidels. By the time of Mohammed's death in 632, Islam, having arisen in the Arabian Peninsula, spread throughout large parts of Egypt, Syria, and Libya. By the early eighth century it had reached North Africa, central Asia, and a large portion of the Iberian Peninsula (Visigoth-controlled Spain). As noted in chapter 6, the Arabs were halted by Charles Martel at the Battle of Tours in 732. (Muslims, under whom art and science flourished, famously contributed to the Renaissance and Western civilization before being driven from Iberia in 1492.)[3] Meanwhile, they continued to pose a threat to the Frankish empire.[4]

The Eastern or Byzantine Empire was constrained largely to Asia Minor and to the areas surrounding the Mediterranean, Sicily, Sardinia, and small parts of the southern and northern Italian Peninsula. The great push of the Frankish empire, however, gave it and the Latin Church control over Western Europe with Christian peoples settled in England, northern Spain, and parts of Eastern Europe. The Roman papacy and its claims were, in other words, in fairly stable condition by the time of Charlemagne's death in 814. But for the next two centuries, critical events would threaten that march to monopoly power in the High Middle Ages. Those events included:

- new pagan threats to Christianity in the form of Viking and Magyar invasions;
- changes in the locus of civil powers protecting (and competing with) the *Roman* papacy;

- emerging monarchies (later to become nation-states) that challenged how economic rents were divided between the papacy and civil authority. These problems involved the split of tax revenues from church-controlled lands, transfers of ownership of such properties and the power to appoint prelates, including bishops, in parts of Western and Central Europe (the so-called Investiture Controversy); and
- a period of papal "bad behavior" wherein a lustful Roman upper class controlled the elections and appointments of the bishop of Rome.

Viking Invasions

Beginning in the late eighth century, Viking raids, first on England, Scotland and Ireland, and later on the western coast and interior of France, had become endemic. Denmark became a Viking state and was a base of operations for the adventurers. Their infamous plundering, murdering, and kidnapping initially had stark effects on the defenseless people, monasteries, and church interests in their path. Vikings used a new type of naval warfare to achieve their aims causing chaos and uncertainty in search of gold, silver, slaves and booty of all types.[5] The principal victims were monasteries and bishoprics, whose repeated destruction and payments of tribute and taxes impoverished large segments of church interests primarily in the late ninth and tenth centuries. Homeless citizens and monks became itinerant travelers as civil properties and monasteries, often considered the same by secular rulers, were captured by Northmen (Normandy in western France is named for the Northmen). Thus the Roman Church's losses were often not only to the Vikings but were to the civil occupants who claimed the property when deserted by the raiders. These raids were a clear threat to the vertically integrated, geographically dispersed Roman Church. The papacy had to control the downstream sale of the Christian good in order to enforce product homogeneity and collect revenues.

Viking raids began to taper off in the tenth century, however, and the political structure in Scandinavia and Western Europe began to stabilize. Just as the Roman imperial government conquered nations by "Romanizing" them—bringing the vanquished to Roman culture, laws, and institutions—so the Latin Church missionaries brought pagans to Christian beliefs and customs. While, for the most part, such Christian exchange (in contrast to Roman practice) was voluntary, force was on occasion used by the Roman Church and their representatives (recall the activities of Martel and Charlemagne). Thus, while Viking and other pagan raiders, such as the Magyars in Hungary, created costs for Western Christianity in the form of lost resources, the losses were temporary, later turning into gains in membership with new Latin Church allegiances.

The Changing Locus of Civil Protection: Opportunistic Behavior

The status of the papacy and its claims to property rights and appointment powers were precarious and even "secularized" between the ninth and mid-eleventh centuries. This state of affairs stemmed from numerous sources, some of them being the decline of the Frankish (Carolingian) empire in the ninth century and the emergence of a new "Holy Roman Empire" in Germany, as well as the Viking and other pagan invasions and the declining "morality" within the papacy. Thus, while the bishops of Rome maintained their claims of primacy over the whole church, their de facto authority in civil matters was being breached. Why were papal claims to authority at the downstream levels of the church so critical to the Roman monopoly? A vertically integrated monopoly cannot function effectively if the lower levels of church organization and the revenues they produce could not be controlled. Secular interventions of civil authorities, especially those claiming rights of clerical appointments and shares of the rents collected as taxes at the local level, challenged the very foundation of Rome's nascent monopoly and could not be tolerated.

One major problem in both the ecclesiastical and secular worlds at the time was the matter of how to handle succession—a problem that lasted for centuries in hereditary monarchies. This problem proved especially difficult among the Carolingians after Charlemagne. His son Louis the Pious (814–840, b. 778 CE) divided the reign of the kingdom in Germanic custom—among three of his sons (Lothaire, Louis, and Charles the Bald). When Louis died, the kingdom's rule degenerated with its power base split four ways. Viking raids and territorial disputes increased over the period. However, one of Louis's sons, Louis the German (817–876) established fairly stable control in Germany, paving the way for a stark shift in the locus of secular power to Germany (from France) in the tenth century. In particular, Otto I ("the Great," 936–973)—son of the German monarch Henry, duke of Saxony and conqueror of the Magyars in 955—became the defender and proselytizer of the Roman Christian church, eventually (by 962) bringing Italy under his influence. Otto, a Saxon, and his successor Ottonian monarchs (Otto II, Otto III, and Conrad II) clearly wanted to resurrect the Carolingian empire of Charlemagne. In February 962, Pope John XII crowned Otto the Great the Holy Roman emperor, a title that lasted until the nineteenth century. But despite the protection and spread of the Latin Church and papacy afforded by the "new" Holy Roman Empire, disputes between secular and papal-religious authorities exploded over the tenth and later centuries. Disputes centered on property, revenue sharing, and appointment powers.

We do not wish to imply that papal-supported power shifted entirely to the eastern part of the Frankish empire. A Carolingian descendant of powerful landowners and a well-connected feudal lord filled a vacuum of power in the western part of the old Frankish empire of Charlemagne. As the most powerful noble in the Western Frankish kingdom, Hugh Capet, was titular founder of a Capetian dynasty in the small region of what had been the great Frankish empire. Constrained on all sides by feudal lords, Hugh nonetheless was proclaimed duke of the Franks, ruling between 956 and 987, and king of the Franks, ruling between 987 and 996. Paris was his base of operations, and although he possessed little military power, he was allied with his cousins, Otto II and Otto III, and was an important defender of Roman Christianity. As with so many rulers of the time, however, Hugh Capet was involved in disputes with the papacy over appointment powers. Moreover, he was the founder of a French dynasty (based upon Roman Catholic Christianity) that lasted into modern times through Capet's descendants.

Papal Opportunism

The papacy was well positioned over the ninth and tenth centuries to engage in opportunistic behavior in civil and ecclesiastical matters. Over the period, all Western emperors wanted a coronation or approbation by the pope. Most often the trade was one of economic reciprocity (credence for protection). We would argue that the same applied to most of the civil governments and feudal lords of Christian Europe. The necessity of legitimization by the head or representatives of the Christian religion was founded in the need for credence on the part of rulers of all stripes. Without it, in many cases, the "faithful" could be inspired to rise up against their governments. One point is clear: the papacy as a monopoly in this activity in Western Europe faced competitive civil aspirants on the other side of the market for credence. The Holy Roman emperor was a protector of the papacy and Roman Christianity at any given time, but the relative strength of that support had to depend on the former's power and authority. The decline of local lords under feudalism and the emergence of the nation-state were a few centuries away, and at this time papal authority and manipulation extended to many levels of civil authority.

Examples abound of papal "interference" (opportunistic behavior) on the part of popes over the period in civil affairs. One example regarding civil authority is related by Collins (2009, 159). Mistresses and multiple wives of earlier Frankish rulers were, for the most part, summarily ignored at a time when the papacy and its properties would have been endangered and required their defense. But in 862, at a time when the papacy was fairly secure, Pope Nicholas I (858–867) intervened successfully against an attempt by Lothar II (855–869) to divorce his childless wife and marry his longtime mistress. A Frankish synod had approved the divorce, but after Lothar's queen appealed to Nicholas, he called a second synod on the matter and sent representatives who were bribed into submission to the pope. When Lothar's brother, Emperor Louis II, marched on Rome, the pope held out in a fort and ultimately prevailed in his threat of excommunication and withdrawal of support of Lothar. Lothar acquiesced.

Forgeries of earlier ecclesiastical documents to support the so-called unbroken Roman papal lineage and documents asserting the divine and total authority of the pope were common. Indeed, the lengths to which the papacy went over this period included the use of clear forgeries to defend the absolute right of the pope to decide cases lodged against other bishops and archbishops. According to Collins (2009, 160), Pope Nicholas "deposed the archbishop of Ravenna in 861 for defying Roman authority and in 864 took on Archbishop Hincmar of Reims, the leading advisor to the West Frankish king Charles the Bald (840–877) and a redoubtable defender of the privileges of his see. As a controversialist, Hincmar was not above falsifying documents in support of the claim of Reims, but in this case he faced an indomitable pope and an even more impressive body of forged texts." The texts used by Nicholas were an impressive body of papal letters, or decretals, that consisted of trumped up rulings on a great number of issues critical to the papacy, including the pope's power of jurisdiction. They were written by Isidore Mercator centuries earlier and were used "to defend the rights of bishops against the authority of the archbishops or metropolitans who had jurisdiction over them. For Mercator, the best counterweight to the archbishops was the pope, and so, using a copy of the *Liber Pontificalis* [itself a medieval hagiographic listing of the "unbroken" line of popes], he concocted letters from many of the popes whose names he found in it" (Collins 2009, 160–161). This forgery was used against Archbishop Hincmar as historical documentation of the authority over both ecclesial and civil authorities in a period when civil authorities were attempting to control the papacy. These examples show that the power of a well-entrenched international religion permits many kinds of opportunistic behavior on the part of a self-proclaimed monopoly (with or without historical antecedents). This kind of monopolistic behavior was used throughout the period.

"Bad Behavior" in the Papacy: A Threat to Credence

The upstream level of authority and *credibility* over the vertically integrating monopoly was threatened also from within. Contretemps between civil and feudal powers were not the only difficulties facing the papacy at this crucial time in its evolution to monopoly power. The issue of succession plagued monarchies for centuries, but it affected the papacy as well. In the first two centuries of the Roman Church, the "election" of the bishop of Rome was a matter left to clergy and the people of Rome. Within this "Roman tradition," candidates came from the lower ranks of the Roman clergy. That system would change later, but it is noteworthy that rulers of the empire, including those of Germany in the tenth century, played leading roles, often *the* leading role, in the appointment and duration of the pope's reign. The degeneration and dissolution of civil society in the late ninth century was accompanied by intense competition among Romans for papal appointments. The period has been termed a "pornocracy" affecting the papal throne, from Sergius III (904) to the death of John XII (964).[6] The papacy's accumulated wealth and power to make lucrative appointments led to ignominious and tragic consequences. Grabs for power and wealth on the part of Roman families and temporal monarchs created havoc so that within the period 896–904 ten individuals (including an unelected "antipope") occupied the throne of Peter. But with the elevation of Sergius III, Rome was in fact controlled by harlots. Marozia, senatrix (i.e., "madame senator") of Rome from the house of Theophylact, whose children numbered one of Sergius's (Chamberlin 1969, 22), was the conduit for this infamous episode in the papacy. Cannon's (1960, 133) description is instructive:

> Theodora [wife of Theophylact of Tusculum] and her two daughters, Theodora the Younger and Marozia, through their charming and enticing harlotry controlled Rome and with it even the church itself in the West. These women sold their bodies for positions, titles, land—the stuff out of which power comes and by means of which great influence is exerted. Marozia, more clever if not more corrupt than her mother, numbered among her amorous relationships one with Pope Sergius III, and out of that illicit affair a son was born who later became Pope John XI.

Marozia had bigger plans for herself. When her son John XI was on the papal throne, she plotted to have herself crowned supreme ruler of the West, an ambition that was furthered by marriage to one Hugh of Provence (a claimant at the time to the imperial title). The intervention of another of her sons, Alberic, thwarted this ambition and led to her mysterious death. The melee continued when Alberic died and willed the papal throne to his son Octavian, who succeeded as Pope John XII (955–964)—the same John that crowned Otto I "holy Roman emperor." Indeed, this particular episode came to an end with the coronation of Otto. After the coronation Otto, enforcing his historical (Carolingian) rights to consent to papal appointments, held a synod that excommunicated John and installed Leo VIII, a German, as pope.[7] John XII and his predecessors were not the only "bad popes," of course. The thirteenth through sixteenth centuries with, for example, the Medici and Borgia families in control of the papacy, witnessed ludicrous behavior and degradation of papal operation.[8]

Despite Roman protestations of "outside interference," Otto established precedent for a "universal" influence in the appointment of Leo. The pope, after all, claimed (and claims) to be head of a universal church. Naturally, the temporal degeneracy of the papacy was not limited to the tenth century, and, indeed, as we will see later in this chapter, yet another member of the house of Theophylact, taking the name Benedict IX (1032–1048), was so venal as to illicit a moral revolution within Roman Catholicism.

At this juncture, however, several important points relating to the ongoing quest for monopoly within the Latin Church should be noted.

Ironically, the disintegration and chaos of the Carolingian dynasty helped strengthen the papacy and the Roman Church establishment. It no longer, at least until the time of Otto the Great, had to depend upon a centralized power for its authority. The church monopoly over belief and credence-providing power to civil governments faced a group of competing monarchs and claimants from whom the church could extract rents. And, despite the shocking behavior of the "bad popes," the essence of Christianity and church membership persisted, despite Viking raids and other disruptions across Europe. Further, property accumulations that propelled the church to become the wealthiest institution in the West after Constantine inevitably altered the focus of the church at all levels. The cycle of abuse-reform-abuse-reform was endemic within the Christian church right up to the Protestant Reformation of the sixteenth century (and afterward as well). The effects of the "pornocracy" of the tenth and early eleventh century were no exception to cyclical changes in church behavior. In almost all cases, the control over property and wealth, the buying and selling of church offices by both secular and church interests (simony), the degeneration of monasteries and clerical behavior, and the outright venality of church behavior were the chief events that brought on these reforms. These events could have had disastrous effects on the Roman Church firm, especially damaging to its credence as a religious institution and its related attempt to become a vertically integrated monopoly. But before turning to the particular reforms that attended church behavior in the eleventh and twelfth centuries, consider the economic nature of some of these disputes.

Property Disputes and the Investiture Controversy

Disputes over property and revenue splits, although common throughout church history, were especially pronounced during the "new dark age." The sources and development of the economic problems are clear. From the beginnings of Christianity, the appointment of church officials, which was theoretically within the exclusive power of the church, became the province of secular officials. Why? Because the accretions of landed property and wealth were income-producing for civil governments. From the third century onward, this conflict between church and state created problems. To put the matter in even bolder relief, as a Holy Roman Empire developed under the Franks, a practice emerged whereby the Latin pope crowned the emperor, and the emperor would appoint or consent to the election of the pope, providing for a mutual dependence in investiture. (Technically, as noted above, the clergy and people of Rome elected a pope, but the emperor had to acquiesce or approve the appointment.)

These appointment powers, from the very top of the religious hierarchy down, carried the most serious implications for the rent flows to temporal and religious interests. The vertical monopoly had to find ways to control downstream agents and to protect church property from taxation or confiscation by civil governments. In practice, this was an ongoing problem. Since the offices of bishops or abbots of monasteries in particular locations carried control over huge and usually growing amounts of land and people, the allegiance of the bishop mattered to temporal leaders as well as to the church. The practice of temporal appointment of bishops, often in return for fees, revenues, or types of fealty became common across the sphere of Latin Church influence. That practice of paying for offices was called simony.[9] The results of secular simony was twofold: (1) rents were redirected from the papacy and church interests, as noted above, and (2) loyalty of prelates to the pope was redirected to prelates' more proximate benefactors—secular leaders. These practices were common over the entire period from Constantine onward. In the dark ages, according to Daniel-Rops (1959, 293), "there was the danger that Christianity might succumb to the general 'barbarization,' that instead of elevating the newly baptized it might slip into violence and vice along with them. This danger was the greater because the laity all too often exercised a disastrous influence upon church affairs, especially in the nomination of bishops. Behaving like real 'bishops outside the church' after the style of Constantine the vast majority of the sovereigns of this epoch considered the clergy as a body of civil servants in their own employ." In addition, confusion reigned when "ecclesiastical provinces were often cut in two by the changing boundaries of the Frankish kingdoms: a bishop who went to his Council was sometimes going into enemy territory."

Even more direct controls existed in so-called proprietary churches as in the German states where a more direct juridical notion of secular-religious property relations took hold. A proprietary church was one on which a monastery was founded by a landowner who then could transfer, mortgage, or otherwise use his property as he saw fit. The landowner had to provide for the priest and prelates so long as the church functioned as a church on his property. As described by historian Uta-Renate Blumenthal (1988, 5):

With the rise of the proprietary church, the bishops lost much of their influence and many of their diocesan rights pertaining to churches and monasteries. The bishops' supervisory functions fell into abeyance, although the
bishops theoretically never abandoned their rights. Their opposition failed to
stem the new developments in the Frankish church that was shaken repeatedly by waves of secularization initiated by rulers to provide for adherents
whose military support was the sine qua non of political power. Increasingly,
side by side with new foundations, old churches and monasteries also came
into the hands of the laity.

Secularization and internationalization of the papacy continued under the Ottonians. Otto I (the Great), as described above, rescued the
papacy from its pornocracy and was responsible for spreading and reju-
venating Latin Christianity but with the pope and church as a partner.
Along with his son Otto II (973–983) and his extremely gifted grandson
Otto III (983–1003), the interests of the Roman Church were defended
and membership expanded. But the advances of the Germanic emperor
for the church were accompanied by both alterations in the nature of
Roman Christian control and in the centralized temporal powers of the
papacy.

Consider two important factors; The German (Saxon) domination of
the papacy wrested control from the Italian-Roman dominance in papal appointments. From the Ottonians onward, the nationality of popes
was universal in character. (It was only after the Protestant Reformation that the papal seat was almost exclusively occupied again by Ital-
ians.) Further, and more importantly from an economic standpoint, the
Saxon domination of the papacy denied the so-called Donation of Constantine to then-pope Sylvester I (314–335) through which the emperor
Constantine allegedly ceded the exclusive and unrivaled primacy to the
Roman pope over all of Christianity. In addition, the donation was interpreted by some to mean that the pope had temporal control over Italy
(the dominion over the Papal States was justified on similar grounds).[10]
In denying the "Donation," the Germans legitimized their control and
occupation of Italy and Rome. Moreover, while serving as protector of
the papacy, the Germanic control involved a much-reinvigorated secular claim on clerical appointments ranging from the nomination of bishops, the receipt of fealty and revenues of knights on church lands, and
the use of church interests to defend the union of Germany and Italy to

the outright assumption of equal control with the pope in the calling and conduct of synods.[11]

Thus, at the early to mid-tenth century, the church's march to monopoly was well underway. The spread of Christianity throughout most parts of Europe and England was a fait accompli. Pagan tribes—Vikings and others—as competitors to Christian religion were for the most part converted to Christianity. The Christian "product" was identified and promulgated. The renewed Holy Roman Empire served as protector of the faith across most of Europe. But challenges remained to monopoly status. In particular, while the church held virtual monopoly power over religious thought, its authority to deal with secular economic interference remained in question. The exact nature of the relations between church and state was malleable depending on the relative power of the two institutions at any given time. Further, the internal operations of the church—for example, papal elections, morality of the clergy, simonical practices within the church—were unsettled, endangering the cohesiveness of the Latin Christian monopoly. Finally, the relations with the Eastern Church, troubled at best since the time of Constantine and Justinian, were coming to an impasse due, ostensibly, to doctrinal differences.[12] Thus, before the Latin Church could emerge triumphantly as a vertically integrated monopoly and effective force against secular authority in the High Middle Ages, some of these issues had to find solutions. Clerical reforms were on the way in a number of forms (in particular the reforms of Pope Gregory VII—the monk Hildebrand—in the later eleventh century). Further, there would be new denouements between religious and secular realms regarding investiture and property control. But before turning to these features of the period and their effects, the issue of East-West church relations deserves close attention in understanding the premier status of the Roman (Latin) Church in the High Middle Ages.

Competition with Byzantium and the "Great Schism"

The split between Roman (Latin) Christianity and Eastern Orthodox Christianity has been deep and abiding almost since the move to Constantinople and the solid establishment of an Eastern patriarchy. The Emperor Justinian put an exclamation point on the fact that Eastern

(Greek) Christians would not recognize the pope (bishop of Rome) as having primacy of authority over a universal church, that is, over all bishops worldwide, a situation that obtains today. The issue, at base, is one of *ecclesiology*, as it concerns the internal hierarchical structure of religion. While the Roman bishop was given special honors by other bishops from the earliest days of Christianity—owing in part to the preaching and martyrdom of Paul and Peter in Rome—the fundamental dispute revolved around the particular form of hierarchical church structure. Roman Church claims for primacy of the Roman pontiff rest upon the belief that scripture enshrines the bishop of Rome as Peter's direct successor, whereas Eastern Orthodox belief that each local city church, which includes bishop, prelates, deacons, subdeacons, and celebrants constitute "the church." All bishops are Peter's successors and, ontologically, all bishops are equal in stature. Roman Church beliefs are in contradiction to this view: the bishop of Rome is the sole successor to Peter and is the actual and functional head of the Christian church. The Eastern Church became schismatic from the perspective of the Roman, but despite repeated difficulties and differences, the alternative authority structure does not invalidate the consecration powers of Eastern bishops or the Eastern Church members as bona fide Christians.

Clearly, from the perspective of evolutionary monopoly, the Roman or Latin Church had to make good its functional claim of monopoly. Cartel behavior, if all bishops had equal voice and influence in synods or councils, would have severely weakened the power of the bishop of Rome, whatever his "special status" might have been. Thus it is critical to understand exactly how Roman Church interests defeated or marginalized the other main claimant to Christian authority. In this spirit, we briefly consider the development of doctrinal and jurisdictional disputes between the two branches of Christianity with an eye on the end result, the ultimate domination of Latin Christianity as the monopoly over religion in the High Middle Ages.

East-West Disputes

Disputes over the primacy of the bishop of Rome emerged as early as the second century. These disputes accelerated as the nexus of political power shifted from the West, that is, from Rome to Constantinople. Five great religious sees developed in this early period, Antioch, Alexandria, Jerusalem, Constantinople, and Rome, but Rome and Constantinople were always accorded special honors due to numerous reasons. For Rome, the city was the initial seat of empire, and the site of the martyrdom of Saints Peter, who was considered the first apostle, and Paul. Constantinople was the locus of power supporting the church, at least for a time. However, for all the rationales considered, Eastern emperors and patriarchs never accepted the *primacy* of the Rome's bishop. He was regarded by the Eastern Church, then and now, as "first among equals." Despite his aggressive sixth-century support of Christianity, the Eastern emperor Justinian was declared anathema by the Latin Church not only for doctrinal reasons, one suspects, but also because he failed to acknowledge the primacy of the Roman bishop—that is the Roman Christian version of ecclesiology. The years between Justinian and the "Great Schism" of 1054 between the western and eastern branches of Christianity were peppered with similar differences. However, we maintain that two of the most critical doctrinal differences between these two branches of Christianity, while nominally of doctrinal importance, were also *pretexts* for the strengthening of the Roman Church's chief assertion of primacy in all matters relating to the content and conduct of institutionalized Christianity. Without credence in that claim, a hierarchical and effective vertically integrated monopoly over Christendom would have been impossible.

Filioque ("and the Son"): The Continuing Issue of Product Definition

The necessity of establishing a cohesive and standardized product or belief system was apparent for Christianity when Christ did not return after the first centuries of the church (see chap. 4 for an elaboration of this matter). That product—including the specification of the books of the New Testament—was presented in brief in the so-called Apostles' or Nicene Creed at the Council of Nicaea. The creed, historically, has numerous meanings. It can recall the original creed from the Nicene Council of 325, the revised creed established at the First Council of Constantinople (381), or the emendations of the latter. The creed, importantly, serves as the sine qua non of being a Christian. In the absence of Christ's return, a strong measure of credence and homogeneity had to be built into the Christian religion. This was necessary in order to restrict entry by those who did not adopt a specific and *well-defined* belief system.

Tentacular disputes raged against parts of the creed within the Western-Eastern community, chief of which revolves around the wording related to the *relative position* of the members of the Trinity (Father, Son, and Holy Spirit). Briefly, the issue is this: The initial creed (Nicaea) ended "and in the Holy Spirit"; the revised creed (Constantinople, 381) ended "and in the Holy Ghost, the Lord and Giver of life, who proceedeth from the Father, who with the Father and the Son together is worshiped and glorified, who spake by the prophets. In one holy catholic and apostolic church; we acknowledge one baptism for the remission of sins; we look for the resurrection of the dead and the life of the world to come. Amen." But, later, ostensibly to counter the Arian heresy, where Christ is considered human, a clause was added that then created a creed that read, "And in the Holy Ghost, the Lord and Giver of life, who proceedeth from the Father *and the Son*, who with the Father. . . ." This addition of the *filioque* ("and the Son") created a centuries-long cause célèbre of discord and dissent between western (Latin) and eastern (Greek or Byzantine) branches of the Christian church. Although some Latin popes were opposed to the addition of the clause (however Charlemagne approved its inclusion),[13] it was retained in Latin practice to the point where the *non*-use of it was regarded as heresy in the Roman branch of the church. For their part, Eastern patriarchs and Christians regarded the use of it as a violation of the expressions of the Councils of Nicaea and Constantinople and later councils that prohibited alterations in the original creed. In other words, Latin Church belief and practice was declared heretical for including the *filioque*.[14]

While some modern theologians find little difference in the underlying belief systems expressed in the two versions of the creed, late first millennium Christians—at least at the upper levels of clergy—took the difference quite seriously. Charlemagne used the assumed heresy to curb the incursions of the eastern empire and Church in the eighth century. In the late ninth century the issue of "appointment power" of the patriarch of Constantinople again involved the *filioque*. The appointment by the Roman pope Nicholas I of a patriarch of Constantinople (Ignatius) was rejected by the Byzantine emperor (Michael III), and in an increasingly familiar story the Roman pope then refused to acknowledge the emperor's appointment (Patriarch Photius I of Constantinople). The Latin Church convened a council (Fourth Council of Constantinople) and condemned, or anathematized, Photius, after which the Eastern Orthodox emperor and patriarch convened their own council reinstating Photius and condemning the *filioque* as heresy. Mutual excommunications followed along with familiar declarations of heresy on both sides.

The issue of the *filioque*, essentially a theological issue concerning the Trinity, would appear to have been relatively simple to solve. But, as some have observed, the insertion, somewhat innocuous in itself, was a symbol of the "legal formalism and logical rationalism" of the Roman Church, a claim that establishes its roots of primacy over Christianity just as the Roman state had maintained over the conquered (Lossky 1951, 87). The debate over the *filioque* was but a stalking horse for the claim of monopoly over Christianity and its interpretation. The Roman Church was able to avoid being "schismatic" itself—not abiding by the council's decisions as to the main articles of faith—by declaring papal infallibility over the interpretations and practices of all of Christianity. The *filioque* was basically a pretext for establishing a *Roman* monopoly over the church.

The Issues of Icons: Product and Credence

A second doctrinal or policy matter related to the issue of iconography. Iconoclasts viewed worship of images (of Christ, Christ on the Cross, the Virgin, saints, and so on) as a violation of the Second Commandment forbidding the worship of false gods or graven images. They supported the breaking or destruction of such images. Clearly, all early religions—Greek, Roman, Near Eastern, and many others—used figures and paintings as integral to worship and ceremony. The Christian church was of course no exception. In the eighth century, however, iconoclasm was taken up around 726 and 730 by the Byzantine Emperor Leo III. Leo ordered the removal or destruction of all images of Christ and the Saints. His son Constantine V (741–775) called a council (the Council of Hieria in 754) to solidify this position. Constantine then expropriated the churches and monasteries relieving them of valuable paintings, statuary, tapestries, and other objects of veneration. Images of Christ were removed from crosses.

Iconoclasm was then denied by the Latin Church, which declared objects and holy representations as material but "venerable" objects that commanded respect but were not "holy" in themselves. The dispute did not end, however, with a Latin-supported council position to this effect. In the ninth century (814–842) a second iconoclastic movement emerged under Byzantine Emperor Leo V, who called a synod to reinstitute the destruction of images. Manufacturers or artists creating sculpture or paintings were not only relieved of their jobs (constituting an opposing interest group) but were declared anathema as well. Paint, wood, or marble are lifeless materials and cannot be claimed to be "holy" in the iconoclast's view. The attempt to do so is the work of Satan.

But once more the Roman branch of Christianity rejected these notions. The Roman Church's rebuttal was essentially that icons, paintings, and statuary represent a *real* Christ or *real* saints whereas graven idols did not represent real persons of real substance (the "Golden Calf," for example). This validation of the use of icons is of course suspect—of the Trinity, for example, only Christ was "of substance." The Holy Ghost was and is often represented by a dove (as represented above the high altar at Saint Peter's Basilica in Rome) and conceptions of God the Father, at least in later depictions, bears a striking resemblance to a famous statue of Zeus. Then there are angels, of course, which have many artistic forms. At all odds, the opponents of iconoclasm, both within the Latin and Byzantine churches (called iconodules or iconophites), won the day. But the dispute is interesting from a number of perspectives. First, it is the case that, absent the return of Christ and his saints, some form of "advertising" is a practical necessity. Representations helped bring to mind the essential persons from which Christianity flowed. It helped sell the product by depicting both the benefits of being Christian, such as God and Christ's beatific vision in a world of eternal salvation, as well as the costs of not belonging, such as the horrors of eternal punishment with depictions of Satan and devils, so prominent in later medieval art.[15] Images were good advertising and, like relics, were good business for Christian entrepreneurs.[16]

More importantly, within an economic context, the Latin support of icons was a blow to the ecclesiology of the Byzantine Church wherein the emperor claimed the right to call a synod and condemn icons. Although the issue of iconography also figured in the Protestant schism, the issue of the East-West debate was not of a magnitude to create schism between the two branches of Christianity especially since a large portion of Eastern Christians wanted icons retained. The icon controversy, like the debate over *filioque*, was actually one of authority and monopoly over the substance and interpretation of Christianity as a religion. These two matters, however, were among the pretexts that led to a final split between the two branches of Christianity. That final split (a continuing split, we might add) was to establish the primacy of the pope as the upstream head of the church, rather than a church ruled by a council of patriarchs as shown in figure 6.1.

The Great Schism: Market Division between
Eastern and Western Christianity

The proximate cause of the ultimate split between the Eastern and Western Churches in 1054 was a debate over another relatively minor matter—the issue of the Latin Church's use of unleavened bread in the Eucharistic service. The contretemps between Patriarch Michael I of Constantinople against Pope Leo IX on this issue resulted in charges and countercharges on the legitimacy of this supposedly Hebraic practice and on the *filioque* as well. A papal bull excommunicating Michael and a retaliatory excommunication of the papal legates that had delivered the bull occurred. Importantly, the Roman charge that the Eastern rite had not remained faithful to the original Nicene Creed was spurious. The Latin rite had added the *filioque* at a council in the late sixth century to the original!

While the *filioque* issue and the additional period of iconoclasm were certain points of difference leading to the formal market division between the two branches of Christianity, they were by no means the only reasons. Celibacy, at least officially, was by this time widely practiced in the Latin Church, but not in the Eastern Orthodox. Divorce and remarriage was also permitted in the East, but, unless protracted and costly procedures are followed, the practice remains forbidden to the present day in the Latin rite. Rather, the chief problem may be described as one of ecclesiology and authority. The Eastern Church was always tied more closely to the state. The Eastern emperor's influence on the patriarch of Constantinople's policies and practices was clear, whereas the Roman Church existed generally as a monopoly facing numerous monarchs and competitors on the political side of the equation. Claims against the papacy, some of them traditional on the part of secular rulers, were strenuously though not always successfully resisted by the Roman Church. Thus the central issue of departure concerned the assertion of Latin Christian organization, in the form of absolute papal authority, as a monopoly over *all* Christians including those in the East. The tight hierarchical structure with the pope at the apex of authority and power was the central reason for the great schism between East and West, a schism that exists today for the same reason. The bishop of Rome might be accorded, for various reasons, a "primacy of honor," but Eastern Christians continue to deny him a "primacy of authority."[17] Western papal interests regard the Eastern rites as "legitimate" and would welcome reunification but only under acknowledged conditions of *Latin* Christian monopoly.

A final question concerns the issue of duopoly in the eleventh century in the matter of Christianity. Put a different way, why did the Eastern Church not represent a viable counterforce to Latin forms of Christianity? The answer is that by the eleventh century the sphere of Eastern Church influence had been sharply reduced by Muslim takeovers of territories surrounding Antioch, Alexandria, and Jerusalem. Latin patriarchs were installed in the East. The areas of Eastern Europe and the Near East controlled by the Eastern emperor (and therefore the Eastern Orthodox Church) were significantly reduced. To cap matters for many Eastern Orthodox Christians, the Fourth Crusade (1204), ostensibly directed against Muslim incursions, included Latin Christian assaults and sackings of Constantinople where Christians warred against Christians. From an economic perspective, the great schism and the events of its aftermath produced enhanced market power to the Church of Rome and helped make it the monopoly provider of religious products until the Protestant Reformation. Geopolitical events kept the Eastern competitive fringe at bay and isolated from the advancing Latin monopoly. Despite attempts at reconciliation between East and West over the second millennium, including some very recent ones, the split between the Roman Catholic and Eastern Orthodox branches of Christianity continues for the foreseeable future.[18]

Roman Church Monopoly Solidifies

By the mid-eleventh century the Latin Church had come to a solution of sorts *within* the Christian religion in its divorce from the Eastern Church. Unable to convince the Eastern Church of its claim to a primacy of authority, it relegated the Eastern Church to the fringe of the control over Christian religion. But, as noted earlier in this chapter, a number of thorny problems remained for the Western Church in the ninth through eleventh centuries. Among these problems were (1) a need for internal reform to provide and restore credence after the shameful takeover of the papacy by Roman aristocrats; (2) a shoring up and reform of the vertical organization and control of the church at the downstream levels, and related to this, (3) clear mechanisms for capturing the property, rents, and control relating to the installation or investitures of prelates vis-à-vis secular institutions.

Internal Church Reforms

As the Christian religion grew from a small and disparate band of believers to the overarching form of European religion in the ninth and tenth centuries, a number of critical institutional accretions to church organization took place. The entrepreneurial power of the missionaries had profound and positive effects on church membership. Doctrinally, an ethos of "Christian behavior" developed, often under the interpretive monopoly claimed by the papacy, with holy scripture as the foundation. A code of behavior was prescribed wherein sin—as defined by the church—was met with particularly vivid and horrible punishment, if not in the present, then definitely in the afterlife. This belief system was adopted hook, line and sinker by illiterate people of all classes and by the literate as well, giving the church an enormous amount of societal control. With this control, however, came abuses. Immoral behavior attended the growing prosperity of monasteries in particular parts of Europe. As wealthy landowners made restitution for their sins in life or through wills, monasteries became relatively large-scale enterprises in agriculture and herding. Such property accumulations altered the focus and internal organization of these religiously based institutions. With wealth came abuses, and abuses engendered reform (Davidson 1995).

Church reforms dotted the landscape of clerical institutions throughout the first millennium. Church reforms and reformers, like the later ones of Saint Dominic and Saint Francis of Assisi, aimed at correcting the worldly life adopted by clergy in possession of wealth and power. They stressed, in contrast, a life of asceticism and poverty with saintly adherence to an imitation of the life of Christ.[19]

The most famous organizational scheme for behavior in monasteries was the Rule of Saint Benedict (followed with variations today by some holy orders), mentioned in connection with Gregory I. Saint Benedict of Nursia (480–550) did not advocate removal from the world as a path to sanctity but espoused communal living and a rigorous routine of spiritual activities, communal prayer (eight "offices" of worship per day), and communal ownership. Abbots were elected, and the "Rule" became the foundation for monasteries throughout the Middle Ages and beyond. A group of Benedictines founded the Abbey of Cluny in 910, which was the standard-bearer of church reform, playing a pivotal role in helping institute the reforms of Gregory VII (the monk Hildebrand). Founded by William of Aquitaine, the Abbey of Cluny, which came to house three hundred monks with two hundred "satellite" monasteries, had a special designation—it was subject and answerable to papal control and not to the bishop of its region. This removed the monastery and its activities from the constant feudal wars that took place between the nobility of Europe—a characteristic of the Middle Ages prior to the formation of monarchical nation-states. Local bishops who often owed their positions to the local nobility were cut out of the rents and revenues that were produced by monasteries. As Blumenthal (1988, 69) reports: "Bishops were gradually discovering that they had lost not only much influence in their sees but also income to the reformed monasteries." In fact, both clerical and secular disputes over property rights raged over the revenues to monasteries, over the nature of "proprietary monasteries," and over the investiture power division between secular powers and the papacy. Again, as we have noted previously, papal control over local-level appointments and revenues was a sine qua non of an efficient and successful vertically integrated monopoly. We therefore return to the issue of investitures.

The Investiture Controversy

The reforms of Cluny, while seemingly confined to behavior in the monasteries, created a grassroots movement to piety within the lay branches of the church and in the papacy as well. But the inevitable accumulations of wealth were bound to cause new conflict. As Scott (1964, 86) notes,

> During the tenth and eleventh centuries donors gave very large quantities of land to Cluniac houses, sometimes mingling the idea of protecting it from encroachment by their neighbours with more pious motives. The order thus became a great landowning corporation with all the responsibilities involved in such a state, such as the possession of serfs and the need to exercise various feudal rights. This led to a large variety of disputes with secular landholders, with other monasteries and with the bishops, who understandably resented the removal of large areas of their dioceses from their own jurisdiction. What had started as a protest against secularization of the Church had itself by the

twelfth century become largely secularized; the time was ripe for another reform.

The whole issue at the beginning of the twelfth century revolved around simony broadly considered—the sale of things holy, including offices, for personal profit—and the division of such rents that could be obtained by monarchs or local feudal lords or, in contrast, by clerics or the papal establishment. Completion of the forward vertical integration of the church had to include elimination or reduced interference from civil authority at the downstream levels.

The foundation of the problems existing between secular and papal interests stemmed from the traditional appointment powers granted the emperor over the pope. By tradition, the Holy Roman emperor had at least "approval" powers over the appointment of the pope, while the pope had similar powers over the emperor. But the degradation of the papacy over the tenth and early eleventh centuries, with simony and immorality rife in the highest office in Western Christianity, weakened the power of the papacy over secular matters. Underlying this problem was the economic issue of claims to revenues, which was part and parcel of the Investiture Controversy. Simony was an important source of income for feudal-secular leaders as it was for local, regional, and papal authorities.

Battles over authority and revenue were endemic to Christianity over the entire first millennium of the church, but the spread of church reforms from the Cluniac movement fomented lasting changes in the eleventh century and beyond. Reforms began in the papacies of Gregory VI (1045–1046) and Leo IX (1049–1054), and in 1059 the election of the pope was declared by a church council to be the sole province of the cardinals of the church (where it remains today).[20] This decree took control over papal investiture from secular leaders. Amid the reforming zeal of the church, already underway, emerged a pope who would create the strong monopoly of the papacy of the central and High Middle Ages.

The monk Hildebrand, who had assisted in the reforming projects of Gregory VI and Leo IX, became Pope Gregory VII. In this pivotal moment for the Latin Church monopoly Gregory attacked simony, the lack of celibacy (many of the clergy, especially in Germany, lived in concubinage), and lay appointments of bishops and other high officials by secular rulers.[21] In particular, Gregory was emphatic in the matter of

defining the rights and relationships between secular rulers and the su-
preme pontiff.

> In both the delineation of its specific principles and the definitiveness of its
> aim, it was new. It represented Gregory's concept of church and state—an im-
> perial theocracy which placed under God's vicegerent all the principalities of
> Christendom. Only the pope exercised universal sway over all governments,
> could use the imperial insignia, possessed the right to depose emperors,
> might annul the decree of any person or synod of persons, was entitled to
> judge everyone yet could himself be judged by no one, and held the power to
> absolve subjects from their oath of fealty to wicked rulers. Gregory expected
> kings and princes symbolically to show their subservience to his will and obe-
> dience to his commands by kissing the papal foot. (Cannon 1960, 165)

The young German King Henry IV was led to action by Gregory's deposition of a Milanese bishop, which was considered a jurisdictional reach
on Gregory's part. Henry was beset on all fronts by a hostile feudal nobility and needed all the secular (economic and military) support he
could get by appointing bishops. Gregory's "new rules" were not to Henry's liking and in January 1076 Henry declared Gregory deposed.[22] In
response Gregory called a synod and excommunicated Henry and, importantly, released all of his Christian vassals from fealty or allegiance
to the king, a prime example of how the papacy played off credence and
certification of secular authority against benefits to the Roman Church.
Ensuing hostilities against Henry by his former vassals encouraged him
to rethink matters and ultimately to seek forgiveness by Pope Gregory, precipitating one of the most famous and dramatic stories of medieval history. Henry crossed the Alps to Canossa in 1077, barefoot and
wearing hair shirt in the snow, begging forgiveness. Although Gregory
lifted the excommunication, Henry's Saxon vassals installed Rudolf von
Rheinfeld as king in Henry's place. Henry, still young and vibrant, ultimately killed Rudolf and marched on Rome to attempt a deposition of
Gregory. Gregory, however, elicited aid from Norman "allies" in southern Italy who rescued Gregory but sacked Rome. Importantly, the papal
claims relative to investiture and the existence of a papal monopoly were
sustained in a process whereby feudal interests were supported against a
recalcitrant monarch.
   Although Gregory died in exile in Salerno, his achievements in establishing papal independence from secular authority—that is, in denying

the claims of theocracy by secular rulers, were the harbinger of papal monopoly in the central and High Middle Ages (and which extends to modern times). Gregory pushed the church in a new direction, one resulting
in the early twelfth-century Concordat of Worms (1122). This agreement
between Emperor Henry V and Pope Callistus II, theoretically at least,
brought the Investiture Controversy to an end. Papal and ecclesiastical
supremacy over the *spiritual* investiture of bishops and other prelates
was established once and for all. This included canonical elections in abbeys and monasteries. Rents from income of massive church properties
were split in effect with retained rights over feudal fees and duties owed
the emperor, who maintained some influence over religious investiture.
But while the details of the direction and amounts of the rent transfers
between feudal interests, medieval religious institutions, and the papacy
remained in flux over ensuing centuries, the principle of papal monopoly
over and independence from secular authority was firmly established by
the beginning of the twelfth century.

Conclusion

An effective vertically integrated, multinational Latin Christian Church
was clearly in existence by the beginning of the twelfth century. Dominance over religious thought extended throughout Europe, including
Germany and Scandinavia, which had not even been part of the Roman
Empire. Most importantly, the church emerged as a papal monopoly by
1100 CE, and the essential means by which this took place have been the
subject of this book and chapter.

A loosely vertically integrated monopoly over Christian belief systems
had been in practical existence since the time of Charlemagne. Elements
of that organization were in place even before Charlemagne. But essential problems remained. First, rent divisions were uncertain as feudal
forces battled with centralized monarchies for power and the ability to
collect taxes and claim revenues. Church interests, including monasteries, abbeys, and ordinary Christian parishes, were caught up in this battle since feudal lords and monarchs had, in long tradition, the power to
at least affect the outcome of clerical appointments and elections, which
affected the church both economically and spiritually. Partly based on
establishing political allegiances from appointees and sometimes based
on feudal contractual obligations, these investitures became critical to

both religious and secular revenues as the church became wealthier. Arguably, the Latin Church owned 30 to 40 percent of all arable land in Europe by the year 1100. The relative rights of church versus secular authorities to revenues from such lands were no small matter. While a permanent solution to investiture was not to be found even in the Middle Ages, the Concordat at Worms and other agreements gave the advantage to the Latin papal establishment.

A second critical issue was central to the success of monopoly, and it too was related to the Investiture Controversy. It was, in effect, the acknowledgment of the papal monopoly of spiritual authority to *appoint* bishops, metropolitans, abbots, priests, and deacons—the entire vertical structure of church power—without the interference of secular authorities as to the individuals selected. (Secular rulers did retain authority with respect to secular issues in dealing with the appointees.) While this issue appears to be identical to the issue of secular investitures, it is even more far-reaching. It is true that even after the Concordat of Worms, feudal lords and monarchs were able to exact or to try to exact their contractual fees and obligations from church properties. But secular powers relinquished all authority to appoint prelates at the upstream or downstream levels of the church. This meant that the traditional appointment power of the Holy Roman emperor to select the pope was nullified. In other words, what had been theocracies, such as those still existing in the Eastern Church, simply became monarchies. The pope became a monarch himself with independent spiritual power and authority just as the secular monarchs were in secular matters.

The disorder and political disruptions of the feudal system might have been a serious blockage in the church's assent to monopoly power, but it was not. States and fiefdoms came and went, but the belief system of Roman Christianity remained a constant throughout the centuries. As Daniel-Rops noted (1959, 534) concerning the post-Frankish period:

> Whereas feudal anarchy would result in virtual destruction of the State, its effect upon the Church would remain superficial. There was the fundamental difference between East and West: the Byzantine Church was part and parcel of the regime, an integral part of political society; but the Western Church managed to preserve its independent life. The effort of the bishops after the death of Charlemagne was not in vain, nor was that of such saints and monks as Benedict of Aniane, who strove for the freedom of the mind. An ideal of

spiritual independence lived on in certain souls, and it was that spirit which, in a word, enabled the Church to right herself and at the same time to prepare a second spring.

That "spring," of course, led to a solidification of monopoly over Christian belief in Europe during the centuries to come. As always, the church was most fortunate in most often being able to pick "winners" among the alternative polities that governed Europe. It gave the papacy the power to manipulate rulers of all kinds through the monopoly it had over the belief system of international adherents.

The Roman Church therefore became a monopoly in all meaningful senses by 1100. It had clear power to support or subvert secular governments and rulers by providing or withholding credence and support. It had the monopoly power to not only define the product of Christianity—means for assurances for eternal salvation—but to interpret the path or alter it as preferences changed. Synods and councils were called, but the Roman pope proclaimed himself supreme in powers of interpreting holy scripture.[23] Moreover, the church became active in preventing entry and in expanding market share by 1100. Gregory's VII's successor, Urban II, called the First Crusade in 1095, which, though only temporarily successful in returning the Holy Land to Christian control, helped blunt the Islamic incursions in Christian territories and Byzantine Christian missionary efforts in the East.

These actions are characteristic of a private interest strategy to achieve monopoly power. Had the church pursued public interest goals, it would have developed a different ecclesiology—one more like the church organizational structure of Eastern Orthodoxy, which emphasized decentralized control and where preferences could be met and adapted to members on a local level. The behavior of the church over the central and High Middle Ages would not be explainable without understanding the evolution of monopoly-building activities over the first 1,100 years of Western Christianity. Naturally, states would vertically integrate in order to achieve policy and revenue objectives. But the Roman Catholic Church was a unique model of international integration and control. It could (and did) trade off credence and legitimization between nations, and it was the only institution to be able to do so. It became, in effect, a superstate with outposts and representatives all over Western Europe within the vertically integrated structure it created. No single civil government could match its reach and influence or match its ability to form alliances and collect revenues for its various products. The apex of that monopoly occurred with the assertions of monopoly power by Pope Gregory VII and the follow-through by later popes who expanded upon the private interests of the Latin Church across Europe and beyond.

CHAPTER EIGHT

Conclusion: The *Roman* Church Monopoly Triumphant

Introduction

The Roman Catholic Church achieved monopoly status in terms of domination over most of Western Europe by the opening of the ninth century. Product definition, although evolving in interpretation, was all but secure. The Eastern Church, while presenting problems in terms of recognition of the Roman bishop as primate of the whole church, was at bay due to a multitude of problems, not the least of which was the successful military campaigns by Muslims from the East. But multiple difficulties stood in the way of the church's business plan. The disintegration of its main protector, the Frankish empire, in the ninth and tenth centuries, the many Viking sieges, the internal corruption of the papacy, and other factors could have caused a fatal erosion in the "business plan" of monopolization. But the church was able to overcome all of these obstacles by 1100 or so. The distinguished medieval historian James Westfall Thompson (1931, 598) once described the situation for the papacy at this point in time as an "enormous development of papal power, culminating in the pontificate of Innocent III (1198–1216). But the church in general, simultaneously with the papacy, increased in authority, in power, in wealth. Indulgences, the inquisition, the privileges of the crusaders, donations, new taxes like the Saladin tithe, enlarged jurisdiction of ecclesiastical courts, were the means by which these results were achieved."[1] The analysis of this book is an attempt to explain how, in economic terms, the church reached this apex.

How the Church Reached Monopoly Status

The appearance of Christianity in the first century created a competitive opportunity for the new belief system. In monotheism it offered a simpler, more cogent, and unified organon of religious belief than did the plethora and pantheon of Roman and other cultures' gods. While it is correct that Judaism was also monotheistic, Christianity offered *clear* and *projected* security or assurances of a happy afterlife and a philosophy of love and societal peace in the present. These factors, we have argued in this book, created a lower full price for the Christian religion, permitting it to actively and aggressively compete with the belief systems of the times. The lower full price is of course net of some costs to early Christians, such as possible ostracism by neighbors and others associated with other sects. The Roman state, moreover, was in fact relatively tolerant of most belief systems and did not engage in serious repressions until the middle of the third and the early fourth centuries.

The tendencies of particular institutions, including religion, to monopolize is the key to understanding the ascendance and authoritarian ecclesiological nature of Christianity, as with earlier temple societies in ancient civilizations. An economic theory of networking and consumption externalities goes far in explaining the rapid spread of Christianity as it does circumstances supporting the nature of the product. The product being sold by Christianity and all religions was metacredence in nature—one whose qualities could never be determined objectively either before or after purchase. After all, no one has ever returned from Shakespeare's "undiscovered country" to tell about the promised product, excepting the testimony based on Christian *faith* that Christ was resurrected from the dead. Thus, credence in the promised product had to be established in demanders and potential demanders. This was accomplished, as we note in chapters 2, 3, and 4, through numerous means. Chief among these means was an extremely fortuitous group of able entrepreneurs such as those working in the Jewish communities (e.g., Peter), but most especially the apostle to the Gentiles, Paul (Conybere and Howson 1997 [1889]). In addition, the demand for this metacredence good was a function of the risk-adjusted full price, including time, money, and "ritual" costs, income, and the full price of substitutes. Further, as with the demand for all religions, demand was influenced by social and political stability and education, the state of scientific knowledge, and other factors such as an inherited environment and personal endowments (the religion of one's parents, state religious institutions extant at the time, among other factors). The full price of "assurances of eternal salvation," the chief product sold by the early Christians and most other forms of religion, was the money price plus the time-ritual-doctrinal price for some degree of certainty and quality of an afterlife. There is a direct relationship between that full price and certainty or assurances against risk, other things equal (see chap. 3).

Thus early potential Christians were faced with a choice between the risk-adjusted full price of Roman or other pagan religions and Christian membership. While Christianity initially arose as a monotheistic Jewish sect, the central thrust of the new religion was, particularly later, in conversion of Gentiles (pagans and believers in cult-like religions). Paul was enormously successful, through preaching and letters, in bringing both Jews, especially Hellenized Jews, and non-Jews to Christianity and in establishing, with Peter's ultimate agreement, the position that one did not have to convert to *Judaism* to become Christian. His critical legacy to Christianity and its growth is manifested in the fact that a large portion of the New Testament adopted at Nicaea is composed of his epistles or letters.

Providing credence, of course, must take on other forms. The periodic persecutions levied on Christians—most importantly, their murders, including those of Peter and Paul, in Rome—actually added much credence to the new religion. Persecutions of the third and early fourth centuries appear to have been particularly effective in increasing consumers of the Christian product. The willingness of believers to be put to death, in famously horrible fashion, rather than acknowledge that the emperor was a god, merely added credence to potential converts that they would be saved by Christ upon his return and would be given an eternal and glorious afterlife. Of course, tales of the severity and pervasiveness of the persecutions may have been partly the result of Christian apocrypha. The growth of Christianity was therefore and very largely a function of the assurances of eternal salvation provided to believers by the leaders of the movement. These and other factors provided the credence necessary for the new religion to flourish and, if the available evidence on growth rates is even close to accurate, entrepreneurship, networking, and the provision of credence for a metacredence product were enormously successful.

Problems for Christianity, both internal and with civil government, remained throughout the early period. The centuries before Constantine were difficult and familiar ones for civil government. Rome's imperial adventures, sumptuary spending, and maintenance of conquered lands were enormous drains on the fisc. These weaknesses and the quasi-constant barbarian threats at the borders of the empire, along with the growth of the new religion within Rome and the major cities of the empire, put the Roman government on the defensive. Internal problems also plagued the Christian religion. Christ had promised to return "to judge the living and the dead," but his return became less certain as the years passed. Able entrepreneurs continued to extol the faith product, and Christians underwent cyclical persecution that added to credence, but there were many unanswered questions among potential demanders. A substantial number of variants of Christian belief prospered at this time, and the quest was on to define the elements of "true Christianity." The response to these problems by Christian entrepreneurs in the first three centuries was to attempt to codify the Christian religion with a canon of writings. Yet, these writings often presented conflicting fundamentals of the religion.

The appearance of the emperor Constantine (272–337 CE) and his assessment of the civil and religious situation provided a fortuitous solution for both Roman government and Christian religion. Constantine was "converted" to Christianity and gave it political legitimacy within the empire. Economic theory offers a clear explanation for this civil approbation. Christianity's fundamental tenets of love, forgiveness, and moral behavior lowered agency and policing costs within the Roman constellation as we describe in chapter 5. The Roman emperors had much on their plates with having to repel barbarians at the fringes of Roman influence. Resources devoted to internal security were clearly lower under Christian religious influence. Cultural and moral homogeneity helped solidify the state and gave it a wedge against nonorthodox enemies.[2]

There was a happy coincidence for Christianity when it was legitimized by Constantine, and it related to the central internal problem of the religion besides persecution (which had recently resumed under Emperor Diocletian)—namely, *which Christianity was the "real" and legitimate Christianity, given all of the variations being preached and given the fact that Christ had, by the early fourth century, failed to re-*

turn? This problem was solved, at least in substance, with Constantine's calling of the Council of Nicaea in 325. That council was the essential ingredient in defining the Roman variant of the Christian product, although there was later disagreement over aspects of its content, and for establishing credence in the Christian religion by clearly defining the product. The books and content of the New Testament were established once and for all for "orthodox" Christians and provided the basis for the Christian monopoly going forward and a handle for the Roman part of that monopoly and its claims for monopoly over interpretations. The exclusive and orthodox product definition laid the groundwork for the coming Christian monopoly and its abilities to punish with annihilation, excommunication, interdict, and other tools any and all nonbelievers in the orthodox version of Christianity established at Nicaea. The hunted became the hunters as *exclusivity* of belief was established.

Property began accruing to the bishop of Rome after the legitimization of Christianity by Constantine, who looted pagan and nonorthodox Christian temples of their wealth and treasure in order to support both the government and to establish the "true" orthodox church. The Lateran Palace in Rome was a major donation of the emperor Constantine, but pious and wealthy Christians, as well as those seeking forgiveness for sins *intervivos* or at the time of death, meant that the Christian church was amassing huge amounts of property and wealth throughout the first centuries of the early Middle Ages. The Roman half of Christendom needed and received protection of its property and wealth from the Eastern emperors. Indeed, the origins of the Papal States occurred when the Byzantine Eastern Church reconquered large parts of Italy from the Ostrogoths under the leadership of the Eastern Roman emperor Justinian. Control of these lands was ultimately divided between Eastern and Western (Roman) interests, but Eastern protection of the Western Church was greatly diminished after the death of Justinian.[3]

More fundamentally, the patriarchs of the Eastern Church, organized in hierarchical but conciliar form, did not accept the bishop of Rome as primate but only as one who was deserving of "special honor" and conducted a Christianity that was closely tied to the emperor and civil government. The varying ecclesiology of the two branches of Christianity— wherein the eastern branch governed by "councils" with more autonomy for the individual branches—was clearly destined for conflict. The authoritarian, episcopal (top-down) nature of the Roman Church, although nominally embracing a conciliar form of governance as well, with the

Roman bishop as unchallenged monopolist over spiritual matters, engendered many conflicts. There were mutual excommunications and declarations of anathema between the bishops of Rome and Constantinople, especially after the problems of the Eastern emperor meant less protection for Western Church interests. Threats led to a great schism between the eastern and western branches of Christianity in the eleventh century—a schism that exists to the present day.

The Frankish kingdoms, Merovingian and Carolingian, came to Rome's rescue at this critical moment in the development of Roman Christian monopoly. Charles Martel, Clovis I, and their great successor Charlemagne bowed to the *primacy* of the Roman pontiff even as they maintained certain rights over clerical appointments and property rights. They became protectors of the papacy and de facto competitors with the claims of the Eastern Church and patriarchs. Frankish and other leaders also benefited from the credence supplied by the church. And self-generated claims for Roman papal monopoly had long existed. Gregory I (the Great), one of the last great "fathers" of the church, made those claims in the late sixth and early seventh centuries, but it was several centuries later when his successor Gregory VII, the monk Hildebrand who was bishop of Rome between 1076 and 1085, made the strongest assertions by when he became a monarch in effect, in addition to a spiritual leader, but one who certainly regarded himself as above civil rulers.[4] Balkanization of civil authority after the quasi cohesion of the Frankish empire, far from being an entirely negative aspect for the Roman papacy, was the occasion to use Christianity to manipulate civil governments through the church's power to confer credence on particular civil leaders and their realms.

Gregory VII's assertive and idealized papacy was finally realized by 1100, although there were numerous problems for the church in getting to this point. Throughout the "Dark Ages" the church was beset by both civil and spiritual competitors even as the church was highly successful in evangelizing invading and "occupying" barbarians, pagans, and peoples of territories conquered by Western civil polities. Missionaries were successful in Christianizing England, Germany, and Hungary, and conversions were forced in a "top-down" manner as well. These successful evangelizing efforts were a fundamental key to the establishment of monopoly. Not only did they establish political bases for the church in far-flung lands with high information and transportation costs, they made the Roman Church independent of civil governments and helped

develop a vertically integrated church. Civil leaders required approbation of the church, but civil rulers came and went. The church's ever-
expanding base of "purchasers" was *the constant* in any institutional rift
with kings or civil leaders of any kind. The church provided products demanded by consumers at the local level and received tithes and donations in return for them; civil governments generally just levied taxes in
return for military protection and security. Within this environment the
church met the challenges of the feudal system, the rise of cities, and the
rise of nation-states by supporting and giving credence to civil leaders
that would protect church property and interests and, most importantly,
who would accede to the self-proclaimed monopoly of spiritual authority.[5] Disputes between kings and popes over the High Middle Ages—
such as the investiture controversies—continued, as did internal difficulties such as when, in the fourteenth century, the papacy was moved to
Avignon. But the absolute spiritual authority was firmly established by
the beginning of the 1100s. Manifestations abound of that monopoly authority and what was done with it.

The purpose of this book has been to argue, with much help from sociological and historical accounts, that the most basic economic theory
of monopoly applies to the evolution of the Christian church after it had
received the sanction of the Edict of Milan in 313 CE, the Council of Nicaea in 325, and the creation of Christianity as a state religion later in the
fourth century. By 1100, the Christian church

- was a single, vertically integrated provider of a homogeneous product with no
  close substitutes, that is, a pure monopoly with only fringe competition in the
  western European sphere;
- created monopoly barriers to entry in the form of moral restraints, violence,
  excommunication, and civil enforcement of Christianity;
- possessed market power and the ability to raise the price of salvation;
- developed efficient output of religious product(s) by using a discriminatory
  pricing scheme in which service was provided to all but at discrete rates based
  on income and wealth;
- became international in scope and, through its international reach, dominated civil governments due to its power over orthodox Christians;
- divided markets on a geographical basis;
- masterfully created name brand capital to maintain the credibility of its primary product—assurances of eternal salvation; and
- developed innovations that related to profits and economic policy, for ex-

ample, manipulations of the usury doctrine to gain revenues both when the Church was a lender and when it was a borrower.

In sum, the church evolved from a mass of competitive Christian sects in the first three centuries CE to a full-scaled monopoly in seven centuries (fifth through twelfth). How it did so, we believe, is a fascinating story. What happened after it had created the monopoly and the devolution to competition after a new Christian competition reemerged is also of critical import to the long saga of historical evolution and characteristics of a vertically integrated monopoly power.

Roman Monopoly Processes and Market Entry

The processes through which the Roman Catholic Church achieved and maintained monopoly over spiritual and some temporal interests over the first millennium continued unabated throughout the High Middle Ages. The church's ability to manipulate the risk-return trade-off in order to find new demanders for Christianity was accompanied by the punitive methods used by monopoly to thwart entry and to elicit compliant behavior. The unparalleled growth in Roman Christianity reached new heights in this period also. Around 1300 England contained over 50,000 priests, deacons, and subdeacons (about 1 percent of its population) and, according to Mundy (1973, 284), similar figures attached to Catholic countries on the European continent where there were over seven hundred episcopal sees, or bishoprics, along with a large number of monasteries as well. The building of massive cathedrals competed in importance only with castle construction. Gilchrist (1969, 3) argued that the medieval church was "a richly endowed corporation whose income made it the wealthiest of societies. Through their revenues churchmen disposed of a great part of the liquid capital of the Western world."

This monopoly over Western religion was rigidly hierarchical in nature and, as we have noted in this book, was fairly well established by the time of Charlemagne's crowning by Pope Leo III in 800. The assertions of Hildebrand (Gregory VII) merely put the exclamation point on the top-down and powerful papal monopoly, a vertically integrated monopoly with downstream, geographically separate sellers of the product elaborated upstream. But in order to ensure membership growth and maintenance, the medieval church engaged in more than a business plan that maximized its wealth. The church manipulated the risk-return tradeoff to potential and existing members in numerous ways.

Most importantly, the church manipulated the means of attaining the final product of Christian belief—the conditions for assurances of eternal salvation—to its advantage. Marriage, in early times a civil matter, was co-opted from civil authority as a religious contract. Doctrinal changes were made by the church with conditions attached to the simple civil contract that gave the church a legal monopoly of determining legitimacy of marriage or children. Endogamy regulations, blood relationships, were instituted to create barriers to marriage and financial rewards when in the church's interests. Individuals were required to exchange vows in front of a priest for payment, religious bans had to be posted, and so forth. To willingly avoid these regulations carried maximum punishment for the so-called sinful behavior. Excommunication—elimination from the church and sacraments—was often the punishment, but the church had a whole menu of possible retributions. Divorce and marriage dissolution, possible under conditions laid down and often favorable to the papacy, were similarly treated as they are today—dependent on the income and position of petitioners. Usury and "just price" concepts were manipulated beyond recognition as well. When the church was a debtor, the prohibitions on usury applied, but not when the church was a creditor. Similar manipulations of monastery tithes, taxes, benefices, and subsidies, often in perpetuity to families, bishops, and cardinals, were common practice (see Davidson 1995).[6]

The church used many kinds of punitive measures to attack those who did not adhere to its dictums and conditions for attainment of the final product sold. Most severe, and possibly the oldest stricture, was excommunication, a total separation from the Catholic Church and its product. But excommunication carried the negative aspect of condemnation to hell as well, a factor that created a self-policing mechanism up to the present day. Interdict, often levied against the Jews when conditions warranted, condemned the "sinner" to be shunned by other Christians. (The American Puritans used similar devices.) There were even more severe entry control measures taken as well. The many crusades were regarded as a Christian device to recover Christian property (the Holy Land in the First Crusade in 1095) or to defend Roman Christianity against external or internal enemies. These bloody adventures included wars against enemies of all kinds including Cathars, Albigensians, Baltic "heretics," and dissidents from orthodox Catholic teachings as interpreted by the upstream papacy. Many were wars that involved conversion (the German crusades), but some crusading had the impact of reducing the influence of Eastern Christendom. Reconciliation of belief in Christ and violent crusading against Eastern Orthodox Christians and other Christians is difficult to conceive.

The economic interpretation of the high medieval church is that it was, in form and content, a monopoly organization with all that it implies. If the church were a public interest organization, it would have ministered to individuals by providing spiritual goods, information, and social goods to the poor at marginal cost. Even a cursory examination of the medieval monopoly activities of the Roman Catholic Church casts doubt on this premise. The medieval church was to a large extent wealth-maximizing and characterized by private interest activity, and the road to this activity, if not the motive, is to be found in first millennium events.

Further and far more alarming, the bellicosity exhibited by the Roman Catholic Church through the Crusades, the various inquisitions, and the assault on "witches," which several modern historians and many Roman Catholic defenders would like to minimize, underscores an important point.[7] There was and is a natural desire of Roman Christianity, *and a number of other modern religions*, to monopolize, since it taught and continues to teach that its form of religion is the "one true way" to paradise or at least to credible assurances of eternal salvation. Other ways must be condemned or eliminated. This "natural" tendency to exclusivity did and sometimes does lead to political strife and is a basis for violence.[8] Cartelization is or would be the result of ecumenism in any religion, and it would carry those implications for any religion. It would seem that a competitive playing field and an effective separation of church and state constitute the only antidote to these tendencies. That began, in the case of Christianity, with the entry of Martin Luther and the Protestants, some of whom imposed a uniting of church and state. While state-sponsored Christian religions remain, the number of stand-alone, differentiated Christian sects in the United States alone is staggering, numbering in the thousands.

Protestant Entry

Changes in the behavioral means to obtain the final product, long-term assurances of salvation, were at the heart of innovations introduced by the church in the twelfth through the fourteenth centuries. There were a number of aspects to these innovations. Confession of one's sins was no longer a group practice, but became a one-on-one auricular activity. This permitted, certainly in small village contexts, a priest to become closely acquainted with the individuals in his flock, including their income and economic status (Murray 1981, 303–304). Another important innovation, the doctrine of purgatory, which was earlier suggested in religious writings, took to the main stage of promulgated beliefs of the faithful. This halfway house from earthly life to heaven was designed as a holding tank for individuals who must fully expiate their earthly sins. The key to mitigating the time spent in purgatory—interestingly defined as human time though clearly signifying some "eternal" time—was through earthly prayers and good works, but also through the use of indulgences. Some of these indulgences could be paid for in money as well as in prayer, and official church documents, papal bulls dealing with indulgences, sanctioned differential pricing for these tickets out of purgatory. Vatican records provide clear and surprising pricing schemes for these benefits, price schedules with multiple tiers. The most elaborate scheme was developed by Jasper Ponce, the papal agent to England during the papacy of Alexander VI (1492–1503). Ponce's schedule included three categories of givers, with each category containing four to seven separate tariffs based upon ranges of annual personal income (see Lunt 1962, 60–64, 494, 586). This coterie of product innovations and most especially the use of plenary indulgences, expiating all time in purgatory, was the tipping point for Luther's successful entry into the Christian market in the early sixteenth century.[9] Increasingly intricate monopolistic price discriminatory schemes in the sale of indulgences brought Roman Catholic Christian demanders to the margin of purchase. Luther's innovation stresses a lower entry price—salvation was determined by faith alone, as had been Roman Catholic teaching prior to the innovations of the High Middle Ages. In contrast to Roman teaching, Luther maintained that "Everyone is a priest"; this worldview dispensed with the need for priestly mediation between man and God. Luther used Protestant simplicity and the flagrant financial abuses of the church to make good his entry into the market for Christian religion with reformers such as Zwingli and Calvin following with similar entry strategies.

Protestant entry was essentially a *process* of entry into many areas of Northern Europe (England was a special case). Southern Europe, including Spain, Italy, and parts of France and Germany, remained Roman Catholic. It is critical therefore, given our arguments for the Christian breakaway from Roman and pagan god systems, to understand the nature of the risk profile and the risk-adjusted full prices faced by those that broke away. One essential characteristic of early and modern Protestantism is that every man is a priest. Behavior grounded in the Holy Bible, available to be read by each believer in his or her language, together with a just and virtuous life, meant that the ultimate product—eternal salvation—could be attainable. Contrast this view with that of the highly ritualized toll road to heaven sold by the Roman Church. Careful adherence to the central church's *interpretation* of scripture, together with, in the modern period, strict adherence to marriage laws, avoidance of birth control, embryonic stem cell research, prohibition of gay marriage, and the prohibition of women in the priesthood are some of the necessary elements for attainment of the final product of the church.[10] The point is that the Protestant contract contained less certainty and more risk, whereas the Roman Catholic contract offered and offers in contrast to modern Protestant faiths more certainty and less risk.

But were more certainty and less risk demanded? Successful Protestant entry took place in the sixteenth century because the risk-adjusted full price of Protestant adherence was lower than that offered by the Roman Catholic religion. Those individuals who could accept a riskier religious portfolio faced a lower risk-adjusted full price than those who could not. The question then becomes: why were many Northern Europeans and the English eventually willing to switch from the Roman Catholic form of Christianity? Clearly, the full price was lower under Protestantism. There was less ritual offered on the supply side with Protestantism, meaning that there was greater leisure or market time to consume. For these buyers, the time costs and, most probably, the money costs were lower than the Catholic alternative.

Naturally, the degree of certainty offered by the various sects of Protestantism and the full price charged also affects religious choice. The steps leading to membership in alternative forms and the different rituals involved lead to higher or lower costs to demanders and more or less certain contracts. Baptism, a requirement of most Protestant faiths, may be highly ritualized. Severe clothing, attendance requirements, and ritualized ceremony may be part of some Christian sects but not others, as Iannaccone explains (1992). Costs and the certainty offered in religious contracts obviously have an enormous impact on the risk-adjusted prices of belonging to particular religions. The variance in the contract is also critical. Presbyterianism, adhering to strict forms of predestination, whereby the knowledge of salvation is determined by God after death, has far greater variance than some forms of Methodism and other Protestant sects, which emphasize both faith and temporal good works as linchpins for ultimate salvation. The point is that the form of the contract accepted by buyers is a function of the risk-adjusted full price of the final product.[11]

Does the Economics of Early Christianity Relate to Contemporary Religion?

Our discussion of early Christianity, its solidification of product definition, and its appeal of a lower price has taken us full circle from an initial market structure of competition in the first three centuries of Christianity to the high monopoly of the Middle Ages to a mature competitive structure of Christian religion in most countries today. Does this journey and the economics we have attached to *early* Christianity (through 1100 CE) have relevance for contemporary events in religious markets? We believe that it does. All of the important elements of early Roman Christianity have relevance for the course of modern and mature Christianity of many varieties. These include credence and metacredence establishment (an issue for all religions), product standardization, market structure, and the institutional structure of the church itself—all interrelated factors in ongoing Christianity. In short, the essential problems are identical to those we have discussed concerning first millennium Christianity: to maintain "product purity" in a top-down hierarchical structure; to prevent credence-reducing behavior; to attempt to eliminate opportunistic behavior in the downstream church through censorship, excommunication, and other means; and to attack "secular" and other competition for membership and membership retention.

Obviously the Roman Catholic Church is no longer a monopoly in most areas of the world in the sense that it was over the High Middle Ages. However, it clearly retains the institutional structure of a vertically integrated church, now in competition with other sects with different internal structures. Tensions between the upstream Roman Church, which defines and interprets doctrine, ritual, and practice, and the downstream church have erupted periodically and are quite active today.

Consider the market structure of Christianity which may be described as monopolistically competitive in the terms of modern economics (lots of sects, with different beliefs, easy entry and exist, emphasis on advertising). For the Roman Catholic Church, market structure at the retail level (roughly competitive) is intertwined with the internal structure of that Christian church.[12] The door to market entry was flung open for Christian religion after Luther's successful penetration of the market and the Protestant Reformation (1517). Despite a so-called Counter-Reformation, inquisitions and attacks on heresies and "secularism" continued throughout the post-Luther period. The orthodox product and Roman papal interpretations of it were staunchly defended. The Council of Trent (1545–1563) was called to address Protestant entry. The Vatican created the Holy Office (formally the Supreme Sacred Congregation of the Roman and Universal Inquisition or, simply, the Roman Inquisition) in 1542 in the wake of Protestant entry and launched an attack on then-extant forms of "secularism" including censorship of books, art, and science in addition to religious writings—a response to the Renaissance and, later, to the Enlightenment.[13] We have elsewhere (Ekelund et al. 2004) argued that the Roman Church cleaned up the retail side of the sale of the chief product, assurances of eternal salvation, by addressing such matters as the competence of the clergy and their sale of indulgences, but did little to make significant alterations in the upstream church regarding such matters as simony, nepotism and the operating of hereditary "benefices" claimed by bishops and cardinals. Those reforms would not be actualized for several centuries.

The newly competitive market structure is also related to product definition and the internally vertically integrated church. Attacks on Protestants were accompanied by inquisitions focusing on the purity of the orthodox (Nicene, Pauline) product. The Roman Inquisition famously burned scientist Giordano Bruno at the stake in 1600 for theological reasons, that is, for expanding on the nature of the product of Roman Catholicism, and for arguing that life might exist beyond earth and for an ecumenical belief in the unification of religions.[14] The latter was a clear violation of the "one way" thesis of Roman Christianity. These inquisitions were a means of controlling product definition for downstream purveyors of the product in "top-down" vertically integrated fashion. Such activities, without the burning faggots but with excommunication as punishment, also attend the contemporary Roman Church's downstream enforcements. The role of women in Christian worship has expanded in traditional Protestant churches. However, the contemporary official distaste for enhanced women's role in church ceremony, a product of the Vatican II conciliar reforms, has gone beyond traditional conservatism to the heart of women's attempt to reform the Roman Church: the church excommunicates women who dare, against historical church policy, to be ordained priests of the Roman rite, leading to increasing defections of women from the church in advanced counties, many to the Episcopal Church, and to the formation of a women's ordination conference dedicated to changes in church laws.[15] U.S. nuns suspected of straying too far from doctrinal guidelines set by the upstream church have been placed under extensive investigation by the upstream papacy in order to ensure doctrinal purity at the downstream level.[16]

Containment of schism on the left may not be easy in the developed world, where church attendance and membership is in decline (except for participation by immigrants) given the church's "traditional" treatment of women. In the face of an almost worldwide shortage of priests and a precipitous decline in female vocations, except for some growth in Africa and Asia, Benedict XVI, acting through the Congregation for the Doctrine of the Faith, issued an "excommunication order" for women who participate in the ordination of women to the priesthood (excommunicants cannot receive the sacraments). In March 2009, the archbishop of Saint Louis excommunicated three women for submitting to ordination. While excommunication has been lifted from a Holocaust denier, Bishop Richard Williamson (Wensierski and Winter 2010), and despite the lack of penalties on bishops who facilitated child abuse in the clergy, women who attempt ordination remain under the penalties of excommunication. Women's ordination has been identified on a list of the gravest moral wrongs along with pedophilia, heresy, apostasy, and schism (Donadio 2010c).[17] Naturally, such actions may be a *cause* of schism or "switching," and pressure on the Vatican by women's groups has not been stilled.[18] In June 2010 women's ordination groups marched on the Vatican and had to be restrained by Vatican police (Winfield 2010a). Traditional downstream policies in church vertical integration are being maintained but at an increasing cost to credence and (possibly) membership.

Constant attempts to maintain doctrinal purity riddles many Christian denominations, including Roman Catholicism and the Anglican Communion. Sporadic attempts at monopoly control through competition and doctrinal manipulations continue to be the object of Roman and other Christian religions, and our theory of religious contracting through the first millennium CE may also be applied to a number of empirical phenomena observed in the contemporary economics of religion.

The divide between advanced world and third world religious trends is well known.[19] That divide, that is, differing *demands for the products of religion*, is essentially a divide in risk aversion, with the political instability and low education levels in the third world underlying a highly risk-averse profile for many.[20] In the advanced world, with politically stable governments and generally high incomes and educational levels and social integration, Christians have tended to pick and choose among formal parts of the religious contract.[21] This is often the source of the so-called "cafeteria Catholics," but it applies to all cafeteria or generic Christians as well.[22] This suggests that there is a defined spectrum of risk profiles *within* as well as *between* particular faiths. Perhaps this spectrum of risk aversion has always been and will always be the case, and it may be that *each and every* Christian (or Catholic or Lutheran) has a singular profile that differentiates his or her demands for assurances of eternal salvation and other products. No two Mormons or Jehovah's Witnesses carry the *exact* same views on theology, cultural matters, or politics.

Likewise, so-called cafeteria Christians existed both before and after the Council of Nicaea. That council, which purported to define the irreducible minimum of beliefs for Christians, was itself a visit to a cafeteria. Dozens, perhaps hundreds, of "Christianities" existed at the time with a multiplicity of then-extant writings. Some literature—for example, the Books of James, Mary, and Judas, together with epistles and essays purportedly written by apostles and evangelists—were examined and/or rejected and completely ignored by the bishops gathered at that council. The Nicene Creed reflects a particular notion of Christian theology. Modern-day visitors to the Christian (Roman Catholic specifically) cafeteria would include arch-conservative members of Opus Dei, liberation theologians, and liberal thinkers such as Hans Kung, folk Catholics, and actors like Mel Gibson. But, while it might be true that a pre-Nicaean Christian had genuine choices in the matter of Christian theology, that is likely not true for contemporary Christians. And our discussion of the approach to Nicaea and its aftermath tells us why. At Nicaea, an exclusive and essential minimum of doctrines were established to form the product of Christianity. That product, assurances of eternal salvation, has evolved to mean for Roman Catholics the principles of Nicaea along with the interpretations of pope and councils. The pope has been declared "infallible" in terms of faith and morals since 1870, and he calls and dominates Roman Catholic councils exercising the right to interpret conciliar activities.

Being saved means adherence to some body of doctrine and *interpretation* that corresponds to "unalterable principles" for each Christian religion. Product purity is a goal to be maintained by the Roman Church as evidenced by principles found in encyclicals of the pope and of policies directed at doctrinal purity. Just how far this irreducible minimum or spectrum of belief must go for membership or salvation is a matter of interpretation, just as it was at Nicaea and in the ensuing centuries of the early Middle Ages. Indeed, behavioral and interpretive issues over "literal and inerrant" biblical teachings are what is in dispute. Can one remain a Roman Catholic and support embryonic stem cell research, birth control, women in the priesthood, or gay marriage? Theologians may differ in private on these matters, but not in public, as evidenced by the papal requirement of the censorship of Catholic theologians and universities by area bishops who have adhered to the hard line of the upstream church. Again, the vertical system of preventing opportunistic behavior in the downstream church, developed and invented by the church in the early Middle Ages, is being used to bring dissidents from Roman orthodoxy into line.

The central issue, as has been the case since Nicaea, is interpretation. Literal and inerrant interpretations of the Old and New Testaments and earlier church teachings will not bear scrutiny in the modern age, slavery being but one example. Science does over time create a reinterpretation of scripture. The account of the Creation of the world in Genesis was in doubt within the Roman Catholic Church due to developments in geological science even before the appearance of Darwin's ideas. Slowly, it would appear, some Christian churches have come around to a belief that a reinterpretation of "creation" is required by the level and status of scientific experimentation, evidence, and method (see Coyne 2010). Others hold to a literal interpretation. One of these groups have developed a Creation Museum in Kentucky, which depicts dinosaurs and modern-day humans together in dioramas. Unsurprisingly, many scientists and faiths believe it to be a travesty against science as well as religion. Emerging biological and psychological studies on the heritable as well as environmental nature of homosexuality are also creating problems and turmoil in religion markets. Organizations associated with conservative Christian religions, such as the Family Research Council and Focus on the Family who join traditional Roman Catholics as well on some issues, routinely attempt to influence, however indirectly, electoral politics in the United States by so-called Judeo-Christian biblical opposition to abortion and gay rights, including same-sex marriage. Such religious groups choose to interpret scripture relating to homosexuality literally (it is not condemned by Christ in the New Testament) and are willing to fuel cultural and political divide on the issue, condemning rights for gay persons. Demographic trends in U.S. opinion on this issue does not favor these interpretations.[23]

Naturally, in the modern context, as opposed to post-Nicaean first millennium Christianity, schisms are common. Schisms and divisions of Christian religion continue apace, with thousands of Christian divisions around the world today. (Some estimates count as many as 23,000 brands of Christianity worldwide.) Schisms reflect different demands and underlying risk profiles among believers in Christ and his divinity. *Changes in any of the demand determinants we identified for the early church— education, the state of science—or changes in full price will cause "switching" of religions and/or schisms from existing sects.* Most countries of the world, such as the United States, include a nonestablishment clause in their constitutions guaranteeing religious freedom and allowing many forms of "schism."[24]

Schisms of a formal sense will vary with church organization and the strength of rule-making and enforcement within a particular Christian church. Two of the largest hierarchical Christian religions are Roman Catholicism and Anglicanism. Outwardly, given the so-called conciliar form of church governance in both, they may appear to be similar or identical in form. This is not so, however. The Anglican Communion is led by the archbishop of Canterbury, who administers a truly conciliar church (of which the Episcopal Church is one major segment). The Roman Catholic church is also conciliar—run by councils—but it is only nominally so. The pope calls councils at irregular intervals and makes rules and interprets their results according to his own directions. There is little or no input from the downstream church, including laity, local priests, and other prelates. The Eastern Orthodox Church, as we mentioned in chapter 7, in contrast to the Roman Church, is organized in conciliar fashion by a number of "patriarchs" and bishops. Both churches are highly centralized, and use the power of the upstream church to dampen the prospects of schism. Nonetheless, in either church, policy is formulated collegially, and as such is more likely to be in line with consensus and constant for long periods of time. By contrast, in the Roman Church the pope may decide policies based on his personal preferences. As opposed to colle-gial choice, such idiosyncratic choice by popes will lead to a greater vari-ance in church policies over time, depending on the pope's preferences and interpretations of scripture and council decisions. The spirit of the Vatican II Council (1962–1965), for example, has been weakened by sub-sequent papal-curial interpretations of its conclusions and directives in the direction of liberalization. Likewise, congregational churches (such as Presbyterian, Unitarian, and many Evangelical churches), many ap-pearing in the wake of the Protestant Reformation, are "bottom-up" in orientation providing a more immediate response to changes in all of the factors affecting religious demand, with schism being a more common and predictable event given the church structure.

The present administration of the upstream Roman Church and parts of the worldwide Anglican Communion takes a "tighter" view of the tra-ditional belief system. There is a problem with "tight" interpretations of theology and necessary behavior to attain the final product. The tight-ening of theological and behavioral constraints must always take place within a spectrum of changing demands—changes that may demand more (or in some cases less) liberal bodies of necessary belief. When that spectrum reaches a critical value, schisms occur.

Particular faiths have been able to accommodate skewed profiles for long periods of time without schism. The Roman Catholic Church in the United States and Western Europe, for example, has so far been able to provide services that assuage risk for highly conservative Roman Cath-olics such as those of the organization Opus Dei. It has, on the liberal side of the spectrum, often invoked draconian penalties for less risk-averse groups sponsoring women, gay rights, or married priests and so on, avoiding *formal* schism. On some issues and in some locales, despite attempted enforcement at downstream levels of the church, the church has failed.[25] Despite vehement opposition, the Roman Church was un-able to stop civil legalization of same-sex marriage in such countries as Spain or Portugal (or in Mexico City) or divorce in Italy.[26]

The official definition of "Roman Catholic" in terms of ritual and doctrinal mandates or interpretations has become a much-debated ques-tion and, for its part, the Roman papacy appears ready, with some excep-tions, to impose strict traditional-conservative guidelines and conditions for salvation on members in advanced parts of the world. Membership shifts, however, may substitute for schism in these cases. Changes in membership in the U.S. Catholic Church may be a factor. According to research conducted in 2007, "Catholicism has experienced the greatest net losses as a result of affiliation changes. While nearly one-in-three Americans (31 %) were raised in the Catholic faith, today fewer than one-in-four (24 %) describe themselves as Catholic."[27] Immigration was the major offsetting factor in keeping the U.S. Roman Catholic population from markedly declining in 2007. Italy, nominally the most Roman Catholic of countries, has one of the lowest attendance rates in the world. It goes without saying that the United States and Europe are the principal funding sources of the Roman Catholic Church—a fact that might explain policies in those countries.[28]

This has not been the case for the Anglican Communion. In 2009, U.S. Anglicans (Episcopalians in the Anglican community) chose to separate from the world Anglican community over the issue of gay marriage and the consecration of women and gay and lesbian bishops.[29] This difference in demand profiles and the specifications for conditions for attainment of eternal salvation has, in other words, led to schism in this Christian denomination. It is somewhat unclear if the schism consisted of the departure of conservatives (largely Anglican members in Africa and Latin America) or of the departure of liberals in the advanced world, particularly in the United States and Western Europe. Pope Benedict XVI, in a bid to attract conservative Anglicans to the shrinking ranks of the priesthood, issued a formal program through which disaffected Anglican priests (and members as well) could join the Roman rite. Regarded as "poaching" by some observers, the Anglican establishment has had mixed feelings about both the fragmentation of its own church and the attempt by Roman Catholics to accept the conservatives.[30] These events reveal that the marketplace for Christian beliefs—which are heavily dependent on demand factors—is alive and well. Schisms may occur in strongly hierarchical religions, as the Anglican example shows, but they are far more common when direct demands of congregational religions make policy (Beard et al., forthcoming).

Schism and "switching" might also be avoided by doctrinal adjustment. Our grounding of the market for religion in contract theory helps provide insight into another observed phenomenon relating to schism in the third world—particularly in Latin America. The observation is that there is a distinct movement from Roman Catholicism to cult-like Evangelical sects in those countries (Gill 1998). Christians in these countries would be expected to experience similar levels of risk-aversion. So, why the switch? The Roman Church has, for centuries, emphasized the "sanctity of life," and in 1966 reaffirmed the church proscription of any form of birth control, with one recent exception (see note 31). Growing levels of science and women's rights in Latin America and to a somewhat lesser extent in Africa appear to have caused at least one switch point from one form of conservative Evangelical religion (Roman Catholicism) to another with similar, but not untenable, characteristics related to sex.[31] However, counter measures are being adopted. In 2006, conservative-traditionalist Pope Benedict XVI, who appears sympathetic to the dictum of Pope Pius X that "Modernism is heresy," permitted a return to the Tridentine form of the mass—a highly ritualized form of worship performed in Latin.[32] While the majority of U.S. congregations would not be anticipated to return to such ritual, it is expected to be more popular in elderly populations and in low-income, low-education, and politically unstable parts of the world (e.g., Africa and Latin America). This may be seen as an adapted form of product differentiation to more effectively compete with Protestant Evangelical sects in the third world. The tactic is to increase membership and to maintain as much "integrated monopoly control" as possible, reducing the probability of schism on the right and attempting to contain schism or defections on the left.

Tailoring doctrine and ritual to diverse demanders with ever-*shifting* demands is not only occurring in the third world, but in the advanced world as well. Megachurches with attendance levels of more than 20,000 per week are siphoning members from other Christian sects, both liberal and conservative. The net *gain* in nondenominational and Evangelical religious identification between 1990 and 2001 was 37 percent and 42 percent, respectively.[33] But it would be a mistake to identify the megachurch movement with a unidirectional move toward conservatism in theology. Some of these megachurches are far looser theologically than the churches from which members are drawn. Competitive, modern Christian institutions are being developed, in some cases to "Evangelical-lite" products for particular sets of demanders.

Credence, for all churches (Christian and otherwise) is as much as problem today as it was in early Christianity. Part of the metacredence required of church memberships hinges on the behavior and conduct of the exemplars of that faith or religion. The "bad behavior" of the Roman papacy and clergy in the tenth century and later during the High Middle Ages along with Protestant entry in the sixteenth century, brought

new credence issues to be (ultimately) addressed by the Roman Catholic Church. Such issues remain for many Christian churches. One of
the most dramatic credence issues that the Roman papacy has faced
in perhaps hundreds of years is that so-called pedophilia crisis around
the world. Roman Catholic churches in such countries as Ireland, Germany, Brazil, and most notably, perhaps, in the United States, has had to
contend with charges of many thousands of abuse cases by hundreds of
priests and other prelates, leading to a credibility crisis that some theologians label the worst for Roman Catholicism since the Reformation
(Küng 2010). Beyond that, and perhaps of greater import for credence,
is the alleged "cover-up" by unpunished bishops and (possibly) by Pope
Benedict XVI himself when he was archbishop of Munich and Freising
and then leader of the Congregation for the Doctrine of the Faith under
Pope John Paul II (Bennhold and Kulish 2010; Donadio 2010a, 2010b;
Goodstein and Halbfinger 2010).[34] The accusation is that bishops and
other facilitated child abuse by moving pedophile priests from parish to
parish, thus allowing their abuse to continue. These matters have and
will have a negative credence effect on church members and, perhaps,
on church contributions from which hundreds of millions of dollars have
been paid to abuse victims in the United States alone.[35]

The Roman Catholic Church is certainly not the only Christian church
to inherit such credence issues. Traditional congregational churches have
had problems, as have the strictly conservative Evangelical churches and
associations. Pedophilia, child pornography, illicit affairs with church
members, and gay sex solicitations have all been associated with Evangelicals and other Christian church officials, some of whom are in the
business of preaching against and collecting money to fight such activities.[36] Hypocrisy and disgrace in such cases ordinarily reduce membership and strain credence in particular churches. Thus credence and opportunistic behavior are not only issues with top-down organizations
but exist in congregational Christian churches as well. In such communities, correction tends to be swift as membership shifts and contributions respond quickly to malfeasance. For vertically integrated organizations such as the Roman Church, with legalistic bureaucracies as internal
structures, response may be slowed.

The child abuse issue may be, in part, an example of bureaucratic foot
dragging, but downstream opportunistic and credence-reducing behavior may take on other forms as well. Siphoning church funds has created
serious scandal in particular dioceses in Europe, notably in Germany.

At a time of general financial cutbacks, reducing social and educational programs of the church, it has been reported that "more than €40 million have gone missing in the Diocese of Magdeburg in eastern Germany, €5 million have disappeared in Limburg near Frankfurt, and it was recently discovered that a senior priest in the Diocese of Munster had 30 secret bank accounts" (Loll and Wensierski 2010). Many bishops' sees keep two sets of books, with only one for public consumption. (Overall church wealth is a well-kept secret.) These facts and other reports of opulent spending on bishop's residences and fraud by downstream agents reduce credence and church contributions. Similar problems were part of the vertically integrated church in the first millennium and its attempt to prevent opportunistic behavior.

Reductions in credence due to these and other demand determinants may reflect that self-theologizing and forms of what might be termed "secularism," if that term means abandonment of *formal* religion while possibly retaining a belief in Christ and his teachings, are also dramatically on the rise. Perhaps it may be regarded as the ultimate form of schism where many members of the schismatic sect are merely *one individual.* Naturally, studies vary in quality and reliability. Among the fastest-growing group of self-identifiers between 1990 and 2001 (15 percent) are those claiming "no religion," numbering 30 million individuals (Kosmin et al. 2001, 24). Further, 7 percent of self-reporters in the Religious Identification Survey claim to be "Christian" (with no religious affiliation) and 2 percent as (unspecified) Protestant. These statistics appear to support the fact that risk profiles respecting "religion" are in flux. The fluidity of U.S. Christian affiliation and statistics on the "unaffiliated" has been verified in the most recent and well-executed study by the Pew Forum on Religion and Public Life. More than one-quarter of American adults (28 percent) have changed their faith denomination or have fallen into the category of "no religion at all." Most relevant for the present study, however, is the massive percentage increase in those who are "unaffiliated" in the survey. These include atheists, agnostics, and secular unaffiliated and religious individuals (including Christians formerly affiliated with a church). The Pew study found that those people who are unaffiliated with any faith today is 16.1 percent of Americans, more than double the number who were "unaffiliated" as children. One in four Americans aged 18–29 are in this group.[37] Again, does "secularism" mean non-affiliation with an organized religion, or is it simply a nonbelief in a higher power or supreme being?

The prognosis among some who study religion that the "secularism hypothesis" is dead must be given some reexamination if contemporary data are anywhere near correct and under particular interpretations of secularism. It appears that science and higher educational levels in the United States and elsewhere may indeed be having an effect on religion and on the need for religious affiliation as opposed to self-service, especially in younger age groups. Whether this amounts to "secularism" or not is, of course, open to interpretation. The demand for some spiritual beliefs or for more formal demands for assurances of eternal salvation is probably endless. Religion will not disappear, as some skeptics appear to argue. But a study of the early foundation of Christianity, where competition, *demands* for forms of the eternal product, and institutional arrangements for the product supply provides suggestive insights into contemporary religious behavior.

This book has been an account of the process through which religion, in our case Christianity, became a monopoly that is, and remains, vertically integrated with upstream and downstream segments. It is fundamentally a historical account of how the religious product is sold under these conditions, how it is defined, how it was ultimately manipulated to control civil entities, and how competitive entry was ultimately inevitable due to changing demands and risk functions. Economic theory has much to contribute to the understanding of religion and its primary products. We have argued that the principal good sold by Christian religious organizations is the assurance of eternal salvation in an afterlife. This good is a metacredence good whose qualities cannot be known given any amount of human time or money. The essential economic issue relating to these goods is the nature of the contracting process for this good between buyers and sellers. That contract will depend upon the risk profile of buyers. (We assume that sellers will entrepreneurially adapt products to demands and potential demands under competitive conditions.) Risk profile for the main religious product is a function of a number of variables including education, political and social uncertainty, the state of science, and other variables. When these factors are considered, certain switch points in and aspects of religious markets may be considered and rendered more understandable. Interactions with civil governments, manipulations of civil disputes, and differences with the Eastern Church, which did not adhere to the primacy of the Roman bishop, were all part of the vertically integrated monopoly achieved over the High Middle Ages. We have argued that the movement from Roman gods to mono-

theistic Christianity, the Protestant Reformation, as well as aspects of
the contemporary Christian religious market are all examples of the Roman Church's quest for monopoly control over the market for the chief
(and metacredence) product of religion—assurances of a happy afterlife.

Christianity has also proved to be durable despite recent shifts and
credence-reducing events. Not only did Christianity grow rapidly from
its beginnings, it proved to be an incredibly lasting set of institutions
and beliefs. And the features that made Christianity successful early
on are the same forces that explain its longevity. The Ten Commandments, among other aspects of Christian teachings, are very compatible
with a world of trade and commerce in which complex contracting problems have to be overcome. Most contracts are unwritten, so that trading networks will be made more productive by individuals who follow
the Ten Commandments. Sociologist Max Weber was right, but for the
wrong reasons. The Ten Commandments are compatible with trade and
economic growth, but not because Christians have different preferences
for saving and labor supply. Christian principles allowed the expansion
of trading networks and fostered economic growth as a result. Herein
lies one reason for their adoption by Rome and their power of survival
over time.

While the tendency to monopoly no longer leads to wars, murder, and
mayhem within Christianity, that result is only the product of the ascent
of the religious market from monopoly to forms of Christian competition
in most locales. This result could appear to strongly argue for the competitive provision of religion and for the strong separation of church and
state. A study of the manner through which the early church through
1100 CE achieved market dominance is instructive not only in explaining second millennium events in religion markets, it also provides much
food for thought regarding the contemporary religious environment. To
the extent that we could sum up our "policy implications," they would be
the following: if consumer welfare is the goal, competition and decentralized control trump monopoly and centralized authority in the market for religion, as they do in most other cases. We do not believe that
Adam Smith would disagree.

The Impact of Saint Paul

S tark, as noted in the text of chapter 4, calculates an "index" of cities possessing local Christian churches by the century marks 100 and
180 CE. An index number of 2 represents churches present by 100, 1 by
the year 180, and 0 for cities with no church by 180 CE. The results are
given in table A1 (the rightmost column in the table is our recalculation
of Stark's CHRISTIANIZATION VARIABLE, to be discussed presently). Stark's
analysis gauges the "receptiveness" to Christianization, and there are, as
he notes, many reasons for this result. Those reasons are captured in the
following variables of interest:

CHRISTIANIZATION: as defined above (2 for cities with Christian church by 100
CE; 1 by 180 CE; 0 with none by 180); see column Stark's Code in table 3-2;[1]

POPULATION: Stark's calculation is for 22 (nonrandomly selected) cities; data
are from Chandler and Fox (1974) providing population estimates of Greco-
Roman cities circa 100 CE;

SYNAGOGUES IN CITIES BY 100 CE: a proxy for Jewish population in cities;
Stark uses the existence of synagogues as a proxy for the size of the Jewish
community;

MILES FROM JERUSALEM: proxy for ease of Christian conversion (calculated by
Stark; for description of procedure see 1997: 136);

MILES FROM ROME: proxy for ease of Christian conversion (calculated by Stark: for description of procedure see 1997: 136);

ROMANIZED: ratio of distance to Jerusalem to distance (of city) to Rome; and

GNOSTICS: Stark identifies a three-level categorical variable equal to 2 if a city was known to have had active Gnostic groups before 200 CE, 1 if Gnostic groups were present before 400 CE, and zero if no active Gnostic groups were present by 400 CE.

Clearly, as mentioned in chapter 4, the Stark model of early Christianity would include the following expected direction of the variables. An inverse relation between population and Christianization would be expected. The number of synagogues by 100 CE and the number of Gnostics would be expected to be positively related with Christianization, although negative relations would be expected on simple distance from Jerusalem and from Rome.

We have replicated all of Stark's conclusions from his data but believe that a model that introduces an explicit element of entrepreneurship would provide some advantages. We consider the case of Saint Paul. Since Christian entrepreneurs were critical to the establishment and spread of the religion, we have entered a variable to proxy Paul's travels (a dummy equal to 1 if he preached at least once in a city on his three voyages and 0 if he did not) in Stark's basic model (see table A3 below for the journeys of Paul). Statistically, moreover, one would be inclined to use an ordered probit model given the fact that the dependent variable is categorical (as Stark presents it). But two difficulties prevent that: (a) the small sample size, which, combined with maximum likelihood estimation, would cause biased coefficients, and (b) the lack of variation in the dependent variable with the levels of dummy variables of interest.[2] A continuous variable, moreover, can be constructed for CHRISTIANITY. Stark (1997, 133) lists sources of information about whether a city had a church by 100 and 180 (table A1 above reproduces the data), but instead of using all the information about the churches, he creates an index, thus aggregating information. If these sources are added together for each city and then divided by the maximum possible number (10), a new variable may be obtained and used as a proxy for the spread of early Christianity (see column labeled "NEW CODE" in table A1). This new variable (CHRISTIANIZATION) essentially aggregates and weights Stark's sources; for example: Caesarea Maritima and Damascus have the same value in

TABLE A1. **Christian Churches (Years 100, 200, and 300 CE)**

City	Source 1	Source 2	Source 3	Source 4	Source 5	Stark's Code	New Code
Caesarea							
Maritima	2	2	2	2/1	2	2	1
Damascus	2	2	2	2/1	0	2	.8
Antioch	2	2	2	2/1	2	2	1
Alexandria	2	2	2	2/1	2	2	1
Pergamum	2	2	2	2/1	2	2	1
Salamis	2	2	2	2/1	2	2	1
Sardis	2	2	2	2/1	2	2	1
Smyrna	2	2	2	2/1	0	2	.8
Athens	2	2	2	2/1	2	2	1
Corinth	2	2	2	2/1	0	2	.8
Ephesus	2	2	2	2/1	2	2	1
Rome	2	2	2	2/1	2	2	1
Apamea	1	1/0	1	0	2	1	.5
Cordova	1	1/0	1	0	1	1	.4
Edessa	1	1/0	1	2/1	1	1	.6
Syracuse	1	1/0	1	2/1	1	1	.6
Carthage	1	1/0	1	2/1	1	1	.6
Memphis	2	1/0	1	2/1	1	1	.7
Mediolanum							
(Milan)	0	1/0	0	0	0	0	.1
Augustodunum							
(Autun)	0	1/0	0	0	0	0	.1
Gadir (Cadiz)	0	1/0	0	0	0	0	.1
London	0	1/0		0	0	0	.1

Source: Stark 1997, 133, table 6.1, and our calculations in rightmost column.

Stark's index, which is 2, while in our variable they take two different values 1 and .8 because one of the sources maintains that there was no church in Damascus until after year 180 CE.[3] This new variable will take a value of 1 if Christianity was established in a city in year 100, while taking subunitary values for cities for which the sources do not indicate the presence of a church. We interpret the presence of a church in the city in year 180 (CHRISTIANIZATION takes the value .5) as being half the likelihood that the city had a sizable Christian community in year 100 CE. Table A2 presents a summary of the data.[4] Similarly, we interpret lower values, for example, .1 for Londinium (London), as furnishing information about the likelihood that a Christian community was present by 100 CE. The assumption here is that once a Christian community is established in 100 CE, it does not get smaller by 180 CE, and that information about a city at 180 CE can be linearly projected back to 100 CE. Consequently, our dependent variable can be interpreted as the probability

TABLE A2. **Data Summary**

Variable	Obs	Mean	Std. Dev.	Min	Max
POPULATION (in 100ks)	22	1.21	1.42	.3	6.5
CHRISTIANIZATION	22	.69	.34	.1	1
STARK'S CHRISTIANIZATION	22	1.36	0.79	0	2
MILES FROM JERUSALEM	22	1016.36	807.66	60	2565
MILES FROM ROME	22	1108.41	501.22	0	1775
SYNAGOGUES (DIASPORA)	22	0.41	0.50	0	1
GNOSTICS	22	1.00	0.93	0	2
ROMANIZATION	22	1.68	2.15	0.04	7.31
PAUL VISITS	22	0.32	0.48	0	1
GNOSTICS200	22	0.41	0.50	0	1
GNOSTICS400	22	0.18	0.39	0	1

that a city had a sizable Christian community (a church) by year 100 CE. The ROMANIZATION variable was computed by Stark (1997, 135–138) by dividing the distance in miles from a particular city to Jerusalem by the distance in miles from Rome, and consequently implies sacrificing one observation (for Rome). In order to avoid losing this observation, we replace the ROMANIZATION observation for Rome with the highest value in the sample, the one for Milan (7.3).[5] Nevertheless, we proceed to estimate two models, one including ROMANIZATION and one without; the results are presented in table A3. We will discuss the results from model 2, which includes the ROMANIZATION variable.

The positive and significant (at the 1 percent level) sign on Paul's visits appears to indicate that the intensive proselytizing among the Gentiles (and others) in the first century affected Christianization as measured by Stark.[6] Holding constant the other factors, and if no significant Jewish congregation existed (SYNAGOGUES takes the value zero), a visit by Paul in a particular city increases the likelihood that a church was established by 100 CE by 58 percent (or 70 percent in the first model). While this should surprise no one, it offers a bit of evidence that the success of early Christianity in the first century was not simply the result of cultivation of the Jewish Diaspora. The positive and significant sign on SYNAGOGUES appears to corroborate the view that the Jewish Diaspora contributed in some measure, with the existence of a sizeable Jewish community in a city increasing the likelihood of a city having a church before 100 CE by 21 percent, assuming that Paul did not visit the city. We would expect both variables—PAUL'S VISITS and SYNAGOGUES—to be positive. These results are certainly true for the marginal effects taken separately; there

TABLE A3. **The Determinants of Spread of Early Christianity: OLS Models**

Variable	Model1	Model2
PAUL VISITS:		
Coefficient	0.70	0.58
Standard error	0.09***	0.12***
P-value	0.00	0.00
SYNAGOGUES (diaspora):		
Coefficient	0.29	0.21
Standard error	0.09**	0.09*
P-value	0.00	0.04
POPULATION (in 100ks):		
Coefficient	−0.02	0.03
Standard error	0.02	0.03
P-value	0.43	0.33
GNOSTICS200 (200 CE):		
Coefficient	0.41	0.33
Standard error	0.12**	0.12*
P-value	0.00	0.02
GNOSTICS400 (400 CE):		
Coefficient	0.29	0.17
Standard error	0.10*	0.13
P-value	0.02	0.20
SYNAGOGUES* PAUL VISITS:		
Coefficient	−0.57	−0.44
Standard error	0.11***	0.14**
P-value	0.00	0.01
ROMANIZATION:		
Coefficient		−0.04
Standard error		0.02*
P-value		0.02
INTERCEPT:		
Coefficient	0.30	0.41
Standard error	0.09**	0.12**
P-value	0.01	0.00
OBSERVATIONS	22	22
F TEST:		
Statistic	18.25	46.05
P-value	0.00	0.00
R-SQUARE	0.78	0.82
ADJUSTED R-SQUARE	0.70	0.73

Legend: * $p<0.05$; ** $p<0.01$; *** $p<0.001$
Note: The reported standard errors are the heteroskedasticity-robust standard errors.

was a dual positive impact on Christianization in the first century. Both the Jewish Diaspora (measured by SYNAGOGUES and not simply by distance from Jerusalem) and the tenacity of Saint Paul in his visits to Gentiles and others (Jewish communities as well) had important impacts on the adoption of Christianity. The sign on population is not significant.

This means that the entrepreneurial hypothesis is a better explanation of the spread of Christianity than alternative hypotheses such as market size or transportation costs. The algorithm of Paul's travels was more complex than, for example, simply minimizing transportation cost. Yet another interesting result is the positive and significant effect of Gnostic activity by 200 CE, an effect that diminished with time (by 400 CE, the effect was positive but not significant at the 5 percent level). This suggests, in contrast to Stark, that Gnosticism was a complementary movement with Christianity, one arising from Judaism (in Stark's term, it was a "Jewish heresy").[7]

A gauge of the relative influence of Jewish synagogues versus Paul's preaching to the Gentiles and others may be determined utilizing an interaction variable. The marginal effects for each of the models are presented in table A4. If Paul visited a city (PAUL'S VISITS is equal to 1), the marginal effect of having a sizable Jewish community in the city is negative 0.23 and significant at 10 percent level. Here SYNAGOGUES changes from zero to one, holding constant the POPULATION, GNOSTICS activity, the degree of ROMANIZATION, and the effect of Paul visiting the city. This would imply a degree of rivalry between the two religions. For Paul to visit a city with a sizeable Jewish community, his effect on the spread of the Christianity diminished, to 0.14, still positive but barely insignificant at the 10 percent level. Reported Gnostic activity in a city in year 200 (as a proxy for Gnostic activity around year 100) increases the likelihood of the existence of a Christian community by 100 CE by 33 percent. The effects disappear if Gnostic activity appears between 200 and 400 CE. Population has a positive but insignificant impact. The important variables in question are the relative impact of sizeable Jewish communities

TABLE A4. **Impact on Christianity of Paul's visits and Synagogues: Marginal Effects**

| | | PAUL VISIT/SYNAGOGUE (Jewish Diaspora) | | | |
| | | Model 1 | | Model 2 | |
		Present	Absent	Present	Absent
PAUL VISIT	Marginal effect	0.13	0.70	0.14	0.58
	Standard error	0.08	0.09***	0.08	0.12***
	P-Value	0.14	0.00	0.10	0.00
SYNAGOGUE	Marginal effect	−0.28	0.29	−0.23	0.21
	Standard error	0.13*	0.09***	0.13	0.09*
	P-Value	0.05	0.00	0.09	0.04

Legend: * p<0.05; ** p<0.01; *** p<0.001
Note: The reported standard errors are the heteroskedasticity-robust standard errors.

and Paul's visits to the highest population cities. Table A3 and A4 clearly show that both Paul's visits and the presence of synagogues are important, but that the impact of Paul on CHRISTIANIZATION appears to be stronger.

These results are intended as suggestive of how Stark's model could be expanded and strengthened. While the statistics suffer from a variety of problems outlined previously, we believe that they are nevertheless important, confirming evidence on Paul's role as an entrepreneur. Indeed, the results could be expanded to include Paul's letter writing. What, for example, was the relative importance of direct versus indirect marketing?

Notes

Chapter One

1. Other estimates put growth at about 40 percent per decade (Stark 1997: 7), claiming that in a mere century (from 250 to 350 CE) Christians as a percentage of the population rose from about 2 percent to 56 percent. For an estimation of the process, see MacMullen (1981, 1984), who used both Christian and non-Christian sources. Mormon and atheist growth rates have outpaced the estimates for Christianity in the twentieth century. Stark (1997, 7) estimated that the growth rate for the Mormon Church is 43 percent over the past hundred years. The point is that similar or even higher growth rates might be observed in comparison to early Christianity. Analyses of the first millennium of Christianity and its remarkable evolution have been, almost exclusively, within the perspective of the areas of history and sociology.

2. Technically, forms of religious pluralism existed prior to the Reformation. The distance between Rome and the "retail" parts of the church around Europe led sometimes to alternative interpretations of church rules and theology by monks and lower-level prelates. The central church eliminated such dissidents by establishing noncompeting "franchises" in the form of monastic "orders." In addition, there were (unsuccessful) attempts at entry into the Roman religious market by such dissidents as John Wycliffe (c. 1325–1384), who questioned papal authority, and Jan Hus (1372–1415). The latter was tortured and burned by the church for his "heresy." Both of these early dissenters were precursors of Martin Luther.

3. These and other contemporary contributions are discussed in chapter 2.

4. Some social scientists dispute a ubiquitous tendency of institutions, guided, after all, by self-interested individuals and groups, to eliminate competition. Economists dispute this claim. The Roman state as the premier institution of its time, certainly during the advent of Christian sects, drove out competition in every possible manner. Religions of the time (and currently) compete for dom-

inance, particularly when the central precept is "only one way" to salvation or
to some stated goal. It is not surprising, then, that Christian sects competed
for dominance even in the earliest periods of Christianity. That Roman Catholic monopoly took centuries to establish in no way suggests that all possible
means to destroy competitors, Orthodox Eastern Christians, heretics, and other
Christian sects, were not employed. Such is the behavior of the attempt to create monopoly.

5. Note that monopoly may be dictated or created by government as in the
regulation of entry by such agencies as the Food and Drug Administration or
the Federal Communications Commission as part of the process of regulation.
Our conception of "process" is broader in that we wish to consider how, historically, a religious institution engendered monopolization through a directed
"business plan" involving whole political regimes and a multitude of policies and
practices.

6. There is also the normative or social cost issue of rent seeking and its effect
on economic welfare as an addition to the usual deadweight cost of monopoly.

7. Two points should be remembered when characterizing the Roman Church
as a monopoly. First, the dominance achieved by the Christian church was not
subject to the kind of "creative destruction" through competition that Schumpeter (1981 [1911]) described. Church power eroded slowly and not significantly
until the competitive entry represented by the Protestant Reformation in the
early sixteenth century. Second, unlike today, there were no antitrust laws or
measures to maintain or support the erosion of monopoly, even though such regulations do not apply to religious entities.

8. See Toynbee's magisterial twelve-volume study (1934–1961), which is a
global analysis of the rise and fall of civilizations featuring dominant (though)
minority creative classes interacting with internal and external proletariats.

9. The historical granting of monopoly rights by a monarch, king, or pharaoh
has a long history because pure monopoly (or granting cartel rights to a group
of entrepreneurs), in contrast to taxation, is effective in raising revenue for the
state. Mercantilism, a form of economic organization that dominated Western
Europe between the sixteenth and eighteenth centuries, involved widespread
and detailed regulation of both the domestic and international economy. This
regulation took the form of creating monopoly rights for favored individuals in
numerous productions and trades. As democratic institutions began to evolve
in England and elsewhere, competition to grant these rights led to a period of
deregulation and, ultimately, to forms of laissez-faire (Ekelund and Tollison
1981, 1997).

10. A temporary monopoly is simply one whose power is reduced or eliminated by competition. A Schumpeterian monopoly, named for economist Joseph
A. Schumpeter (1883–1950) (Schumpeter 1939, 1943) is, similarly, one whose
profits induce entry into a never-ending process of creation and destruction in

markets. Technological advance and innovation are the essential ingredients in creating these results.

11. Certainly, Judaism and Buddhism have longer histories as religions, but the history of the church in the West is remarkably well documented after the early period.

12. There is, moreover, a "great debate" as to whether Roman Catholicism fostered or impeded economic growth and scientific progress over the first millennium and a half of Western civilization. Certainly there were elements on both sides of the debate, which we completely eschew in this book. An excellent account of some of the achievements of the church in the course of Western society may be found in Woods (2005). We are principally concerned with the church as the exemplar of a particular form of economic organization.

13. Acceptance of the canon of writings laid down at Nicaea and after—including the belief that the Old and New Testaments were written through the direct divine guidance of God by the evangelists—was the sine qua non of being a traditional (Pauline) Christian. This is, of course, at variance with some other Christian beliefs at the time and with some contemporary views that the Bible (Old and New Testaments) is a human document written by humans as metaphor or allegory.

14. The Roman Catholic Church is officially directed by councils of bishops (as in Vatican Council II of the early 1960s), but it is the pope who calls and convenes a council, interpreting the policy results of them as well. Thus, the pope, aided by the Curia, his Roman administration and ambassadors, is the guiding authority of the Roman Catholic Church, issuing directives, some in the form of encyclicals, to the lower clergy and lay members. There is therefore a "tension" between the conciliar form of organization and the singular leadership of the pope in church affairs.

15. These principles may be applied *between* types of Christian denominations in the modern world. Those religions providing a public good with "exclusivity" may have different views on the necessary conditions to attain afterlife consumption. While open bellicosity between such faiths is rare, open competition for membership is not, as in the Roman Catholic versus Evangelical competition in Latin America (Gill 1998). On a larger scale it may perhaps be the case at some point that once zero-sum circumstances are reached, conflict between monotheistic religions might be inevitable as well. But for an alternative and happier scenario, see the excellent study of Wright (2009), which argues that the three Abrahamic religions will move to a high and complementary moral plane.

16. Details of these empirical tests are placed in an appendix at the end of the book.

17. Note that this structure is not unlike integration in some modern industry. The structure of the steel industry, for example, might include ore mining, refining the steel, and the retail selling at steel yards. Complete vertical integration

would mean that a single company would go backward to own the ore extraction part of the business and forward to own retail yards as well. The steel company could partially integrate by owning either the upstream business (ore extraction) or downstream business (retail steel mills). Consider in contrast that another company, McDonald's restaurants, is *not* vertically integrated, since the company franchises its retail outlets by contract (that is, it does not own them at the geographic level).

18. As noted previously, we frequently use the inherited term "Dark Ages" for the period 400–800 CE with the full recognition that contemporary research, archeological and otherwise, challenges the pejorative adjective "dark."

19. The term "secularism" has many meanings. Dictionary definitions of "religious skepticism or indifference" or as a view that church and civil affairs or education should be separated are somewhat question-begging. These views depend on a definition of what a "religion" is. If it is affiliation with a church, attendance, or formal religion, the definition is problematic. For example, Italy is, in percentage terms, one of the most Roman Catholic of countries. However, it has one of the lowest participation (church attendance) rates in the world (see Stark and Iannaccone 1994). Is lower church attendance an indication of secularism? Further, all surveys have measurement problems and deficiencies: questions such as "Do you believe in God?" will receive high responses, but that says little about "secularism" if that is defined as participation or as affiliation with churches or religious *institutions*. It may be the case that particular formal religions that impose stricter rules of conduct over its members are growing in numbers at the same time that secularism is growing in the aggregate. For one perspective on survey design, see a Baylor Study funded by the John Templeton Foundation in 2006 (www.baylor.edu/content/services/document.php/33304.pdf). We will discuss this issue more fully in chapter 8. (Also see Beard et al., manuscript).

Chapter Two

1. A demand curve, perhaps the most famous tool in all of economics, is a graphical depiction of the quantities of the good or service that an individual (or group of individuals) would purchase at alternative full prices, holding all other factors constant.

2. As we make clear, assurances of eternal salvation (assuaging fears of death with promises of a happy afterlife) are certainly not the only services produced by most religions. Social welfare services, consolations in the present life, and many other products and services are produced by most religions as well. But there is competition in temporal life for these latter goods and services (government, private charity, psychologists, familial bonds, and so on). There is no "temporal" competition for sale of the ultimate and unique religious product that we

call assurances of eternal salvation. This does not mean, of course, that personal philosophy and magical and cult beliefs cannot substitute in some measure for religious services—these are religious beliefs as well. We only suggest that the central and unique product sold by organized religion concerns eternal life.

3. Smith's brilliance is nowhere better on display than when he noted "if politicks had never called in the aid of religion, had the conquering party never adopted the tenets of one sect more than those of another, when it had gained the victory, it would probably have dealt equally and impartially with all the different sects, and have allowed every man to chuse his own priest and his own religion as he thought proper. There would, in this case, no doubt, have been a great multitude of religious sects. Almost every different congregation might probably have made a little sect by itself, or have entertained some peculiar tenets of its own" (1776, 744).

4. Comte's British followers, including early adherent John Stuart Mill, were aghast at Comte's willingness to embrace what they regarded as "secular religion" (see Ekelund and Olsen 1973). Mill, in fact, deleted all references to Comte in his later work.

5. See Ekelund, Hebert, and Tollison (2006), chap. 8, for further discussion of these issues.

6. Gary Becker (1930–) is an economist at the University of Chicago who won the Nobel Prize in 1992. He has, famously, applied the tools of rational behavior—those that guide economics—to areas heretofore believed to be in the province of anthropology, history, sociology and other social sciences. He and those who accept his approach have analyzed myriad institutions. See, for example, Becker's analysis of dating, marriage, divorce, polygamy and other institutions in his *Treatise on the Family* (1981). Our work on religion, in addition to that of others (for example, Lawrence Iannaccone), owes much to Becker's insights on implicit markets.

7. This is not to deny that some time-intensive and strict groups, such as the Mormons, have grown rapidly, as discussed previously. Iannaccone (1992) offers important insights into some of these cases.

8. Recent evidence presented in the *Pew Forum on Religion and Public Life* in 2008 suggests a fairly high degree of sect infidelity and switching, however. (See chap. 8 for discussion of this point.)

9. McBride (2007) presents an intriguing analysis of the Mormon Church as an extension of "club behavior" as described by Iannaccone. Free riding is limited and a "menu-based" enforcement system is employed.

10. These kinds of goods were identified by Rosen (1981) in a somewhat different context. See chapter 3 below.

11. As Miller notes, "Differentiation can increase per capita organizational resources by exploiting switching costs across subcultures. Hence, a strategy of focused differentiation may result in more loyal participation, with loyalty

expressed in terms of longevity of involvement as well as resource commitments" (2002, 435). A study that is also related to the organizational structure
of religious denominations is the so-called property rights approach to religion.
Exemplified by economist Douglas Allen (1995), the approach emphasizes how
the particular organizational structure of a church, be it congregational, denominational, or hierarchical, is determined by particular theologies and transaction
cost problems within given sects. As such, the theory of clubs and organizations
may be considered "supply-side" approaches to religious behavior.

12. Cell biology, the mapping of the human genome, and stem-cell research,
innovations that could change views on human reproduction or issues such as the
biological basis for homosexuality, may alter the demand for religions relying on
literal interpretations of the Bible or imposed interpretations of "when life be-
gins," increasing them for those sects that accommodate scientific advances.

13. The invention of the printing press and the development and growth of
literacy had a major positive impact on the successful entry of Luther and other
Christian sects into the Roman Catholic market in the first half of the sixteenth
century. Unable to halt this development, the church took to banning and burning books during the various inquisitions that followed, ultimately to no avail.
The Index of "forbidden" books (formally, the *Index Librorum Prohibitorum*),
initiated in 1559 and published in twenty editions, was a device to censor and
prohibit books that, in the opinion of the clerical censors, diverged from Catholic theology, teaching, or interpretation. The *Index*, which ended only in 1966, at
one time or another included prohibitions on reading by Catholics of books constituting a virtual history of Western philosophy, science, and literature. Censorship and "ranking" of motion pictures by American bishops in the twentieth century, established by a "Catholic Legion of Decency" in 1933, attempted
similar censorship for Catholics. The legion's power was curtailed by a Supreme
Court decision, but the rankings by a consortium of bishops exists to the present
day and owes its origins to earlier forms of censorship by the church.

14. Granovetter argues strongly that "[w]hile economic models can be simpler if the interaction of the economy with noneconomic aspects of social life
remains inside a black box, this strategy abstracts away from many social phenomena that strongly affect costs and available techniques for economic action"
(2004, 9). A number of other writers in the neoinstitutionalist tradition focus on
the various methods through which Becker's "rational actor" model of institutions may be integrated with culture and sociological constructs (see Powell and
DiMaggio 1991; Bobbin 2004).

15. The present book deals almost exclusively with the microeconomic origins and organizational form of Christianity. A sizeable and important literature exists that furthers understanding of the macroeconomic impact of religion
and religious participation. A study that stems directly from Max Weber has reemerged in the contemporary literature. The issue is an important one: how do

particular institutions—in this case, religion—affect economic variables of interest, for example, GDP, measures of economic growth, and so on. There are a number of avenues in these extensions: (a) studies related to how religious state monopolies affect religious behavior; (b) how and in what way economies and participation rates are affected by particular religions; and, most importantly, (c) how particular religions affect measures of economic growth. This literature has been led principally by Harvard scholars Robert Barro and Rachel McCleary. See Barro and McCleary (2003, 2004, 2005) and McCleary and van der Kujip (2010).

16. Even more tantalizing is the view that the demand for religion is an evolutionary response to meet challenges where collective action is necessary. Religion, as human beings or art, is constantly evolving by meeting constraints. See, for a readable account, David Sloan Wilson's *Evolution for Everyone: How Darwin's Theory Can Change the Way We Think about Our Lives* (2007).

17. Sociologists, for their part, accuse Becker of using overtly stylized cases rather than real world ones (Granovetter 1985).

Chapter Three

1. The debate between the metaphysical explanation for a near death experience and physical scientific explanations rages on (see http://health.yahoo.com/experts/yeahdave/5066/near-death-experience).

2. The possibility that religion—specifically, a "supernatural punishment mechanism"—played a role in establishing and enforcing property rights in early hunter-gatherer societies is explored in a fascinating paper by Manuel Mueller-Frank (2010).

3. These effects are a focus in a stimulating book by Robert Wright (2009). Wright chronicles the evolution of concepts of God and religion from a "materialist viewpoint," which Wright describes as the explanation of the origin and development of religion "by reference to concrete, observable things—human nature, political and economic factors, technological change, and so on" (2009, 4). Wright also discusses the economic phenomenon of "positive network externalities" noting (2009, 290) that economists do not generally apply the concept to religion. Economists have in fact done so (see Iannaccone 1992; Ekelund et al. 2006, 67 et passim).

4. Muir, chastising Stark for exclusive reliance on Christian sources in this regard, argues that "Stark's theories about the attractiveness of Christianity because of its superior capacity to explain disasters and the reduction of constraints for pagans entering Christianity during crisis periods are problematical. They reveal an inadequate understanding of Greco-Roman religion and of the ways in which persons in antiquity thought and acted" (Muir 2006, 230).

5. Credence can diminish, as the fallout from the clerical abuse scandal in the United States and elsewhere may suggest.

6. The essential product of the Roman Catholic Church, assurances of eternal salvation and the means to achieve it, has remained virtually unchanged since the Middle Ages. The doctrinal imperatives of natural law (derived from Aristotle) developed by Thomas Aquinas in the thirteenth century have been merely extended to the contemporary technology of life issues, as in stem cell research, in vitro fertilization or birth control. Naturally, extreme cases of witch hunting have disappeared with the development of modern Christianity (see chap. 8), but the assault on some forms of science and the interpretation of sacraments, miracles, and sainthood continues virtually unaltered. The church's attack on secularism is fueled by the Congregation for the Doctrine of the Faith, successor to the Roman Inquisition (which originated in the sixteenth century). The name of the agency was changed to the former in 1908, but censorship remains the role of the Congregation. Its crusades against individualism and recourse to one's own conscience continues to be a part of rule making in the church. Philosophers and theologians teaching in Catholic universities are subject to censorship, as are books by Catholic authors relating to Catholicism. Roman Catholic theology and rule making today would not be a shock to any late medieval member of the upstream church (that is the rule-making pope and his board of advisers, the Curia).

7. The nature and interpretation of transubstantiation was given a neo-Platonic gloss in the Middle Ages, which softens but does not eliminate the charge that the practice has "magical" (nonprovable) qualities. In this interpretation, the substance (Platonic inner reality) of the bread and wine are transformed into the body of Christ, whereas the "accidents" or external qualities that we perceive through the senses (e.g., appearance and taste of the bread and wine) remain unchanged. Such a belief requires faith (credence), but in a positivist sense this proposition remains untestable.

8. Sainthood status requires miracles, but the papacy has become less stringent in terms of the quality of proof. A "Devil's Advocate" no longer plays a pivotal role, which has caused questions concerning the canonization to sainthood of Josemaria Escrivá—founder of Opus Dei, an elitist and ultraconservative movement in the Roman Catholic Church. Other forms of magic have been practiced by Catholic priests in third world countries, much to the consternation of the Vatican. In August 2006, African bishops had to warn Catholic priests about adopting the traditional African practice of calling on ancestors for healing. (See http://www.cnn.com/2006/WORLD/africa/08/16/africa.catholic.witch craft.reut/index.html).

9. Most religions promise some form of afterlife or a cycle of existence. For example, some forms of Buddhism teach that we return—the form based on our compassion in the present life—over and over. Unless one puts credence in the

astonishing revelations of those dealing in "Spiritualism," a greatly popular movement at the end of the nineteenth century and the beginning of the twentieth but still very much alive today, the point is not provable.

10. The Christian tradition in art through the High Middle Ages is, in the main, composed of illustrations from both Old and New Testaments. Scenes and illustrations from Christ's life, miracles, death, and resurrection fill the canon of Western art until the Middle Ages.

11. This chain of succession in the early period, theological and apostolic, has been subject to many disputes and interpretations that do not relate to our thesis. Those interested may profitably consult Bart D. Ehrman (2003, 191–197), who provides an interesting discussion of the "proto-orthodox" activity in the early church and the many disputes over what Christ "really meant" He stresses the importance of the interpretation of early writings, noting that "[i]n the ancient world there was no more unanimity about how to interpret a text than there is today" (195). Also see Wand (1937) and Wagner (1994).

12. *How* these determinants affect the demand for temporal assurances of eternal salvation is a matter for empirical testing, which we do not conduct in this book. A number of studies are oriented toward such testing (however, see Iannaccone 1998; Beard et al. manuscript, and many other empirical excursions into these areas). Most studies reveal that there is a clear positive relation between religious participation and age, gender (females), and married individuals and a negative one with males, the young, and educational level.

13. Even under forced exchange, no one can control an individual's thought. This aspect helps gives rise to the idea that risk profiles vary within all religions, producing varying belief systems within each religion (the "cafeteria" approach to religion).

14. A recent study of northern European countries with state religions found the populace "culturally religious" rather than actually religious (Zuckerman 2010), although this does not mean that those areas that are religiously observant did not experience higher scores in "life satisfaction" (see Clark and Llelkes 2005).

15. The risk-uncertainty-insurance model of religious choice is only one of several possible metaphors for religious behavior, although it is widely used. Self-protection is another way of responding to uncertainty—it involves resource expenditure to reduce the probability of an undesirable outcome (for example, buying insurance against house fire). Self-production is the expenditure of resources in the present to reduce the probability of a "bad outcome" in the future (see McGuire et al., 1991; Ehrlich and Becker 1972). The self-protection model, unfortunately, has no unambiguous relation to risk profile, although it is a very useful metaphor for studying religious behavior (Beard et al., manuscript).

16. This line of reasoning is often related to Pascal's wager. French mathematician and physicist Blaise Pascal (1623–1662) believed that the expected value of

believing always dominated the expected cost. Since the existence of God could not be determined by reason, the "payoff" to acting in the present as if a "good outcome" (heaven?) existed in the future always carried a greater payoff than assuming the opposite (bad behavior in the present with God's punishment in the future). If one wins the wager, one gains everything—eternal happiness; if one loses, you lose nothing. This of course leaves no room for agnosticism—one must choose—for one must live in some manner. Contemporary atheists contend that Pascal neglected opportunity costs—the costs attributable to time spent in church, and other activities required to "be good" in this life. These views introduce the notion of probability and game theory as well. Further, the use of Pascal's idea does not comport well with standard notions of a "continuum of outcomes" in probability theory.

17. Importantly, Durkin and Greeley base the identity of their "product" partly on expected quality of an afterlife *and* on an increase in "lifetime utility," the latter being implicit in our "assurances of eternal salvation."

18. Some have argued that religious belief in an afterlife cannot be analogized to the purchase of insurance because, unlike insurance, the probability of a positive or negative outcome cannot be estimated by a third party like an actuary. There are, of course, no data with which to make such an estimate and other metaphors such as self-protection have great merit in leading to an understanding of religious behavior. However, the insurance metaphor is appealing from a behavioral perspective. Individual believers (and nonbelievers) can and do make such subjective calculations; that is, they behave as if they were purchasing an insurance policy. Heaven and hell may not exist probabilistically for an actuary, but religious believers and nonbelievers behave in response to their estimates of the relevant probabilities of the two outcomes over their lifetimes. The issue of heaven and hell is not the scientific proof of whether or not these dominions exist, but rather, do individuals believe that they exist and act accordingly to purchase insurance against negative outcomes.

19. Generally speaking education and income are positively correlated. The income variable, as a traditional argument in a demand function, may be difficult to analyze in the context of religion, brand of religion, or belief system, however. While some studies show types of insurance to be a normal good (where increases in income lead to higher quantities demanded of it), the impact of income on religion may be positive or negative. This is so because higher incomes, suggesting higher opportunity costs of ritual participation, may stimulate higher monetary expenditures on religion, substituting for time-consuming religious participation. Higher incomes, in other words, may create substitutions in the manner of paying the full price of assurances of eternal salvation.

20. There is a whole continuum of risk profiles *within* particular church denominations, with, for example, more liberal Catholics ("cafeteria Catholics") being higher risk takers and "Evangelical Catholics" (such as most of those in

third-world countries) being more risk-averse. The same kind of continuum exists within the "Evangelical" movement. See chap. 8 for further discussion of this issue.

21. Risk aversion, for example, explains the difference between short-term and long-term interest rates. Such rates differ because a long-term investment is riskier than one in the short term. Investors will demand higher interest rates for long-term undertakings because more things can go wrong over the extended period. The higher risk requires a higher return. More generally, as risk increases, prices of underlying contracts will go up.

22. Benito Arruñada (2004) provides an interesting alternative interpretation of the institution of confession.

23. Purgatory, for example, was an invention of the Roman Catholic Church, as was "limbo."

24. Note that there is no "race to the bottom" in choices. Demand for benefits and a "strictness continuum" from religion will be dependent on those factors affecting risk profile, and the type of religion chosen will be determined by the relative benefits and costs to the consumer. Sociologists make similar arguments (see, e.g., http://www.jknirp.com/stark.htm).

25. A formal and more complete discussion of expected utility is presented in Durkin and Greeley (1991, 194–195).

26. As noted above, Durkin and Greeley (1991) use a rational choice model under uncertainty to derive interesting theoretical (and empirical) results regarding variations in expectations of an afterlife. One of them is that there is a whole continuum of believers, depending upon these expectations, a conclusion that dovetails with our own.

27. Also see McBride (2007).

28. But there are testable implications of the analysis that are interesting. For example, are the portfolios of Protestant denominations riskier than those of their Catholic counterpart? There are data on church portfolios, and the techniques of modern finance allow calculations to be made with respect to how "risky" given portfolios are. If we are correct about the nature of religious contracts, perhaps one could find the footprints of our argument in the realm of church finances.

29. The ability of "pagan" pantheons of gods to successfully compete with Judaism is a complex matter. Ethnic, racial, and traditional elements enter that explanation—one that we do not attempt to analyze here.

30. Some of this complexity has only been reduced in modern times. The Roman Catholic pope Benedict XVI formally eliminated the concept of "limbo" in 2006 (see Woodward 2006). Limbo was the place where unbaptized souls, such as infants who died without being baptized, spent eternity.

31. Ferrero (2008), citing some literature on Christian sects between the first and third centuries, argues that some factors (political instability) explain some

of the early demand for monotheistic religions. The multiplicity of early Jewish-Christian-related sects and the existence of the pagan panoply meant, according to Ferrero, a more exclusive membership policy coupled with greater theological pluralism in the early church. But, as Ferrero maintains, supply factors created a reversal of this organizational/theological tactic on the part of the primary Christian supplier. This interesting analysis relies heavily on the supply-driven model of Iannaccone (1992).

Chapter Four

1. Details of these empirical tests are shown in an appendix to this chapter appearing at the end of the book.

2. Atheists, of course, do not support this assumption. We fall back on the assumption of religious belief, noting only its prevalence in virtually every known society, including our own. See Fletcher (2007). Recent writers do not make our assumption: see, for example, Dawkins (2006) and Hitchens (2007).

3. Norris and Inglehart (2004) present an extremely interesting analysis of how secularism (commonly defined) must be amended as a cause of the decline, predicted by so many thinkers of the past, of religion, and of religious behavior. As we have argued elsewhere in this book, existential dread often leads to some form of belief, however personal, ephemeral, or philosophical. That, of course, does not mean that atheists do not exist within populations. The *form* of belief or nonbelief, as we also argue, is a function of particular demand factors including scientific achievement, education, and other demand "shifters," given acculturation and childhood instruction and experience.

4. Contemporary religious disputes are filled with examples of schism or near-schismatic situations. The Southern Baptist Convention, part of a larger Baptist organization, split off due to the "liberal" stance of other Baptist churches in the United States. Conservative U.S. Episcopalians are aligning themselves with African bishoprics in the Anglican Communion, and a full-scale schism is expected. The same was the case under Greco-Roman systems and within early Christianity. Factors affecting risk preference and demand are the initiating elements in many of the changes labeled "schism."

5. From the first, moreover, Christians had an advantage over competing interest groups such as the cult of Isis or Roman god cults. They were organized in the beginning with a cartel of twelve disciples, eleven excluding Judas. These disciples had already borne the fixed cost of organization. As a small group, the apostles were able to control activities at low cost. Once organized, the marginal cost of using their organization for other purposes was zero. The cartelized structure gave them an advantage over the pantheon of Greco-Roman gods,

which had no such structure. The Jews were organized but, from a New Testament and Roman perspective, they were unpopular and made high demands (the adoption of Jewish ethnicity) on prospective converts. In addition, the term "Christianity" took on many meanings as multiple sects adopted new (and alternative) forms of the new religion.

6. Secular monotheism based on Platonic principles was also known to exist (Lee 2006, 165).

7. Evidence, its purposes not undisputed, for belief in an afterlife occurs in the middle and late Paleolithic period. Careful burials by *Homo sapiens* (as early as 60,000 years ago) and by *Homo neanderthalensis*, with flowers over the deceased appear to signify some belief in an afterlife. Early belief in animal gods and parallel but unseen universes also accompany some of the early practices of *Homo*. Wood spirits, echoes, and artistic representations of animals (such as those at Altamira and elsewhere dating to 39,000 BCE) are at least suggestive that sentient humans had a penchant or a necessity to look beyond the purely physical world.

8. According to Cicero (*On His House*, 1.1 cited in Warrior 2006, 42), "Among the many divinely inspired institutions established by our ancestors, nothing is more outstanding than their desire to have the same individuals in control over worship of the gods and the vital interests of the state. Their objective was to ensure that the most eminent and illustrious citizens maintain religion by their good government of the state, and maintain the state by their wise interpretation of religion." Marriage of religion and state existed in virtually all of the early temple societies. In the early days of Christianity as upper-class citizens began to be converted, the tie between the state and "the gods" loosened, only to be joined again after Constantine.

9. Their role was to use a particular form of augury to determine the wisdom of particular state activity. Many other forms of magic and divination were used by the state—for example, using flights of birds as "portends"—some of which were officially sanctioned by Roman government. Magic, the occult, and astrology were commonly practiced as well.

10. We do not mean to imply that the Roman government did not, on important and significant occasions, banish the Jews from Rome and engage in all-out war in Jerusalem (which they ultimately did).

11. We have argued this from the beginning of our investigations into the economics of religion.

12. There is a kind of "dualism" in the Islamic view of an afterlife, offered centuries later. Body is separated from "spirit," which is shaped by man's earthly deeds. Bodies die but spirits go on to exist either exalted in paradise or punished in hell. Islam does not believe in bodily reincarnation but in a "day of judgment" when the full realization of good or bad deeds meets fruition (see http://www .muslim.org/islam/int-is35.htm).

13. Note that the Old Testament predicts the coming of a "messiah," but that Orthodox Jews did not and do not believe that Jesus Christ was that person. Further, Judaism does not *clearly* postulate an afterlife and its characteristics.

14. This discussion relies on information from the Jewish library (http://www.jewishvirtuallibrary.org/jsource/History/sadducees_pharisees_essenes.html). Also see Driscoll (1911).

15. Speculation concerning the omission centers on the rejection by Jews of the Egyptian religious tradition wherein death takes the central and controlling role of behavior.

16. Also see http://www.jewishvirtuallibrary.org/jsource/Judaism/afterlife.html.

17. Afterlife beliefs were part and parcel of prehistoric and all historic societies, as noted earlier in this chapter. Rituals relating to these beliefs died hard even in the case of the shift from Roman to Christian traditions. Wells (2008, 171–173) provides an anthropological explanation with archeological illustrations of how Christian burials (as late as the sixth century) combined elements of Roman traditions and Christian locales (for example, burials under the choir of the Cologne Cathedral). The Romans believed that particular places were "haunted" by the spirits of people buried in the region. Wells, in this regard, notes that "[b]eliefs surrounding early saints in the Christian church were much like ideas about local spirits inhabiting the countryside in earlier times."

18. A similar switch point for Christian believers came with the lower full price offered by Protestantism over Roman Catholicism in the early sixteenth century. Protestantism offered simpler rituals and no intermediary between believers and God ("every man a priest").

19. Again, we do not mean to imply that Christianity did not liberally borrow from Greco-Roman and pagan doctrines and beliefs. Hell had its precursors, for example, in chthonic gods of Greek mythology, such as Hades and Persephone. Mother goddesses permeate virtually all historic cultures and belief systems providing a platform for the "Virgin and Child" of Christianity. Depictions of God the Father in early Christian art recall early sculptures of Zeus. Propitiation of the god(s) through sacrifice is yet another practice common to most historical religions. The adaptations are endless, suggesting a commonality of religion, ritual, spirituality and myth through time (Campbell 1991).

20. Note that the full price must be adjusted for accompanying risks that might have heightened fear of death or punishment in an afterlife. Christians were persecuted at various periods and risked discovery and punishment. But those risks also applied to Jews at certain times and other religious sects who had run-ins with the state. Christian persecution was most serious in the mid-third to early fourth centuries. Also note that in the early period there were many Christianities (Jenkins 2010a).

21. Stark argues (2006, 7) that "the Jewish leadership demanded that all 'nations' become fully Jewish; there was no room for Egyptian-Jews or Roman-Jews, let alone Germanic or British-Jews, but only for Jewish-Jews . . . this ethnic barrier to conversion probably was the sole reason that the Roman Empire did not embrace the God of Abraham." Note, however, that this observation conflicts with that mentioned in the text by Casius Dio (c. 160– c. 235 CE), a Greek who wrote a history of Rome up to his own time.

22. We acknowledge here that we do not agree with the emphasis, shared by Stark, that the early Christian sects were cults as those defined by Iannaccone (1992). A cult employs rigorous standards and sanctions on its members in order to enforce group behavior and to prevent free riding. The spread of early Christianity was the result of *inclusiveness*—Christian entrepreneurs were attempting to grow rather than limit numbers. Clearly, there were net benefits to memberships but with little censure—forgiveness and repentance were and are hallmarks of early and, indeed, most Christian religion.

23. The Jews, while monotheists, did offer heterogeneous alternatives with regard to such matters as biblical interpretation, Hellenism, and the afterlife. Three major groups, the Pharisees, Sadducees, and Essenes, held varying positions on these matters, and only the Pharisees believed in "resurrection." Resurrection was not included in the Torah, however, and resurrection and afterlife consumptions were not a central part of the sale of the Jewish product. See http://www.hjewishvirtuallibrary.org/jsource/Judaism/afterlife.html and http://www.jewishvirtuallibrary.org/jsource/History/sadducees_pharisees_essenes.html. Regarding the general discount and deemphasis on an afterlife in Jewish thought and practice, it might be argued that the Jewish experience in Egyptian society that so clearly emphasized the identity of religion and state totally immersed in particular and ritualized visions of an afterlife, often at the expense, peril, and suffering of Jews, was a possible cause.

24. Contemporary suppliers (for example, fundamentalist preachers of all types) are, like their Roman counterparts, claimants of multiple interpretations of Christian ritual. Snake handling, total baptismal immersion, and many other rituals were invented by preacher-entrepreneurs.

25. An interesting and provocative paper (Gotsis and Drakopoulos 2008) applies the New Testament epistle of Saint Peter (2 Peter) to the reduction of "free riding" by Christian-based "deviants" (competitors). The epistle, with Peter's authorship questioned by Biblical scholars, attacks "false" teachers and explains that Jesus did not return immediately to give sinners time to repent. Gotsis and Drakopoulos argue that the epistle was a warning aimed at dissident Christian entrepreneurs and communities and threatening their afterlife rewards for not adhering to the principle traditions and orientations of the dominant Christian communities and entrepreneurial teachings.

26. According to Perkins, "Peter's faith . . . grew out of the experiences he had with Jesus, himself. Unlike Paul, a Pharisee from the Greek-speaking Diaspora, Peter shared the world of the Galilean peasants and craftsmen with Jesus. Like Jesus, he had grown up in the Judaism of the Galilean synagogues and had probably participated in annual pilgrimages to Jerusalem. When Peter encountered the risen Lord, he met a friend, and a hope that had appeared dashed was reborn" (Perkins 1994, 13). On later pilgrimage to the Holy Land, see Hunt (1982).

27. Others are even less kind concerning Paul's teachings, calling him a "mythmaker," whose fashioning of Christian doctrine was not of whole cloth. Worse, Paul has been accused of being a Gnostic. In this latter role it is claimed that he went along with the view that women were inferior and, thus, were to have a much diminished role in the Christian church (see Pagels 1989).

28. A clear distinction must be made between "the Vatican" or "Vatican City and the Holy See." The Holy See—the place where (now) more than a billion worldwide Roman Catholics are directed—existed from the early days of Christianity (see our chaps. 5 and 6). Vatican City, or more properly, the State of Vatican City, an ecclesiastical state within the city of Rome, was created by the Lateran Treaty between Italy and the papacy in 1929. The primacy of the Holy See and the existence of Vatican City are not to be confused with the Papal States, existing under the direction of the Holy See between 756 and 1870. These states were absorbed into Italy during the nineteenth-century unification led by Garibaldi.

29. In the case of Roman Christians, the expectation of a speedy resurrection was often elaborated on the ceilings of niches in the catacombs, some of which may be seen today.

30. Stark (http://www.jknirp.com/stark.htm) argues, in contrast, that "the early Church [was] a quite literate group. When you read the New Testament, for example, ask: Who are these people talking to? The language there is the language used by educated people." Hopkins (1998, 212) disagrees, arguing that extremely few literates were part of the house-cult communities in the first two centuries of the church. Communications between such groups and between cities does not imply high literacy for all. Hopkins, furthermore, doubts "mass conversions" in the early church—such conversions may well have occurred later after the marriage of church and state under Constantine, when non-Christians were subject to property confiscations, punishments, and even death for "heresy" or when Christian persecutions were in high gear in the third century.

31. As virtually all writers point out, speeches and dogma later attributed to the early apostle-entrepreneurs were based upon both fact and apocrypha (see, for example, Perkins 1994, 34–35). This fact set the stage for the primal disputes over the proper official canon of Christianity.

32. We believe that historian Roger Collins (2009, 20–21) correctly assessed the matter when he argued that the "early primacy of members of Jesus' family, together with the expectation of an imminent Second Coming, limited the need

for institutional structures and authority. It is only after the destruction of the Temple in AD 70 that the first Gospel, Mark's, was written, followed by those of Matthew and Luke within another ten to twenty years. It is in their narratives that the Apostles as a group first take on a special role in the revelation and spread of Christ's teaching. This may reflect the growing sense that the End was not nigh and that Christian communities, some of which were now claiming special links with particular disciples, saw an apostolic transmission of Jesus' words as a source of direction and authority."

33. Consider the problems that emerged with multiple gauge sizes for railroad tracks. After a period of competition, a standard gauge was adopted for efficiency. For most railroads, that standard remains applicable. (New gauges have been developed for high-speed trains in Europe and Japan.)

34. Cases such as the alleged superiority of the Dvorak keyboard (for typewriters, and so on) over the standard QWERTY keyboard have turned out to be bogus (see Liebowitz and Margolis 1990). Liebowitz and Margolis argue that the dominance of the QWERTY keyboard was not a "natural monopoly" in that a superior technology would have enabled market entry. There are important differences between the difficulty of penetrating networks such as Microsoft or the QWERTY keyboard and the ease with which Christian networks could be penetrated. A relatively minor change in doctrine or interpretation, for example, could create a whole new brand of "Christianity."

35. In addition, we do not make the assertion that all individuals demand religion or even a degree of "spirituality." Atheists and agnostics certainly exist without the services of organized (or unorganized) religion.

36. In the Middle Ages, the building of magnificent Romanesque and Gothic cathedrals helped provide "awe and grandeur" capital and credence to the religious products of the Roman Catholic Church. Priestly celibacy in the Roman Catholic case, clerical behavior, and "living standards" of clergy of all faiths are other forms of credence building for believers. Naturally, credence can be destroyed as well with religious scandal.

37. As the impact of martyrdom lessened, other credence-providing devices emerged. As suggested to us by medieval scholar Thomas Kuehn, the adoption of ascetic forms of community and worship (and later celibacy) became the "new martyrdom." These forms became institutionalized as the foundation of reform movements and successful missionary entrepreneurship in England and Germany.

38. See appendix 4.1 at the end of the book for full details of Stark's model and tests and our extension of it.

39. From Conybere and Howson (1977).

40. For a list of the cities Stark analyzes, see appendix 4.1.

41. We do not know whether Paul was a church founder or a sort of consultant who advised existing churches with respect to certain matters, such as rites and procedures.

42. Stark's assessment was that early Christianity was based significantly, but not exclusively, upon the membership of the privileged classes who acted as patrons to the lower classes. Others clearly disagree (MacMullen 1984). Further, Stark reasons that if Christianity had been a large proletarian movement, the state would not have been as tolerant as it was in the beginning, fearing social uprisings. A different reason was that Christianity stayed under the radar and that the Roman government was relatively tolerant of "dissident" religions— until, that is, individuals began to refuse homage (and contributions, ostensibly) to the official Roman gods late into the early Christian period. Persecution of Christians, when it occurred notably in the third and early fourth centuries, was less for "sedition" than for this refusal to renounce Christ and "pay up" to the established Roman religious bureaucracy.

43. The impact of Christianity on the "fall" of the Roman Empire has been much debated. It appears, however, that the general decline from the late empire to the sixth century was due to a multiplicity of economic and political factors (McCormick 2001) and not to the emergence of Christianity. Some of the issues relating to the interface between Christianity and the Roman state over the first three centuries are developed in chapter 5.

Chapter Five

1. This section draws on Anderson and Tollison (1992).

2. We note that the following interpretation appears to differ from Iannaccone's (1992) strict church club model. Without doubt, some subset of individuals will demand self-imposed restraints on their behavior—timed refrigerator locks, Christmas club accounts, demanding personal trainers, and religious strictures among them. But these self-imposed constraints are subject to individual demand determinants. Iannaccone is undoubtedly correct, empirically, that Mormons in the United States and Evangelicals in Latin America are demanding stricter religions. They are doing so due to particular demand determinants, however. Joining a Pentecostal religion, which requires sacrifice in contrast to other religious possibilities, is, other things equal, a product of demand determinants, including (in this case) low income, low levels of education, risk profiles, and the like. Proselytizing entrepreneurs offer these strict alternatives in packages to create conversions. The *same* theory of demand also explains the trend to lower demanding belief systems in advanced countries where stricter religious growth is stalling out, and self-administered Christianity and spirituality (as well as atheism) is growing, as evidenced by a number of surveys (see, for example, http://religions.pewforum.org/reports).

3. In our view various forms of religious supply arise to meet variations in demand, often through schism. Myriad and numerous forms of the "major sects"

exist with, for example, forty-six main denominations of Baptists alone, each selling a differentiated product. See http://www.thearda.com/denoms/Families/F_96.asp, for examples.

4. Throughout the chapter our frame of reference is *organized religion*, as opposed to individual, nonaligned religious practice.

5. In Latin America, the shift from Roman Catholicism to strict Evangelical religions, supported by entrepreneurial efforts, may be explained by preferences. While both religions contain rules that would appeal to the same set of adherents with similar risk profiles, Evangelicals permit unrestricted birth control, a growing practice in many Latin American countries (e.g., Mexico).

6. Moral order as a public good does not apply to all categories of behavior. The immorality of murder, theft, fraudulent dealings, nonpayment of taxes, and hostility to foreigners is the kind of moral order we refer to here. Culture wars concerning issues like abortion or gay marriage are not part of the concept.

7. A modern example of this is the loss in credence that may have attended the pedophilia scandals in the Roman Catholic Church in countries such as Germany, Ireland, and the United States.

8. Demonstrably, the Roman Catholic Church was a wealth-maximizing entity in part during the post-Constantine era and, most particularly, during the Middle Ages. But as noted in previous chapters, many different motives attend church behavior. These include missionary activities with no hope of immediate profit other than increased membership, reputation, and so on. The early pre-Constantine church, personified by the entrepreneurial activities of the apostles, may well have been motivated by the spiritual spread of the Christian message. Clearly, however, the church became, at least partly, a wealth-maximizing organization after it became an instrument of the state and, later, when it became a multinational power and a vertically integrated monopoly firm. We discuss some of these issues in chapters 6 and 7.

9. Here the opportunistic manner in which the medieval church handled the "usury doctrines" may be an example (Ekelund et al. 1996).

10. The Gnostics who also believed that Biblical writings were a metaphor and not literal managed to escape persecution (Collins 2009, 19).

11. Our argument here is the same as that of Buchanan (1973) concerning the mafia.

12. Naturally, these were costs of becoming Christian that tended to raise the price to the individual, but reciprocity by other Christians mitigated these costs. Further, there were costs associated with the probability of persecution, but according to Hopkins (1998, 196), persecutions were few and spasmodic until the third century because "Christians were protected from persistent persecution, but by the Roman government's failure to perceive that Christianity mattered, and by its punctilious legalism, which prohibited anonymous denunciation through the courts." Hopkins also argues that Christians needed persecutions

or stories thereof "to nurture a sense of danger and victimization, without there ever having been a real danger of collective exstirpation" (1998, 197).

13. We are certainly not the first to note that Constantine's conversion and adoption of Christianity was due to his "perception of Roman interests" (see Hopkins 1998, 226, for example). Our emphasis, however, is on the economic benefits that came from such actions.

14. This relationship has in fact been tested with U.S. state-level data, finding strong negative relationships (see Lipford, McCormick, and Tollison 1993).

15. A host of writers point to astonishing economic growth in the Roman economy during the first century CE. Temin (2006, 135) notes that "that GDP per capita in Roman Italy was between that in 1700 in the Netherlands, Italy, and Spain, the most advanced European economies a century before the Industrial Revolution."

16. A Gini coefficient is a number between 0 and 100 calculated to estimate the degree of inequality in the distribution of income; the larger the number, the *less* the degree of equality.

17. Enforcement of taxation in the provinces, especially for politicians representing particular areas, helped create the problems of lower productivity and skew income distribution. One observer notes that "[i]t is the corrupting of the whole process of distribution and collection, not absolute weight, which distinguishes taxation in the decline from taxation during the Principate; for the change appears to date to about the turn of the fourth century. It affects the yield ultimately delivered to the emperors; it affects the development and exercise of rural patronage (*patrocinium*), as well as real and fraudulent landownership" (MacMullen 1988, 42).

18. Mikhail Rostovtzeff (1926, 473), perhaps the greatest of all Roman historians, provides the following picture of the decline in the third century in his magisterial work: "This tremendous depression in business activity was due in large measure to the constant danger to which the most progressive and richest provinces were exposed. We have spoken of the repeated invasions of Gaul by the Germans and in particular of the catastrophe of A.D. 276. when the richest parts of Gaul were pillaged and devastated and most of the cities lost all power of recovery. The Danube lands repeatedly suffered similar devastation. We have mentioned the capture of the largest and richest cities by Goths and Sarmatians: the fate of Philippopolis was typical. The rich and flourishing province of Dacia was finally given up by Gallienus or Aurelian, and the population had to emigrate to the other Danubian provinces. Even in those cities which had not been pillaged and destroyed by the Goths we observe a rapid and disastrous decay."

19. As noted in chapter 4, these persecutions from the third and early fourth centuries must have had enormous credence-producing effects on conversions given the high growth rates of the church over this period. Cyclical persecutions were reported as wonderful acts by Christian martyrs going to their deaths for

Christ (MacMullen 1984, 29–30). Persecutions were, in all periods between 60 CE and the era of Constantine, relatively mild but much was made of them and Christian entrepreneurs were not above "manufacturing" their severity (Hopkins 1998, 195).

20. Diocletian also "reformed" the tax structure and collection system making the large estates responsible for collection. Workers, moreover, were bound to their land (*colonus*), a policy that was a precursor to medieval institutions. The wretched conditions of such laborers were not lessened by their being required to pay taxes and tribute on their produce.

21. There may be other reasons why Christianity was adopted under Constantine and not, say, under Diocletian, who persecuted Christians in the not-too-distant past. In addition to the "critical mass" of economic problems in the period surrounding and immediately after Diocletian's reign, Constantine's entrepreneurial network was markedly different than Diocletian's. Diocletian's circle centered on Rome, and he had a large number of Roman generals. Constantine, in contrast, was based in the eastern part of the empire where Christian networks were more likely larger. Many of Constantine's generals were Christians as was his mother. Such pressures might help explain the timing of the Edict of Milan and the Council of Nicaea.

22. We note that crime is not the only example of the possible efficiency effects of Christianity. As noted above, during the recurring plagues over the early centuries, Christians demonstrably provided better care for fellow Christians, raising their survival rates (see Stark 1997, 73–94), although Christians were not the only groups engaged in such welfare activities (MacMullen 1997). This provision of health insurance was a practical demonstration of the potential economic value of the new religion.

23. Something of this nature might have happened in contemporary times when the Southern Baptist Convention broke away from its larger coalition due to its "hard line" view of the role of women (subservient to their husbands in all things). Historically, the breakaway of Roger Williams from the Puritan sect might constitute another example, in this case, on matters of dogma.

24. Again, it is far less certain that Constantine himself accepted Christianity at this point (or ever). Constantine, at least apocryphally, promised God that he would institute Christianity if he won the battle. A sign from outer space—an asteroid or comet—sealed the deal for Constantine, according to some scientific accounts. The influence of Constantine's Christian mother (Saint Helen), who went on successful "relic hunts" in Jerusalem and elsewhere, cannot be denied either in this regard. Many of these relics (e.g., the "holy steps") found their way to Rome, linking the eastern and western parts of Christendom.

25. A highly readable account of the "survival of the fittest Christianity" and Constantine's role in it may be found in Wright (2009, 288–302). Also see Ehrman (2003).

26. The controversy ensued for several hundred years, however, only being settled by Augustine who argued, theologically, that sacraments were valid notwithstanding the "state of grace" of those who administer them.

27. The whole issue of the relation between the Jewish Old Testament and the New Testament and the more fundamental issue of whether the Old Testament should become part of the "new" religion—Christianity—was addressed by the mid-second-century Christian, philosopher, and teacher Marcion. He was the first to produce a canon of scripture, but he, following Paul according to Marcion, eliminated the Old Testament and its prescription of the details of Jewish law. Marcionism was later declared to be a heretic sect. The sect, however, survived into the early Middle Ages (Wright 2009, 293–295).

28. We admit that a three-hundred-person collusive agreement on doctrines and politics (not counting nonattendees) involved numbers not usually associated with cartel function. This is mitigated somewhat by the fact that the bishops represented territories so that geographic variation in doctrines would have been relatively easy to detect and sanction.

29. Note that the councilor form of church governance is firmly established in the Nicaean Council with special reverence to be accorded the Roman (and Alexandrine) bishops. The tension between the Roman bishop as "primate" of the Christian church and the organization of the church in councilor fashion remains both within the Roman Catholic Church and outside it even today (see chap. 8).

30. We are grateful to Professor Rachel McCleary for calling our attention to these issues.

31. There was disagreement over theological interpretation among Jews, who were also exclusivists but who espoused different interpretations of Scripture. The groups adopted a live and let live attitude at this time.

32. Ehrman (2003, 2005), without apology and with broad agreement on his textual exegesis from the documents of Nicaea from Biblical scholars, emphasizes that no original texts of the New Testament exist. Copy after copy meant that errors and intentional changes of the so-called writers of the "word of God" became the canon of Christianity at Nicaea. What was "left out" includes a mass of credible and noncredible material from orthodox Roman and later versions of the Christian religion. He argues that contradictions riddle the books of the New Testament and that "literalism" is actually not possible. Modern Evangelicals and Roman Catholics are, of course, not supportive of Ehrman's beliefs.

33. It is the difference in *interpretations* of both Old and New Testaments that forms the ground for the great diversity among Christian religion, both in the first millennium and in our own time. Clearly, early Christians accepted slavery (Depeyrot, 2006, 232) since slavery is nowhere condemned in scripture. That position would not be accepted or acceptable today. Those fundamentalist sects (including conservative-traditional Roman Catholicism) demanding a "literal"

interpretation of the testaments are forced to "cherry-pick" around issues that cannot be taken literally (if indeed they ever were).

34. In the extremely prescient words of Hopkins (1998, 223–224): "In the long-run, Christianity gave to the Roman state a degree of symbolic unity and exploitable loyalty, which it had previously lacked. Christianity had more combinatory power and more power to demand self-sacrifice than the previous combination of localized polytheisms, vague henotheism, and emperor cult. Christian rulers and the henchmen now had the legitimacy and authority of a powerful and interventionist God to support their authority and the enforcement of state regulations. The Roman state endorsed and then borrowed Christian intolerance."

35. The concept of a "trinity," moreover, was foreign to the Greco-Roman classical logic, a fact that may have hindered conversion of this group in the post-Nicaean era.

36. The structural differences between Roman and Orthodox Christians remain. Only the Croatian Church allies itself with Rome today. Further we certainly do not suggest that some kind of total monopoly over Christian Europe was established by the Roman Church. Roman interests lost out to Orthodox in large parts of the East, including Russia and the Balkans. Nonetheless, the structure of the Roman Church is in strong contrast to Eastern Orthodox organization.

37. Explanations for the rise of Christianity—lower full price of membership, provision of social services in response to declines in the Roman economy, proselytizing of the religion by apostolic entrepreneurs, Darwinian survival due to Christian beliefs, and so on—are only a few of the reasons for the rise of the new religion.

38. It was alleged, in a creative forgery written in the eighth century, that Constantine established the imperial (political authority) of the papacy, giving the pope in Rome authority over secular monarchs (the power to "crown," and so on). The interpretation was sometimes based on the baptism of Constantine in the Lateran Basilica in Rome—which became a "gift" of Constantine to the pope and (supposedly) an acknowledgement by him that religious and political power belonged to the pope. (Constantine allegedly offered the pope his crown but the pope refused it.) Most writers (Lieu 2006, 301, 305) recognize these allegations as apocryphal. It is noteworthy that Eusebius, the great church historian, also grossly exaggerated the role of Constantine in the founding of the Christian Church.

Chapter Six

1. Roman imperial governments and earlier temple societies faced similar issues in management of conquered territories and tax collection. Christianity, in many respects, mimed Roman administrative practice. Many modern organiza-

tions have used this system as well, including legitimate and illegitimate businesses (the Mafia).

2. Civil authorities, as we will see in chapter 7, were prone in many areas to seek revenues from church bishops and monasteries by claiming tithes as taxes owed the government and, importantly, by claiming rights to "invest" or choose individuals to take posts as bishops or abbots.

3. The cameral branch of the Roman papacy became a sophisticated arm of church government over the High Middle Ages. It was the papal bank, and it functioned as a court as well. It consisted of a director (the *camararius*) and locationally dispersed regional and local fiscal agents (rent collectors and cartel submanagers). A host of prelates, papal nuncios, and legates assisted in local enforcement, including cameral merchants (e.g., the Medici in the Middle Ages). Armies of functionaries, accountants, notaries, tax collectors, and lawyers were associated with these rent collections and malfeasance, such as clerical delinquency in payments, was treated harshly: excommunication was a common tool to force compliance.

4. Readers acquainted with the economics of industrial organization will recognize the above description as a forwardly integrated monopoly firm (Blair and Kaserman 1983). It is also worth noting that, under conditions of fixed proportions, the site of the monopoly (upstream or downstream) makes no difference in that monopoly profits will be collected under either circumstances. Further, it is important to note that the upstream church enforced relations with the downstream sellers under conditions of fixed proportions (i.e., a person redeemed by the "retail" monastery equals one saved by the upstream church). Technical details may be found in the classic paper by Spengler (1950) and Ekelund and Tollison (1981, 99–103).

5. An excellent discussion of the monasteries' role in church organization may be found in Davidson (1993, 1995), who clearly notes the role of these institutions in the vertical organization of the church.

6. If five patriarchies had remained in existence, it is difficult to see how the Roman monopoly over Western Christianity could have developed or persisted. We are grateful to Professor Thomas Kuehn for these and many other insights.

7. Myth making (or credence building, if you prefer) about the exploits and achievements of Constantine with respect to Christianity began with church biographer Eusebius (263–339), who was the "father of ecclesiastical history" (and friend of Constantine's) who described Constantine as "the mighty victor . . . pre-eminent in every virtue that true religion can confer . . . [who] won back their own eastern lands and reunited the Roman Empire into a single whole, bringing it all under their peaceful sway, in a wide circle embracing north and south alike from the east to the farthest west. Men had now lost all fear of their former oppressors" (Eusebius 1965, 413). Certainly, Constantine's military-political successes were less "mythical" than myths about his piety.

8. The *filioque* dispute —the source and ordering of the Holy Spirit vis-à-vis the Father and the Son—is very much alive today. Recent attempts by the pope and the Eastern patriarchs to come to agreement have been met with hostility on the part of some Eastern Christians.

9. The claim of primacy (not equality) of the bishop of Rome over the entire church and that of the pope's infallibility is based on several claims. Roman claimants to primacy rely on an interpretation of scripture (specifically, Matthew 16: 18–19 and John 21: 18–19) that suggests that Peter is the "rock upon which Christ founded his church" (and, by implication, Peter and his successors are absolute leaders). These claims are also embroiled with the "Petrine tradition"—the fact that apostles Paul and Peter came to Rome and were martyred there around 60 CE. In reality, there was no "bishop of Rome" until the second century, and the supposed "unbroken line" of popes that existed from the beginning is largely hagiographic and apocryphal. The alleged presence of the bones of Saint Peter's under the high alter of Saint Peter's Basilica in Rome is also adduced as evidence of the "primacy" of Rome. The archeological dig, authorized by Pius XII in 1939 did not produce firm results, although in 1968 Pope Paul VI proclaimed the bones to be Peter's. Also, one authority believes that the weight of evidence that the bones found there are not those of the saint (Collins 2009, 1–10). Many, including Protestants and Eastern Orthodox Christians, disagree with this interpretation of papal power. For example, did Christ's charge to Peter apply only to him or to all bishops?

10. It is perhaps noteworthy that the office of "bishop of Rome" did not exist until the middle of the second century. Collins (2009, 14) notes that most scholars agree that the individual was Anicetas whose episcopate likely covered the years 155–166 CE. In an attempt to add credence to a Roman papacy, the "cult of martyrdom" was associated with bishops of Rome. Roman bishops (around the time of Constantine) began to associate themselves with the cult of martyrs that had arisen as a credence device for Christian religion per se. They also associated themselves with buildings in Rome. But, as Collins notes (2009, 14, 20–21, 55), very few of these bishops were martyred.

11. Available at http://www.newadvent.org/cathen/06780a.htm.

12. The Italian city of Ravenna was the "western" geographic seat of the Eastern Emperor's authority, a jurisdictional unit called an exarchate.

13. Gregory "regularized" and systematized the rules and regulations that became the belief system of the medieval monopoly. This included the establishment of the notion of purgatory (which was only implied in the writings of Augustine), which suggested a prolongation of "earthly life" and purification (before reaching heaven) that could be "started" and mitigated by the practice of prayer, good deeds, and Christian conduct while on earth. (This "system" of delayed reward was not in full effect until the eleventh or twelfth centuries.) He also developed the notion of the importance of private penance as a corollary

to the institution of public penance. Both of these developments would be expanded and manipulated later in the High Middle Ages to extract rents from believers (Ekelund et al. 1996).

14. Again we are very grateful to Professor Thomas Kuehn for directing us to this point.

15. According to Collins (2009, 104), "The churches in the Anglo-Saxon kingdoms looked to Rome for guidance and direction to a degree unmatched in any of the other much longer-established churches of the West. They also developed a special reverence for the person of Gregory, so much so that the first ever 'Life' of him was written about a century after his death in Northumbria, in the joint male and female monastery of Whitby on the north Yorkshire coast."

16. Such behavior also tended to limit the size of secular polities as well, as it did with the ultimate size of the Frankish empire under Charlemagne.

17. The Encyclopedia of World History, http://www.bartleby.com/67/407. html.

18. Cannon (1960, 55) recounts this "gift": "Pepin gave outright to the Roman church and its bishop all the cities won by him from the Lombards including the exarchate of Ravenna in its entirety—that is, the country situated between the Apennines and the sea, the Po and Ancona . . . What Pepin did he did for the glory of God, the honor of the apostle Peter, and the salvation of his own soul. As a result of his action an entirely new commonwealth [the Papal States] was added to the map of Europe, a commonwealth which was to continue in existence from 756 until the unification of Italy in 1870."

19. The Roman Church was, for many centuries, both a spiritual and temporal property owner in Italy. Areas "owned" and administered by the papacy between the sixth century and the unification of Italy in 1870 were known as the Papal States, giving the pope territorial as well as spiritual sovereignty. The areas governed depended upon the ability of Rome to engage and support successful defenders of these properties. The Frankish and Ottonian Holy Roman emperors were, in general, protectors of these papal property rights, but actual control fluctuated over the centuries ending in the wave of Italian nationalism in the nineteenth century. Modern-day Vatican City, enclosed by the city of Rome, was established as a functioning national government in 1929. The Roman Catholic Church remains a civil as well as a spiritual institution.

20. A strand of historical interpretation has Charles angling for the crown all along, just not wanting to receive it in Rome from the Pope.

21. In addition, the church apparently supplied a quid pro quo to Charlemagne in the form of "housing" his sons and daughters from his ten marriages or from concubines. Daughter Theodrada (born 784) was made abbess of Argenteuil; daughter Ruodhaid (775–810) was made abbess of Faremoutiers; Drogo (801–855) became bishop of Metz from 823 and abbot of Luxeuil Abbey; and son Richbod (805–844) the abbot of Saint-Riquier.

Chapter Seven

1. It is perhaps worth noting again that these early European unifiers were fundamentally bloodthirsty, self-interested killers whose protection of the Roman Church gave them its support. In the case of Martel, who confiscated church lands and possessions in order to garner support for his military to keep the Muslims out of Europe, was (and is) chastised for the taking of church property rather than his more egregious crimes against humanity. The contemporary position on Martel, explained in the *Catholic Encyclopedia*, is ambiguous, noting that the lands with which Martel bribed his supporters to fight (to save Europe and Christianity) were, after all, church property in the end and that the so-called vision of Saint Eucher "showed Charles in hell, to which he had been condemned for robbing the Church of its property." The entry also notes that Charles had "not only tolerated but perpetrated many an act of violence against the Church, [but also] set about the establishment of social order and endeavoured to restore the rights of the Catholic hierarchy" (Kurth 1908; http://www.newadvent.org/cathen/03629A.htm).

2. Charlemagne was ruthless in forcing "pagan tribes" to accept Christianity. According to one source, "The Saxons on his eastern frontier were pagans; they had burned down a Christian church, and made occasional incursions into Gaul; these reasons sufficed Charlemagne for eighteen campaigns (772–804), waged with untiring ferocity on both sides. Charles gave the conquered Saxons a choice between baptism and death, and had 4500 Saxon rebels beheaded in one day; after which he proceeded to Thionville to celebrate the nativity of Christ." See http://www.chronique.com/Library/MedHistory/charlemagne.htm. The use of violence to "convert" pagans during the first millennium was adopted by the church in the second millennium as well. Missionaries accompanying Spanish conquistadors forced native Indians in the Americas—initially regarded by the Roman Church as subhuman—to convert to Roman Catholicism. For example, the Indians of the North American Taos Pueblo were forced into Catholicism and slavery in order to "civilize" them in the early seventeenth century (1619), a practice that engendered a revolt there in 1680. The Roman Catholic conquest was ultimately successful in establishing Christianity in many parts of the world, sometimes through violence, but often as a veneer over local religions and practices. (The often-curious mixture of Roman Church practices with earlier "pagan" ones characterizes much religious practice in Latin American and other areas today). This process naturally destroyed priceless historical documents of many peoples. The glorification of this process by Roman Christianity is questioned by many modern scholars.

3. Monks, in fact, brought back the intellectual treasures from Spain preserved from antiquity by Islamic scholars. The flowering of Western culture under the Roman Church was, in fact, derivative of these developments.

4. The classic work on the relations of Islam and the West is that of Henri Pirenne (1937).

5. Blumenthal (1988, 1) writes: "Highly mobile, the Northmen, who were wont to operate in bands of between three and four hundred men, had great tactical advantage. Their fast, light ships equipped with oars and sails took them swiftly within reach of their target—and, when necessary, just as swiftly out of reach of any would-be pursuers. Their ships turned up on every coast in the region between the Rhine and the Somme, as well as on the Seine, the Loire, and the Garonne. When they began to winter in England and Francia around 850 and to use horses to raid the countryside, it was difficult for anyone to find a safe haven."

6. The term "pornocracy" was not coined by Chamberlin, who wrote of the "bad popes," but by a sixteenth-century papal historian and prince of the church historian Cardinal Caesar Baronius (1538–1607) (Chamberlin 1969, 27).

7. John, not to be outdone, excommunicated Leo, but before Otto could return to exact retribution, John was murdered. The assassin, as described by Chamberlin (1969, 60), was a champion of Christianity and "was an outraged cuckold who had caught his Holy Father in the act and cudgeled him so severely that he died three days afterward." But in typical fashion the story was remade into a morality play by Christian interests in which "the injured husband was transformed into the devil himself, come to fetch home his most faithful servant."

8. See Chamberlin (1969) for an interesting account.

9. *Simony* is a general term for taking money for office or privilege. It may also be considered, somewhat cynically, as a method of tax farming for the church. Assuming that the church controlled the payee once in office, it could contribute to the solution of the principal-agent problem. But where transactions and information costs are high (as they would be in faraway locations), the simoniac could divert church revenues to himself or to secular powers.

10. The donation was shown to be an eighth-century papal forgery and was admitted to be such in the fifteenth century.

11. The Ottonians were followed by other Saxon monarchs in the first part of the eleventh century—Henry II (1003–1024) and Conrad II (1024–1039).

12. For and excellent discussion of conditions in the Eastern Empire between 500 and 1000 CE, see Wickham (2009, 255–348).

13. The clause was added by a synod directed by Charlemagne's people, which made him imitative of the Eastern emperor (who judged images correct or incorrect, depending on himself), while deliberately creating a distinction from the East and the possibility of appearing Greek Orthodox in contrast.

14. We do not wish to minimize the complexity of the theological debate. Our purpose here is only to note the importance of the dispute to the two major branches of Christianity and to the crucial roles of product definition and papal primacy.

15. One function of most representational art is propaganda, and Christian art through the ages is no exception. Pictorial forms of advertising Christianity by the Roman Church proceeded through the centuries. The acceptance and defense of icons was as much an "advertising gimmick" as it was a philosophical defense of the "Catholic understanding of and appreciation for the created world" (Woods 2005, 115). Indeed, the early history of Western art is a history of illustrations from both Old and New Testaments often used to educate the illiterate with "secular" art, which was, in the earlier periods, condemned. A whole era of subsidized religious art (the Baroque) followed on the heels of the Protestant Reformation. Caravaggio, the font of this movement, used "street people" with "dirty feet" to illustrate vignettes and stories from the Bible to appeal to the common people. The massive (and resource-using) cathedrals of Europe were, in addition to artistic high points, forms of "awe and grandeur capital," providing credence to illiterate and poor members of society.

16. Christian imagery, just as that of the religions of ancient temple societies, emphasized a panoply of saints who were specialized in function (Saint Joseph, the patron saint of carpenters, Saint Cecilia, the patron saint of musicians, and so on). This advertising served to increase the interest in and spread of Christianity among diverse professions and interests in the population.

17. Steps to reunify with Eastern Christianity by John Paul II (1978–2005) and Benedict XVI (2005–) have been unsuccessful, not the least due to Eastern objections.

18. The Syrian Orthodox Church (now called the Syriac Orthodox Church) parted ways with Orthodox (Nicene and Chalcedonian) Christianity, along with the Coptic Orthodox Church and the Armenian branch, over issues debated at the Council of Chalcedon in 451. These eastern branches remain in general communion with Orthodox Christianity, however. The Russian Orthodox Church is also affiliated with Eastern Orthodoxy and is said to be second in membership size only to Roman Catholicism among Christian Churches. Patriarchs head these religions as in early Christianity.

19. Papal "reformers" who were often interested in lives of poverty, nonetheless on occasion issued admonitions to virtue and to chastity. For example, a council at Pavia (in 1022) issued a prohibition on clerical marriage, but such decrees "were issued in order to protect ecclesiastical and monastic property and not to raise ecclesiastical morals" (Blumenthal 1988, 71).

20. This reform was accepted over time, and secular rulers still had some influence in elections.

21. The requirement of celibacy may be thought of as a means of support for vertical integration in that it ensures that offices are not transmitted by inheritance and that "survivors" have no claims on the church or diminish the wealth of the church.

22. The dictatorial mandate espoused by Gregory (*Dictatus Papai*), compiled about 1087, and included such articles as "12. That with him is the power to depose emperors. . . . 16. That no general synod may be called without his command. . . . 18. That his decree may be annulled by no one, and that he may annul the decree of anyone. 19. That he may be judged by no one. . . . 22. That the Roman Church has never erred and will never err, to all eternity. 24. That by his command or permission subjects may accuse their rulers. 27. That he has the power to absolve subjects from their oath of fidelity to wicked rulers" (Thompson 1931, 440).

23. A modern example is Benedict XVI's reinstatement of renegade right-wing bishops, who defied the dictates of Vatican Council II and maintained traditional practices of church worship. The formerly renegade bishops include one who denies the Holocaust (see chap. 8).

Chapter Eight

1. The Saladin tithe, a response to Saladin's capture of Jerusalem in 1187, was the highest revenue-producing tax in England up to the end of the twelfth century. It was a 10 percent tax on revenues and moveable property (excepting the clergy and joiners of the Third Crusade) assessed and collected by individual Christian dioceses. There was much resistance to the tax, and the Third Crusade failed to restore Jerusalem to Christian control.

2. One may identify noncompeting arguments for Constantine's actions based on social and familial pressures surrounding him in the Eastern part of the Empire. Constantine's Christian generals may have ruled the army and rejected persecutions. Further, Constantine's Christian mother may have also pressured her son to become Christian.

3. Parts of which became the Papal States which were not relinquished to civil government until the nineteenth century.

4. This "Roman imperial style" papacy continued throughout the Middle Ages. Assertions of all manner of authority—the exclusive appointment of bishops by the papacy and a separate system of laws (canon law), for example—were claimed by the Roman Church throughout the centuries. As such, organizational claims, not to be found in scripture or Christ's teachings, became part of the "theology" of the church that is received and promulgated today.

5. Indeed, the church may well have been aided in maintaining its monopoly control by the feudal systems that characterized countries in one degree or another at this time. France and Germany were Balkanized by assortments of fiefs, bishoprics, and warring feudal dukes. These conditions left the field open for the church to use opportunistic behavior on the part of the various factions to gain revenues, favors, and protection (e.g., leverage to fight crusades). In Norman England, William the Conqueror supported papal ambitions and projects,

and in Italy, the pope himself was the temporal master. The papacy held the balance of power given its monopoly over religious belief by the mass of the citizenry of these countries, especially those in "decentralized" nations.

6. There are many other examples as we (with others) have shown in *Sacred Trust* and *The Marketplace of Christianity*.

7. Witch hunts were episodic and were not limited to Roman Catholicism. Other religions participated as well. However, *Malleus Maleficarum*, the "how to" book on the treatment of witches, was written by two Roman Catholic inquisitors in the late fifteenth century. Others downplay the severity of witch hunts as well as the various "inquisitions," deeming them of far less importance than is commonly thought (Woods 2005).

8. We do not here pretend to investigate all of the implications of the "natural conflict" among religious demanders.

9. Indeed, the granting of indulgences is being revived in the modern-day United States. In a reversal of the simplicity suggested in the Second Vatican Council (early 1960s), some bishops are granting indulgences, which release, either partially or totally, time in purgatory in exchange for prayers or "pilgrimages." Modern uses of these indulgences are associated with "confession" (as in the High Middle Ages) and are "not for sale" (monetary transactions were eliminated in 1857). Charitable contributions are welcome of course and the toll road (confession and return to the faith) is intended to be especially attractive to Roman Catholics who have left the church and whose return would enhance membership and revenues. See Vitello (2009).

10. Divorced Catholics who remarry without "dispensations" are not allowed to receive "valid" sacraments although *ex post* annulments which carry dispensations are available before remarriage for a price in terms of money and time costs from Rome.

11. Again, historical data could shed light on the risk-adjusted full price of Christian religion in the areas that switched to Protestantism and in those that remained Roman Catholic. Property ownership characteristics and the distribution of industry size and structure would be expected to favor sole proprietors, shopkeepers and independent businesses. Economies becoming Protestant could be expected to be more democratic (with greater citizen participation) than hierarchical with less rent seeking and fewer guild movements within the laboring class. Saving, investment, innovation and a work ethic would have characterized those economies that ultimately settled Protestant. Historical data, in short, could offer evidence concerning the risk profiles of European nations prior to and after Protestant entry.

12. Actually, the Roman Catholic Church still approaches a pure monopoly in some parts of the "developing" world today (e.g., the Philippines).

13. The Roman Inquisition (Roman Holy Office) is not to be confused with the Spanish Inquisition (1478–1834), formally the Tribunal of the Holy Office of

the Inquisition. It was the Roman Inquisition that prosecuted Galileo for example, not the Spanish Inquisition.

14. A number of contemporary Christian writers who wish to portray the church as a leader in science point to the famous case of Galileo as proof that the church "was not so bad" in its general condemnations (see Woods 2005, 69–71). While Galileo challenged accepted beliefs about the universe, he is alleged not to have had "proof" that the universe was heliocentric. The church condemned his view as "false and contrary to Scripture," using a theological argument rather than providing any scientific evidence that Galileo was wrong. (Jesuit astronomers of Galileo's time in fact formed an "interest group" in opposition to his amazing achievements.) And, critically, while the monasteries of the time provided real advances in what can only be termed "agricultural technology," the church came down hard on theories and evidence relating to the physical world, especially if science seemed at variance with a literal interpretation of the Old and New Testaments. As testing methods improve, it has become more difficult to make such allegations against science and in favor of "supernatural" arguments. Indeed, the Roman Church established the Pontifical Academy of Science, housed at the Vatican since 1936, to counteract the common impression that the church has waged wars on science. Despite weak apologies from the Vatican establishment, Galileo himself remains the champion of science and reason against superstition, regulation, and suppression and will likely remain so.

15. See http://www.womensordination.org.

16. See http://ncronline.org/news/women/vatican-investigates-us-women-religious-leadership for the *National Catholic Reporter*'s analysis of the nun investigations in the United States.

17. A poll of North American Catholics from 2010 revealed that 59 percent favored ordaining women, while 37 percent opposed ordination. American bishops, moreover, have been quick to point out the important role women play in the church—a clear attempt to assuage the downstream church in the United States (Donadio 2010c).

18. Formal schism in the contemporary Roman Catholic Church is extremely rare, but challenges to hierarchical control and declarations of schism are not unknown. The issue of schism, revolving around monetary and property issues as well as progressive theology, was raised in the case of a Polish parish, St. Stanislaus, in St. Louis, Missouri. A unique aspect of the parish was that it was owned and run by a lay board of directors governing the parish. Further, the parish congregation owned the property and the monetary assets of the church. In 2003, the archdiocese moved to take over Saint Stanislaus. When the congregation refused—fearing a close-down of their church—the archbishop removed the diocesan priests from the church, leaving the congregation without sacraments or ministers for two years. To the rescue came Polish Reverend Marek Bozek, who not only ministered to the flock but also espoused liberal policies

for married, women and gay priests. Bozek was excommunicated for schism by the archbishop (Raymond Burke, made a cardinal in 2010) of St. Louis and the excommunication was affirmed by the Vatican. However, Bozek continued his ministry and, in spite of continued attempts to buy out the congregation's property, the bishop's proposals have been refused. Despite his progressive views and his excommunication, Bozek (as of 2010) had a large following whose confidence and credence in the hierarchy of the church is less than their confidence in Reverend Bozek and his ideas. (See Gay 2010).

19. Anthony Gill (1998) argues, persuasively, that the Roman Church has behaved in clearly opportunistic fashion in its policy toward dictators and authoritarian regimes in Latin countries. In a sample of twelve Latin countries he shows that those in those with significant fundamentalist and animistic sect competition, the church has been far less amenable to dictators and more supportive of "liberation theologies of the clergy." In those countries without Pentecostal and other competition, the church has been supportive of authoritarianism.

20. Sanneh (2003, 15) notes that "Christian Africans came predominantly from the poor and marginalized. By 1985 there were over 16,500 conversions a day, yielding an annual rate of over 6 million. In the same period (i.e., between 1970 and 1985), some 4,300 people were leaving the church on a daily basis in Europe and North America."

21. That divide also exists within religious groups in the advanced world. Evangelical Protestants predominate in the poorest and least educated parts of the United States—in the South and Midwest (Grossman 2006).

22. Note that the "cafeteria" also exists *within* denominations. While the megachurch movement in the United States is often perceived to be "conservative" in orientation, there is in fact great variation among members. Many of the megachurches are Southern Baptist, such as the Saddleback Church (see www .baylor.edu/content/services/document.php/33304.pdf).

23. In October 2010, a majority of Americans supported civil unions and a growing number of Americans support same sex marriage according to Pew Research (see http://pewforum.org/Gay-Marriage-and-Homosexuality/Support-For-Same-Sex-Marriage-Edges-Upward.aspx). If demographic trends of opinion in younger age groups hold, including those in so-called conservative Christian religions, changes in civil law may be predicted despite the vehement opposition of some conservative Christian groups.

24. Unlike the personal computer market, entry is made easy in the market for Christian religion since a nuance of theology or interpretation thereof can be the occasion for a new sect. We argue that such entry is easier and schisms are more likely in bottom-up Congregationalist organizations. In top-down hierarchical structures with "doctrinal purity" a principal goal of the upstream church, entry is more difficult. What may occur under the latter circumstances, however, is "switching," a degree of which we have observed in such churches (see Beard

et al., Manuscript). That does not mean that particular prelates and/or parish councils have not been declared schismatic and excommunicated in the modern age (see http://www.nytimes.com/2010/08/14/us/14church.html?).

25. The 2010 Nobel Prize in medicine was awarded to Robert Edwards of Britain for his work on the invention of in vitro fertilization, a process that has allowed hundreds of thousands of men and women the opportunity to become parents. This scientific advance occurred despite the condemnation, in 1987, by the Congregation for the Doctrine of the Faith (then led by now-Pope Benedict XVI). The objection was that in vitro techniques separate conception from the conjugal act and is apparently judged "unnatural" under Roman Catholic theological interpretation. There is also an issue of disposal of unutilized but fertilized eggs.

26. As of August 2010, same-sex marriage (with equal legal and civil rights) was legal in Argentina, Belgium, Canada, Iceland, Netherlands, Norway, Portugal, South Africa, Spain, and Sweden. Argentina, Portugal and Spain are certainly in the traditional family of "Catholic countries."

27. See http://religions.pewforum.org/reports.

28. The visit of Pope Benedict XVI to the United States in 2008 provides an interesting example of possible differences in the policy stances of the papacy. Two aspects of the visit were widely hailed, and one was controversial. Benedict's visits with clerical abuse victims was well received as an act of "contrition," while his advocacy of "open borders" with Mexico and Latin America was given mixed reviews. But, in an observationally equivalent sense, Benedict's contrition could have been a response to the reported fast drop in revenues from the United States to Rome, and his advocacy of open borders might have reflected the fact that 80 percent of all immigrants, legal and illegal, to the United States are Roman Catholic (http://religions.pewforum.org/reports).

29. The elevation of a lesbian bishop in 2010 led to the Episcopal Church being removed from committees of the Anglican Communion, a move proposed by the archbishop of Canterbury Rowan Williams. The interesting response, with respect to our analysis of church organization, came from U.S. Episcopal presiding bishop Katharine Jerrerts Schori, who pushed back against the Anglican action, arguing that "Anglicans have always been led by local churches, not a centralized body of powerful clerics" (Burke 2010; also see http://pewforum.org/Religion-News/Episcopalians-booted-from-Anglican-bodies-over-gay-bishops.aspx). Bishop Schori is suggesting that a "bottom-up" organization characterizes the Anglican Communion, an assertion that rejects the conciliar, hierarchical form of Anglicanism since Henry XIII. Perhaps a change in organization will accompany the schism between Anglicans and Episcopalians, at least for the latter.

30. See Ruth Gladhill and Richard Owen, "Pope's Gambit Could See 1,000 Quit Church of England," *London Times*, October 21, 2009, http://www.times

online.co.uk/tol/comment/faith/article6883151.ece. As many as 400,000 new Roman Catholic members may be the result of the switch. Also see Gladhill and Owen (2009b). The volume of potential defections on the matter of women's and gays' role in the church suggests a high elasticity on the part of Christian church members.

31. It would appear to be a simple matter to rescind the rule against the use of birth control—providing a competitive edge for the Roman Catholics in the third world. However, such a change would not, according to some observers, be possible without opening the floodgates in matters relating to sex, "life," and procreation. The acceptability of the use of condoms to protect life inside a marriage when one partner is infected with HIV or is sick with AIDS was an issue at the Vatican in May 2006 (Fisher 2006). Right-wing conservatives in the church were fearful, however, that such an exception would open the floodgates in their application of church teachings regarding "life issues" (e.g., embryonic stem-cell research, abortion, and so on). But in November 2010 Pope Benedict, in a surprise pronouncement, sanctioned the limited use of condoms for AIDS if they are used only as a "lesser evil" to prevent HIV infection. Possible future alterations by the papacy in life and sex-related issues cannot be predicted.

32. In 2009, in order to repair a schism on the right in the Roman Church, Benedict XVI admitted dissident right-wing bishops that were excommunicated by his predecessor John Paul II. French bishop Marcel-François Lefebvre, who died in 1991, refused to accept the liberalization of the church in Vatican Council II and founded the ultraconservative Society of Pius X in 1970, ordaining four bishops in 1988. (Lefebvre was suspended by Paul VI in 1976.) Left-leaning Roman Catholics are regarded as the product of secularism. In order to battle "secularism" (undefined except perhaps for plummeting church attendance in developed nations), Pope Benedict XVI created a new "Pontifical Council for Promoting the New Evangelization" in 2010. The object is to "reinvigorate Christianity in the parts of the world where it is falling by the wayside"—chiefly, presumably, in Europe (Winfield 2010b).

33. Kosmin et al. 2001, 24. This survey, like all surveys, that may contain measurement problems.

34. Roman Catholic traditional conservatives and apologists point out, correctly, that pedophilia is not simply a Roman Catholic problem, citing statistics that many pedophiles inhabit other vocations—public school teachers, Boy Scout leaders, and others. Liberal Catholics and sensational reporting is to blame, in this view, for unfairly stigmatizing the church (Jenkins 1996, 2010b). These groups, however, unlike the pope and bishops of the Roman Catholic Church, do not hold themselves out to be ultimate arbiters of "moral behavior." The more serious issue is that the Roman Church hierarchy continues to refuse to admit any moral or ethical responsibility for transferring rather than punishing accused priests, and the erroneous equation of homosexuals and pedophiles has not been

convincing. (Boy Scout leaders and school administrators do not shuffle miscreants from one venue to the other). Punishment of guilty bishops and other clergy of high rank around the world would appear to be tepid at best. The credence of the church, at least in the past, apparently trumped moral behavior on the part of the entire church establishment. Promises of "reform" in the priesthood, regularly voiced by Benedict XVI, are singularly short on oversight and penalties. The church, according to one observer (Sipe 2010), has had a long 1,000-year history of sexual activity within a system of "celibacy," noting that "Roman Catholic clerical culture favors doctrinal rigidity, conformity, obedience, submission and psychosexual immaturity, mistaken for innocence, in candidates . . . Double lives on all levels of clerical life are tolerated if they do not cause scandal or raise legal problems. Sexual activity between bishops and priests and adult partners is well known within clerical circles." This secret system is a natural refuge for those who would abuse minors. Revelation of this secret of clerical celibacy may lead to a vast reduction in "credence" (as we have described it in this book) or to a reformation within the church.

35. The pedophilia issue is not the only "downstream" credence issue facing the Roman Church. A Vatican bank scandal involving possible violations of the anti-money-laundering regulations of the Italian central bank received media attention in 2010 and a full-scale investigation by the Vatican of its bank (Faris 2010). These allegations at least potentially damage credence in the church and were met with alarm and resistance at the upstream level of church governance.

36. Many examples present themselves. Consider only two. Pastor Ted Haggard, pastor of the New Life Church of Colorado Springs and one-time president of the National Association of Evangelicals, admitted, in 2003, to the solicitation of a male prostitute. George Alan Rekers, a Southern Baptist, cofounder of the Family Research Council and provider of testimony of the ability of homosexuals to undergo "conversion therapy," was discovered in 2010 to have hired a gay male companion to carry his luggage on a European trip. These and dozens of other examples create a lack of credence in the ministries they represent. The response to these and other common and regular transgressions and hypocrisies is that "One cannot judge the 'priesthood by the priest.'" Many observers wonder then how else one is to judge religion. It is unlikely that credence is the product of "faith" alone. It is also premised on the bond or behavior of those selling that particular brand of faith.

37. An even more recent study, the American Religious Identification Survey in 2008, was based upon 54,000 interviews in that year. It found, with a margin of error of plus or minus 0.5, that the third-largest religious group in the United States was "no religion" (after Catholic and Baptist) and that the fourth-largest group was "Christian, generic." Indeed, all religious affiliations surveyed declined from 1990 to 2008. "Nones" were 15 percent of the U.S. population

(Grossman 2009, 6A) with approximately another 15 percent being "generic Christian." For all the attention that growth in conservative-Evangelical sects in the United States (and Europe) is getting, these data apparently reveal a rise in "secularism" (including atheism, agnosticism, self-administered spirituality, and self-determined forms of Christianity) that suggests a lowering of risk preference and a predilection for "self-administered" theology and religious practice. Other studies, such as the one by Baylor University, challenge the growth of "secularism" in the United States (see www.baylor.edu/content/services/document.php/33304.pdf). The growth of secularism in Europe and in other developed nations, if that means non-attendance at religious services and defections, is serious enough for the Pope Benedict to establish a new Vatican Office to "re-evangelize" a secular world (see Donovan 2010).

Appendix

1. No doubt, the fact of the establishment of a church does not proxy the local progress of Christianity perfectly. We simply avail ourselves of Stark's data in this case.

2. We conducted tests using an ordered probit model, but they are highly questionable due to small sample size and the lack of variation of the dependent variable across the categorical right-hand variables. Results are available from the authors on request.

3. We interpret the disagreements among these sources as indicative of the degree of spread of early Christianity. If five sources agree that a church was present in a city by 100 CE, that city must have a higher degree of Christian penetration than a city where only four of the authors report the existence of a church. Adding the values horizontally in table 2 accomplishes exactly this type of ranking.

4. Our dependent variable, being a fractional number, warrants a more complicated econometric treatment. Papke and Wooldridge (1996) develop a fractional regression model that requires maximum likelihood estimation, making it not feasible in our case, due to the small sample size. Also expressing our dependent as a log-odds ratio is prevented by observations for which the dependent variable takes the value of 1. Our model is similar to a linear probability model in interpretation and suffers from the same drawbacks, mainly a lack of robustness around extreme values of predictor variables and heteroskedasticity.

5. The use of the highest value of the ROMANIZATION variable for the Rome observation is a conservative one since it is certain that it should be higher.

6. We have found that these results are robust with respect to the normality of errors assumption. Nevertheless, we used parametric bootstrapping (2,000 repli-

cations) for the model and calculated confidence intervals; there were no significant changes (see Cameron and Trivedi 2005; Efron and Tibshirani 1993). These results are available on request from the authors.

7. An issue we have not addressed due to data limitations is whether Christianization would or would not include the presence of Gnostics. Surely issues of "heresy" were raised early in Christian communities, but the official orthodox canon of beliefs necessary to be called a "Christian" did not exist before 325 CE.

References

Allen, Douglas. 1995. "Order in the Church: A Property Rights Approach." *Journal of Economic Behavior* 27: 97–117.

Anderson, Gary M., and Robert D. Tollison. 1992. "Morality and Monopoly: The Constitutional Political Economy of Religious Rules." *Cato Journal* 12: 373–392.

Arruñada, Benito. 2004. "Catholic Confessions of Sin as Third Party Moral Enforcement." *Gruter Institute Working Papers on Law, Economics, and Evolutionary Biology* 3, article 2. http://www.bepress.com/giwp/default/vol3/iss1/art2.

Asimov, Isaac. 1968. *The Dark Ages.* Boston: Houghton Mifflin Company.

Azzi, Corey, and Ronald Ehrenberg. 1975. "Household Allocation of Time and Religiosity: Replication and Extension." *Journal of Political Economy* 85: 415–423.

Barb, A. A. 1963. "The Survival of Magic Arts." In *The Conflict between Paganism and Christianity in the Fourth Century*, ed. Arnaldo Momigliano. Oxford: Clarendon Press.

Barro, Robert J., and Rachel McCleary. 2003. "Religion and Economic Growth." *American Sociological Review* 68 (October): 761–781.

———. 2004. "Religion and Economic Growth." *Milken Economic Review* (April).

———. 2005. "Which Countries Have State Religions?" *Quarterly Journal of Economics* 120: 1331–1370.

Barros, P. P., and N. Garoupa. 2002. "An Economic Theory of Church Strictness." *Economic Journal* 112: 559–576.

Beard, T. Randolph, Robert B. Ekelund, Jr., George Ford, and Robert D. Tollison. Manuscript. "Secularism, Self Protection and Religious Choice: An Economic and Empirical Analysis."

Beard. T. Randolph, Robert B. Ekelund, Jr., George Ford, and Robert D. Tollison. Forthcoming. "The Economics of Schism," in *Oxford Handbook on the Economics of Religion*, ed. Paul Oslington. New York: Oxford University Press.

Beck, Roger. 2006. "The Religious Market of the Roman Empire: Rodney Stark and Christianity's Pagan Competition." In *Religious Rivalries in the Early Roman Empire and the Rise of Christianity*, ed. Leif E. Vaage, 233–252. Waterloo, ON: Wilfrid Laurier University Press.

Becker, Gary. 1981. *A Treatise on the Family*. Cambridge, Mass.: Harvard University Press.

———. 2002. "Interview with Gary Becker." Federal Reserve Bank of Minneapolis. June 14. http://www.minneapolisfed.org/pubs/region/02- 06/becker.cfm.

Bercea, Brighita, Robert B. Ekelund, and Robert D. Tollison. 2005. "Cathedral Building as an Entry-Deterring Device." *Kyklos* 58, no. 4: 453–465.

Bennhold, Datrin, and Nicholar Kulish. 2010. "As Archbishop, Benedict Focused on Doctrine." *New York Times*, March 27. http://www.nytimes.com/2010/03/28/world/europe/28church.html?th.

Blair, Roger, and David Kaserman. 1983. *Law and Economics of Vertical Integration and Control*. New York: Academic Press.

Bleckmann, Bruno. 2006. "Sources for the History of Constantine." In *The Cambridge Companion to the Age of Constantine*, ed. Noel Lenski. Cambridge: Cambridge University Press.

Blumenthal, Uta-Renate. 1988. *The Investiture Controversy: Church and Monarchy from the Ninth to the Twelfth Century*. Philadelphia: University of Pennsylvania Press.

Bobbin, Frank, ed. 2004. *The New Economic Sociology: A Reader*. Princeton: Princeton University Press.

Boyer, Pascal. 2001. *Religion Explained: The Evolutionary Origins of Religious Thought*. New York: Basic Books.

Boussard, Jacques. 1968. *The Civilization of Charlemagne*. London: World University Library.

Brown, Peter. 1989. *Society and the Holy in Late Antiquity*. Berkeley: University of California Press.

Buchanan, James M. 1965. "An Economic Theory of Clubs." *Economica* 32: 1–14.

———. 1973. "A Defense of Organized Crime?" In *Economics of Crime and Punishment*, ed. S. Rottenberg, 119–132. Washington, DC: American Enterprise Institute.

Burke, Daniel. 2010. "Episcopalians Booted from Anglican Bodies over Gay Bishops." Religion New Service. http://pewforum.org/Religion-News/Episcopalians-booted-from-Anglican-bodies-over-gay-bishops.aspx.

Camerer, Colin, George Loewenstein, and Drazen Prelec. 2005. "Neuroeconomics: How Neuroscience Can Inform Economics." *Journal of Economic Literature* 43: 9–64.

Cameron, A. C., and Trivedi, P. K. 2005. *Microeconometrics: Methods and Applications*. New York: Cambridge University Press.

Campbell, Joseph. 1991. *The Masks of God: Primitive Mythology*. Arkana: Penguin.

Cannon, William Ragsdale. 1960. *History of Christianity in the Middle Ages: From the Fall of Rome to the Fall of Constantinople*. Nashville: Abingdon Press.

Castelli, Elizabeth A. 1998. "Gender, Theory and *The Rise of Christianity*: A Response to Rodney Stark." *Journal of Early Christian Studies* 6: 227–257.

Chamberlin, E. R. 1969. *The Bad Popes*. New York: Dorset Press.

Chandler, T., and Fox, G. 1974. *3000 Years of Urban Growth*. New York: Academic Press.

Clark, Andrew and Orsola Lelkes. 2005. "Deliver Us from Evil: Religion as Insurance." PSE (École normale supérieure). http://www.pse.ens.fr/clark/DeliverDec05.pdf.

Coale, A. J., and P. Demeny. 1966. *Regional Model Life Tables*. Princeton: Princeton University Press.

Collins, Roger. 1991. *Early Medieval Europe, 300–1000*. 2d ed. New York: St. Martin's Press.

———. 2009. *Keepers of the Keys of Heaven: A History of the Papacy*. New York: Basic Books.

Comte, Auguste. 1968 [1851–1857]. *System of Positive Polity*. 4 vols. New York: Burt Franklin Reprints.

Conybere, W. J., and J. S. Howson. 1977 [1889]. *The Life and Epistles of St. Paul*. New York: Gordon Press Publishers.

Coyne, Jerry A. 2010. *Why Evolution is True*. New York: Penguin.

Crossley, James G. 2006. *Why Christianity Happened*. Louisville, KY: Westminster John Knox Press.

Daniel-Rops, H. 1959. *The Church in the Dark Ages*. London: J. M. Dent & Sons, Ltd.

Darby, Michael R., and Edi Karni. 1973. "Free Competition and the Optimal Amount of Fraud." *Journal of Law and Economics* 16: 67–88.

Davidson, Audrey. 1993. "An Economic Analysis of Medieval Institutions: The Church, Monasteries, and the Family." Ph.D. diss., Auburn University.

———. 1995. "The Medieval Monastery as Franchise Monopolist." *Journal of Economic Behavior and Organization* 27: 119–128.

Dawkins, Richard. 2006. *The God Delusion*. Boston: Houghton-Mifflin.

DeLorme, Charles D. Jr., Stacey Isom, and David R. Kamerschen. 2005. "Rent Seeking and Taxation in the Ancient Roman Empire. *Applied Economics* 37: 705–711.

Depeyrot, Georges. 2006. "Economy and Society." In *The Cambridge Companion to the Age of Constantine*, ed. Noel Lenski, 226–254. Cambridge: Cambridge University Press.

Donadio, Rachel. 2010a. "With Scrutiny, Vatican Faces Test of 'Moral Credibility.'" *New York Times*, March 27. http://www.nytimes.com/2010/03/28/world/europe/28vatican.html.

——. 2010b. "In Abuse Crisis, a Church Is Pitted Against Society and Itself." *New York Times*, April 29. http://nytimes.com/2010/04/30/world/europe/30 pope.html?th=&.

——. 2010c. "Vatican Revises Abuse Process, but Causes Stir." *New York Times*, July 15. http://www.nytimes.com/2010/07/16/world/europe/16vatican .html.

Donovan, Jeffrey. 2010. "Pope Benedict Creates New Vatican Office to 'Re-Evangelize' Secular World." Bloomberg (Oct. 12). http://www.bloomberg.com/news/2010-10-12/pope-benedict-creates-new-vatican-office-to-re-evangelize-secular-world.html.

Douglas, Allen. 1995. "Order in the Church: A Property Rights Approach." *Journal of Economic Behavior and Organization* 27: 97–117.

Drake, H. A. 2006. "The Impact of Constantine on Christianity." In *The Cambridge Companion to the Age of Constantine*, ed. Noel Lenski. Cambridge: Cambridge University Press.

Driscoll, J. F. 1911. "Pharisees." In *The Catholic Encyclopedia*. New York: Robert Appleton Company.

Durkheim, Émile. 1915. *The Elementary Forms of the Religious Life: A Study in Religious Sociology*. Translated by Joseph Ward Swain. New York: Macmillan.

Durkin, John T. Jr., and Andrew M. Greeley. 1991. "A Model of Religious Choice under Uncertainty." *Rationality and Society* 3: 178–196.

Efron, B., and Tibshirani, R. J. 1993. *An Introduction to the Bootstrap*. London: Chapman and Hall.

Ehrlich, Isaac, and Gary S. Becker. 1972. "Market Insurance, Self-Insurance, and Self- Protection." *Journal of Political Economy* 80: 623–648.

Ehrman, Bart D. 2003. *Lost Christianities: The Battles for Scripture and the Faiths We Never Knew*. Oxford: Oxford University Press.

——. 2005. *Misquoting Jesus: The Story Behind Who Changed the Bible and Why*. New York: HarperCollins.

Eilinghoff, Christian. 2003. "Religious Information and Credibility." *German Working Papers in Law and Economics* 8. http://www.bepress.com/cgi/viewcontent.cgi?article=1059&context=gwp.

Ekelund, Robert B. Jr., and Emilie S. Olsen. 1973. "Comte, Mill, and Cairnes: The Positivist-Empiricist Interlude in Late Classical Economics." *Journal of Economic Issues* 3: 383–416.

Ekelund, Robert B. Jr., Robert F. Hebert, and Robert D. Tollison. 1989. "An Economic Model of the Medieval Church: Usury as a Form of Rent Seeking." *Journal of Law, Economics, and Organization* 5: 307–331.

———. 1992. "The Economics of Sin and Redemption: Purgatory as a Market-Pull Innovation." *Journal of Economic Behavior and Organization* (September): 1–15.

———. 2004. "The Economics of the Counter-Reformation: Incumbent Firm Reaction to Market Entry." *Economic Inquiry*: 42: 690–705.

———. 2006. *The Marketplace of Christianity*. Cambridge: MIT Press.

Ekelund, Robert R. Jr., Robert F. Hebert, Robert D. Tollison, Gary Anderson, and Audrey Davidson. 1996. *Sacred Trust: The Medieval Church as an Economic Firm*. New York: Oxford University Press.

Ekelund, Robert B. Jr., and Robert D. Tollison. 1981. *Mercantilism as a Rent-Seeking Society: Economic Regulation in Historical Perspective*. College Station: Texas A&M University Press.

———. 1997. *Politicized Economies: Monarchy, Monopoly, and Mercantilism*. College Station: Texas A&M University Press.

Ellison, Christopher G., and Darren E. Sherkat. 1995. "Is Sociology the Core Discipline for the Scientific Study of Religion?" *Social Forces* 73: 1255–1266.

Eusebius. 1965. *The History of the Church*. New York: Dorset Press.

Faris, Stephen. 2010. "Vatican Bank Scandal amid Italian Money-Laundering Probe." *Time*. http://news.yahoo.com/s/time/20100924/wl_time/05992021 19400.

Ferguson, Everett. 2003. *Backgrounds of Early Christianity*. 3d ed. Grand Rapids, MI: William B. Eerdmans Publishing Company.

Ferrero, Mario. 2008. "The Triumph of Christianity in the Roman Empire: An Economic Interpretation." *European Journal of Political Economy* 24: 73–87.

Fisher, Ian. 2006. "Ideals Collide as Vatican Rethinks Condom Ban." *New York Times*, May 2. http://www.nytimes.com/2006/05/02/world/europe/02pope .html.

Fletcher, Winston. 2007. "Render unto Adam Smith." *Times Higher Education Supplement* (London), February 23, 2007.

Fouracre, Paul. 1996. *Late Merovingian France: History and Hagiography, 640–720*. Translated and edited by Paul Fouracre and Richard A. Gerberding. New York: St. Martin's Press.

———. 2000. *The Age of Charles Martel*. New York: Longman.

Fowden, Elizabeth Key. 2006. "Constantine and the Peoples of the Eastern Frontier." In *The Cambridge Companion to the Age of Constantine*, ed. Noel Lenski. Cambridge: Cambridge University Press.

Fox, Robin Lane. 1986. *Pagans and Christians: In the Mediterranean World from the Second Century AD to the Conversion of Constantine*. London: Viking.

Frank, Robert H. 1985. *Choosing the Right Pond*. Oxford University Press.

Frend, W. H. C. 1952. *The Donatist Church: A Movement of Protest in Roman North Africa*. Oxford: Clarendon Press.

Furubotn, Erick G., and S. Pejovich. 1974. *The Economics of Property Rights.* New York: Ballinger.

Furubotn, Erick G., and Rudolph Richter. 1997. *Institutions and Economic Theory: The Contribution of the New Institutional Economics.* Ann Arbor: University of Michigan Press.

Gay, Malcolm. 2010. "Renegade Priest Leads a Split St. Louis Parish." *New York Times,* August 13. http://www.nytimes.com/2010/08/14/us/14church.html?.

Geary, Patrick J. 1990. *Furta Sacra: Thefts of Relics in the Central Middle Ages.* Princeton: Princeton University Press.

Gilchrist, J. 1969. *The Church and Economic Activity in the Middle Ages.* London: St. Martin's Press.

Gill, Anthony. 1998. *Rendering Unto Caesar: The Catholic Church and the State in Latin America.* Chicago: University of Chicago Press.

Glenhill, Ruth, and Richard Owen. 2009. "Pope's Gambit Could See 1,000 Quit Church of England." *London Times,* October 21. http://www.timesonline.co.uk/tol/comment/faith/article6883151.ece.

———. 2010. "400,000 Former Anglicans Worldwide Seek Immediate Unity with Rome." *London Times,* October 22. http://www.timesonline.co.uk/tol/comment/faith/article6884673.ece.

Glimcher P., and A. Rustichini A. 2004. "Neuroeconomics: The Consilience of Brain and Decision." *Science* 306: 447–452.

Goldberger, A. S. 1964. *Econometric Theory. New York: Wiley.*

Goodstein, Laurie, and David M. Halbfinger. 2010. "Church Office Failed to Act on Abuse Scandal." *New York Times,* July 1. http://www.nytimes.com/2010/07/02/world/europe/02pope.html?scp=1&sq=%93Amid%20Church%20Abuse%20Scandal,%20an%20Office%20That%20Failed%20to%20Act.%94&st=cse.

Gotsis, George, and Stavros Drakopoulos. 2008. "Economic and Religious Choice: A Case Study from Early Christian Communities." Munich Personal RePEc Archive. http://mpra.ub.uni-muenchen.de/7097/.

Granovetter, Mark. 1985. "Economic Action and Social Structure: The Problem of Embeddedness." *American Journal of Sociology* 91: 481–510.

———. 2004. "The Impact of Social Structure on Economic Outcomes." *Journal of Economic Perspectives* 19: 33–50.

Grant, Robert M. 1966. *Gnosticism and Early Christianity.* 2d ed. New York: Columbia University Press.

Grossman, Cathy Lynn. 2006. "Americans Define Faith Their Way." *USA Today,* September 12, 7D.

———. 2009. "Almost All Denominations Losing Ground, Survey Finds." *USA Today,* March 9, 1A, 6A.

Gruber, Jonathan. 2005. "Religious Market Structure, Religious Participation and Outcomes: Is Religion Good for You?" *Advances in Economic Analysis and Policy* 5, no. 1, article 5. http://www.nber.org/papers/w11377.

Heath, Will Carrington, Melissa S. Waters, and John Keith Watson. 1995. "Religion and Economic Welfare: An Empirical Analysis of State Per Capita Income." *Journal of Economic Behavior and Organization* 27: 129–142.

Herlihy, David. 1961. "Church Property on the European Continent, 701–1200." *Speculum* 36: 81–105.

Hillgarth, J. N., ed. 1969. *Christianity and Paganism, 350–750: The Conversion of Western Europe*. Philadelphia: University of Pennsylvania Press.

Hinson, E. Glenn. 1995. *The Church Triumphant: A History of Christianity up to 1300*. Atlanta: Mercer.

Hitchens, Christopher. 2007. *God Is Not Great: How Religion Poisons Everything*. New York: Twelve.

Hopkins, Keith. 1998. "Christian Number and Its Implications." *Journal of Early Christian Studies* 6: 185–226.

Hull, Brooks B., and Frederick Bold. 1989. "Towards an Economic Theory of the Church." *International Journal of Social Economics* 16: 5–15.

Hume, David. 1976. *The Natural History of Religion and Dialogues concerning Natural Religion*. Edited by A. W. Colver and J. V. Price. Oxford: Clarendon Press.

Hunt, Erick E. 1982. *Holy Land Pilgrimage in the Later Roman Empire, AD 312–460*. Oxford: Clarendon Press.

Iannaccone, Lawrence. 1992. "Sacrifice and Stigma: Reducing Free-Riding in Cults, Communes, and Other Collectives." *Journal of Political Economy* 100: 271–292.

———. 1995. "Risk, Rationality, and Religious Portfolios." *Economic Inquiry* 33: 285–295.

———. 1998. "Introduction to the Economics of Religion." *Journal of Economic Literature* 36, no. 3: 1465–1495.

Jenkins, Phillip. 1996. *Pedophiles and Priests: Anatomy of a Contemporary Crisis*. New York: Oxford University Press.

———. 2010a. *Jesus Wars: How Four Patriarchs, Three Queens, and Two Emperors Decided What Christians Would Believe for the Next 1,500 Years*. New York: HarperOne.

———. 2010b. "How Serious Is the 'Predator Priest' Problem? We Have No Idea." *USA Today*, June 7, 11A.

Johnson, Stephen. 1982. *Later Roman Britain*. London: Paladin-Grafton Books.

Kennedy, Paul. 1987. *The Rise and Fall of Great Powers: Economic Change and Military Conflict from 1500 to 2000*. New York: Vintage.

Kirzner, Israel. 1973. *Competition and Entrepreneurship*. Chicago: University of Chicago Press.

Klein, Benjamin, and Keith B. Leffler. 1981. "The Role of Market Forces in Assuring Contractual Performance." *Journal of Political Economy* 89: 615–641.

Klutz, Todd E. 1998. "The Rhetoric of Science in *The Rise of Christianity*: A Response to Rodney Stark's Sociological Account of Christianization." *Journal of Early Christian Studies* 6: 162–184.

Kosmin, Barry A., Egon Mayer, and Ariela Keysar. 2001. *American Religious Identification Survey, 2001*. New York: Graduate Center of the City University of New York.

Küng, Hans. 2010. "Church in Worst Credibility Crisis since Reformation, Theologian Tells Bishops." *Irish Times*, April 16. http://www.irishtimes.com/newspaper/opinion/2010/0416/1224268443283.html.

Kurth, G. 1908. "Charles Martel." In *The Catholic Encyclopedia*. New York: Robert Appleton Company. http://www.newadvent.org/cathen/03629a.htm.

Lee, A. D. 2006. "Traditional Religions." In *The Cambridge Companion to the Age of Constantine*, ed. Noel Lenski, 159–182. Cambridge: Cambridge University Press.

Lenski, Noel, ed. 2006a. *The Cambridge Companion to the Age of Constantine*. Cambridge: Cambridge University Press.

———. 2006b. "The Reign of Constantine." In *The Cambridge Companion to the Age of Constantine*, ed. Noel Lenski, 59–90. Cambridge: Cambridge University Press.

Liebowitz, Stanley, and Steven Margolis. 1990. "The Fable of the Keys." *Journal of Law and Economics* 33 (April): 1–25.

Lieu, Samuel N. C. 2006. "Constantine in Legendary Literature." In *The Cambridge Companion to the Age of Constantine*, ed. Noel Lenski, 298–324. Cambridge: Cambridge University Press.

Lipford, J., Robert McCormick, and R. D. Tollison. 1993. "Preaching Matters." *Journal of Economic Behavior and Organization* 21: 235–250.

Loll, Anna Catherin, and Peter Wensierski. 2010. "The Hidden Wealth of the Catholic Church." *Spiegel Online*, June 14. http://www.spiegel.de/international/germany/0,1518,700513,00.html.

Lossky, Nicholas. 1951. *A History of Russian Philosophy*. London: Allen and Unwin.

Lunt, William E. 1962. *Financial Relations of the Papacy with England, 1327–1534*. Cambridge: Mediaeval Academy of America.

Maclean, Simon. 2003. *Kingship and Politics in the Late Ninth Century: Charles the Fat and the End of the Carolingian Empire*. Cambridge: Cambridge University Press.

MacMullen, Ramsay. 1981. *Paganism in the Roman Empire*. New Haven: Yale University Press.

———. 1984. *Christianizing the Roman Empire*. New Haven: Yale University Press.

———. 1988. *Corruption and the Decline of Rome*. New Haven: Yale University Press.

———. 1997. *Christianity and Paganism in the Fourth to Eighth Centuries*. New Haven: Yale University Press.

McBride, Michael. 2007. "Club Mormon: Free-Riders, Monitoring and Exclusion in the LDS Church." *Rationality and Society* 19: 395–424.

McCleary, Rachel M. 2007. "Salvation, Damnation, and Economic Incentives." *Journal of Contemporary Religion* 22: 49–74.

McCleary, Rachal M., and Robert J. Barro. 2006a. "Religion and Economy." *Journal of Economic Perspectives* 20, no. 2 (Spring): 49–72.

———. 2006b. "Religion and Political Economy in an International Panel." *Journal for the Scientific Study of Religion* 45: 149–175.

McCleary, Rachel M., and Leonard van der Kuijp. 2010. "A Market Approach to the Rise of the Geluk School in Tibet, 1419–1642." *Journal of Asian Studies* 69: 149–180.

McCormick, Michael. 2001. *Origins of the European Economy, AD 300–900*. Cambridge: Cambridge University Press.

McGuire, Marin, John Pratt, and Richard Zeckhauser. 1991. "Paying to Improve Your Chances: Gambling or Insurance?" *Journal of Risk and Uncertainty* 4: 329–228.

Milanovic, Branko, Peter H. Lindert, and Jeffrey G. Williamson. 2007. "Measuring Ancient Inequality." National Bureau of Economic Research Working paper 13550 (October). http://www.nber.org/papers/w13550.

Miller, Kent. 2002. "Competitive Strategies of Religious Organizations." *Strategic Management Journal* 23: 435–456.

Mueller-Frank, Manuel. 2010. "The Role of Religion in the Creation of Economic Societies. *ERN Economic History eJournal* 2, no. 82. Available at Social Science Research Network. http://ssm.com/abstract=1684638.

Muir, Steven C. 2006. "'Look How They Love One Another': Early Christian and Pagan Care for the Sick and Other Charity." In *Religious Rivalries in the Early Roman Empire and the Rise of Christianity*, ed. Leif E. Vaage, 213–231. Waterloo, ON: Wilfrid Laurier University Press.

Mundy, John L. 1973. *Europe in the High Middle Ages, 1150–1309*. New York: Basic Books.

Murray, A. 1981. "Confession as a Historical Source in the 13th Century." In *The Writing of History in the Middle Ages*, edited by R. H. C. Davis and J. M. Wallace-Hadrill. Oxford: Clarendon Press.

Nelson, Phillip. 1972. "Information and Consumer Behavior." *Journal of Political Economy* 78: 311–329.

———. 1974. "Advertising as Information." *Journal of Political Economy* 82: 729–754.

Newberg, Andrew, Eugene D'Aquili, and Vince Rause. 2001. *Why God Won't Go Away: Brain Science and the Biology of Belief.* New York: Ballantine Books.

Nicolle, David, and Graham Turner. 2008. *Charles Martel Turns the Islamic Tide (Campaign).* Oxford: Osprey Publishing.

Norris, Pippa, and Ronald Inglehart. 2004. *Secular and Sacred: Religion and Politics Worldwide.* Cambridge: Cambridge University Press.

Pagels, Elaine. 1989. *The Gnostic Gospels.* New York: Vintage Publishers.

Papke, Leslie E., and Jeffrey M. Wooldridge. 1996. "Econometric Methods for Fractional Response Variables with an Application to 401(K) Plan Participation Rates." *Journal of Applied Econometrics* 11: 619–632.

Parsons, Talcott. 1951. *The Social System.* Glencoe, Ill.: Free Press.

Perkins, Pheme. 1994. *Peter Apostle for the Whole Church.* Columbia: University of South Carolina Press.

Pew Forum Faith Angle Conference. 2007. "Religion and Secularism: The American Experience." Conference, December 3, 2007, Key West, FL. http://pewforum.org/events/?EventID=161.

Pew Forum on Religion and Public Life. 2008. "U.S. Religious Landscape Survey." February 25. http://pewforum.org/datasets/.

———. 2009a. "Many Americans Mix Multiple Faiths: Eastern, New Age Beliefs Widespread." Pew Research Center, December 9. http://pewforum.org/Other-Beliefs-and-Practices/Many-Americans-Mix-Multiple-Faiths.aspx.

———. 2009b. "Faith in Flux: Changes in Religious Affiliation in the U.S." Pew Research Center, April 20. http://pewforum.org/Faith-in-Flux(3).aspx.

Pirenne, Henri. 1937 [2001]. *Mohammed and Charlemagne.* New York: Dover Publications.

———. 1956. *A History of Europe from the Invasions to the XVI Century.* New York: University Book Publishers.

Powell, Walter W., and Paul J. DiMaggio, eds. *The New Institutionalism in Organizational Analysis.* Chicago: University of Chicago Press, 1991.

Rosen, Sherwin. 1981. "The Economics of Superstars." *American Economic Review* 71 (December 1981): 845–858.

Rostovtzeff, M. 1926. *The Social and Economic History of the Roman Empire.* Vol. 1. Oxford: Clarendon Press.

Sanneh, Lamin. 2003. *Whose Religion Is Christianity? The Gospel beyond the West.* Grand Rapids, Michigan: William B. Eerdmans Publishing Company.

Schumpeter, Joseph. A. 1947 [1943]. *Capitalism, Socialism and Democracy.* New York: Harper.

——. 1964 [1939]. *Business Cycles*. New York: McGraw-Hill.

——. 1981 [1911]. *The Theory of Economic Development*. New York: Transaction Publishers.

Scott, Martin. 1964. *Medieval Europe*. New York: Dorset Press.

Sherkat, Darren E., and John Wilson. 1995. "Preferences, Constraints, and Choices in Religious Markets; an Examination of Religious Switching and Apostasy." *Social Forces* 73: 993–1026.

Sipe, A. W. Richard. 2010. "Secret Sex in the Celibate System." *National Catholic Reporter*, April 28. http://ncronline.org/print/18075.

Smith, Adam. 1776. *An Inquiry into the Nature and Causes of the Wealth of Nations*. New York: Modern Library.

——. 1976 [1759]. *The Theory of Moral Sentiments*. New York: Liberty Classics.

Snape, Robert H. 1926. *English Monastic Finances in the Later Middle Ages*. Cambridge: Cambridge University Press.

Spengler, Joseph J. 1950. "Vertical Integration and Antitrust Policy." *Journal of Political Economy* 58: 347–352.

Stambaugh, John E. 1988. *The Ancient Roman City*. Baltimore: Johns Hopkins University Press.

Stark, Rodney. 1997. *The Rise of Christianity: How the Obscure, Marginal Jesus Movement Became the Dominant Religious Force in the Western World in a Few Centuries*. San Francisco: HarperOne.

——. 2001. *One True God: Historical Consequences of Monotheism*. Princeton: Princeton University Press.

——. 2003. *For the Glory of God: How Monotheism Led to Reformations, Science, Witch-Hunts, and the End of Slavery*. Princeton: Princeton University Press.

——. 2006. *Cities of God: The Real Story of How Christianity Became an Urban Movement and Conquered Rome*. San Francisco: HarperOne.

Stark, Rodney, and Lawrence Iannaccone. 1994. "A Supply-Side Interpretation of the Secularization of Europe." *Journal for the Scientific Study of Religion* 33: 230–252.

Stigler, George J. 1961 [1968]. "The Economics of Information." In *The Organization of Industry*, ed. G. Stigler. Chicago: Richard D. Irwin, Inc.

——. 1964. "A Theory of Oligopoly." *Journal of Political Economy* 72: 44–61.

Stigler, George J., and Gary S. Becker. 1977. "De Gustibus Non Est Disputandum." *American Economic Review* 67: 76–90.

Telushkin, Joseph. 1991. *Jewish Literacy*. New York: William Morrow and Co.

Temin, Peter. 2006. "The Economy of the Early Roman Empire." *Journal of Economic Perspectives* 20 (Winter): 133–151.

Thompson, James Westfall. 1931. *The Middle Ages, 300–2500*. Vol. 1, 2d ed. Alfred A. Knopf.

Tilly, Charles. 1990. *Coercion, Capital, and European States, AD 990–1990.* Cambridge, MA: Blackwell.

Toynbee, Arnold. 1934–1961. *A Study of History.* 12 vols. Oxford: Oxford University Press.

Tullock, Gordon. 1967. "The Welfare Costs of Tariffs, Monopolies, and Theft." *Western Economic Journal* 5: 224–232.

Vaage, Leif E. 2006. "Why Christianity Succeeded (in) the Roman Empire." In *Religious Rivalries in the Early Roman Empire and the Rise of Christianity,* ed. Leif E. Vaage, 253–278. Waterloo, ON: Wilfrid Laurier University Press.

Veblen, Thorstein. 1934 [1899]. *The Theory of the Leisure Class.* New York: Modern Library.

Vitello, Paul. 2009. "For Catholics, Heaven Moves a Step Closer." *New York Times,* February 10.

Wagner, Walter H. 1994. *After the Apostles: Christianity in the Second Century.* Minneapolis: Fortress Press.

Wand, J. W. C. 1937. *A History of the Early Church to A.D. 500.* London: Methuen & Co., Ltd.

Warrior, Valerie M. 2002. *Roman Religion: A Sourcebook.* Newburyport, MA: Focus Publishing.

———. 2006. *Roman Religion.* Cambridge: Cambridge University Press.

Weber, Max. 1930. *The Protestant Ethic and the Sprit of Capitalism.* Trans. Talcott Parsons, with a foreword by R. H. Tawney. London: George Allen & Unwin.

Wells, Peter S. 2008. *Barbarians to Angels: The Dark Ages Reconsidered.* New York: W. W. Norton & Company.

Wensierski, Peter, and Steffen Winter. 2010. "Bishop Williamson Unrepentent in Holocaust Denial." *Spiegel Online,* February 1. http://www.spiegel.de/inter national/germany/0,1518,druck-675163,00.html.

Wickham, Chris. 2009. *The Inheritance of Rome: Illuminating the Dark Ages, 400–1000.* New York: Viking.

Williamson, Oliver. 1975. *Markets and Hierarchies: Analysis and Antitrust Implications.* New York: Free Press.

Wilson, David Sloan. 2007. *Evolution for Everyone: How Darwin's Theory Can Change the Way We Think about Our Lives.* New York: Delta.

Winfield, Nicole. 2010a. "Women's Ordination Groups March on Vatican." Associated Press, June. http://www.signonsandiego.com/news/2010/jun/08/ womens-ordination-groups-march-on-vatican/.

———. 2010b. "Pope Shuffles Vatican Bureaucracy before Vacation." Yahoo! News, June 30. http://www.newsmeat.com/news/meat.php?articleId=79166804 &channelId=2951&buyerId=newsmeatcom&buid=3281 .

Woods, Thomas E. 2005. *How the Catholic Church Built Western Civilization.* Washington, DC: Regnery.

Woodward, Kenneth L. 2006. "Stuck in the Middle No More: The Church Ends Limbo: What Now?" *Wall Street Journal*, January 13.

Wright, Robert. 2009. *The Evolution of God*. New York: Little, Brown and Company.

Zuckerman, Phil. 2010. *Society without God: What the Least Religious Nations Can Tell Us About Contentment*. New York: New York University Press.

Index